Bilingual Education:
From Compensatory to Quality Schooling

Bilingual Education:
From Compensatory to Quality Schooling

María Estela Brisk
Boston University

IEA LAWRENCE ERLBAUM ASSOCIATES, PUBLISHERS
1998 Mahwah, New Jersey   London

Lawrence Erlbaum Associates, Inc., Publishers
10 Industrial Avenue
Mahwah, New Jersey 07430

Library of Congress Cataloging-in-Publication-Data

Brisk, María
Bilingual education: from compensatory to quality schooling
/ María Estela Brisk
        p. cm.
    Includes bibliographical references and index.
    ISBN 0-8058-2495-2 (pbk.)
    1. Education, Bilingual—United States. 2. Educa-
tion, Bilingual—United States—Curricula. 3. Compensatory education—United States.   I. Title
    LC3731.B68   1998
    370.117'5'0973—DC21   98-16788
                                                CIP

Books published by Lawrence Erlbaum Associates are printed
on acid-free paper, and their bindings are chosen for strength
and durability.

Printed in the United States of America
10 9 8 7 6 5 4 3 2

Contents

Foreword

The controversy that continues to swirl around bilingual education in the United States may appear bizarre to those who view the issues solely from an educational perspective. From the beginnings of history, knowledge of additional languages has always been characteristic of educated and elite groups. Virtually every educational system throughout the world attempts to teach additional languages, and the use of two or more languages as mediums of instruction has become increasingly common during the past 30 years.

Case studies and research from around the world show a similar pattern of outcomes from well-implemented bilingual programs: Students, whether they come from linguistic minority or majority backgrounds, attain extremely good conversational and academic skills in both languages of instruction. As documented in María Estela Brisk's lucid account, for majority language students, there is no cost to their first language (L1) as a result of receiving most or part of their instruction through a minority language; for minority language students, first language skills can be maintained to a reasonably high level and second (majority) language skills developed to grade expectations as a result of well-implemented bilingual programs.

I know of no applied linguist who disputes this general pattern of findings. This volume shows clearly the reason for this virtual consensus: The research itself provides overwhelming support for the feasibility of bilingual education and its potential, when implemented appropriately, to contribute to the goal of a linguistically competent society.

Why then, have issues surrounding bilingual education been debated with such ferocity and venom in the United States context? Clearly, there is abundant evidence of a recurrence of xenophobia and paranoia in regard to the "infiltration" of cultural and linguistic diversity. But the same is true of other countries (e.g., in Europe). In these countries, racism against immigrants is not associated with bilingual education to any significant degree.

A major reason for the difference is that bilingual education for recent immigrant groups (as compared to long-term national minorities) exists only in isolated and usually experimental programs in most countries outside the United States (programs for Finnish minority groups in Sweden represent an exception to this). In the United States, by contrast, bilingual programs have been mandated and implemented to a significant extent across the country. For almost 200 years, the implications of the U.S. constitution for educational equity were largely ignored, but in the 1960s and 1970s, these constitutional provisions became powerful tools for minority groups seeking redress for past discriminatory practices. The Supreme Court *Lau v. Nichols* court case in 1974, and subsequent policy mandates from the Office of Civil Rights, essentially made it mandatory for schools to implement some form of bilingual education unless they could show that alternative approaches would be as beneficial.

Thus, although the rhetoric surrounding diversity in the United States may appear extreme and frequently racist, this rhetoric must be considered in the context of the fact that the United States has gone further than virtually any other country in recognizing the rights of linguistic minority groups to an equitable education. However, in no country does several hundred years of racism disappear overnight just because a handful of judges declared that it shall be so. Linguistic minorities' new "right" to bilingual education, together with significant increases in immigration during the 1980s and 1990s, fueled the perception that minority groups were making demands and were unwilling to assimilate as countless generations before them had done. Diversity was now seen as potentially undermining the fabric of nationhood; it became the "enemy within," far more insidious in its power to fracture national identity than any external enemy. For some, bilingual education has become one of the most prominent manifestations of this threat to national unity, whereas for others it represents a long overdue concrete expression of the nation's commitment to ideals of justice, freedom, and equity.

Thus, for both opponents and proponents of bilingual education, the issues go far beyond education in the narrow sense; each group sees itself as reclaiming the nation, rescuing it from its darker impulses: in the eyes of opponents, this darker impulse is its "death wish," as some have called it, to naively invite diversity into its unprotected bosom, whereas in the eyes of bilingual education advocates, the nation's darker impulse resides in its pandering to the evils of racism, while at the same time paying lip-service to the ideals of justice and equity that were supposed to define the essence of nationhood.

No volume that reviews educational research is going to resolve these issues of national identity. But, what María Estela Brisk's volume does beautifully is show the importance of nurturing linguistic diversity in the context of what she terms *quality schooling*. The research does provide very clear directions with respect to what we can expect from different kinds of programs.

Many bilingual programs across the United States have been undermined because of, at best, ambivalence, and, frequently, strong opposition to their implementation. Many have been based on compensatory frameworks that view the linguistic skills that children bring to school as deficits to be overcome. By contrast, however, those bilingual programs that have implemented what the research highlights as quality education have produced outstanding results.

These quality programs show clearly that schools can prepare students to "navigate difference" in the culturally and linguistically diverse world of the 21st century. They show that preparing global citizens is not possible, but necessary to resolve the myriad social, economic, and environmental problems that our global community faces. They also suggest that the term *culturally deprived* might justifiably be applied to any student who graduates into the 21st century where, in both domestic and international arenas, cultural and linguistic diversity is increasingly the norm, with a monocultural perspective on the world and competent only in one language.

This volume inspires us to articulate what education can contribute both to the social and economic health of our society in a rapidly changing world, and it also challenges us to demand that society fulfill its obligation to acknowledge the right of all children to a quality education.

—Jim Cummins,
Ontario Institute for Studies in Education of the University of Toronto

Preface

Chaos theory, a way of analyzing a phenomenon as a whole rather than merely the sum of its constituent parts, has altered perspectives of science (Gleick, 1987). It also provides a useful metaphor for educational research. Educational researchers confront not only the multiplicity of factors that impact on the learning process—the natural endowments of students, their social and cultural contexts, teaching approaches and styles, shifting goals and curricula, interactions between teachers and students and among students, and so on—but the fact that classrooms are not set up as laboratories, so that results in one classroom do not necessarily ordain similar results in other classrooms. In bilingual situations, the complexity is multiplied by the addition of linguistic and cultural variables. Thus, research results on bilingual students often appear contradictory not only because of the inherent complexity of educational research, but also because most analyses focus on the effects of specific, isolated factors that may or may not be replicable.

Instead of isolating factors, perhaps we should approach research and practice in bilingual education with the perspective that all factors impact on how students learn in schools and that, consequently, teachers themselves need to analyze and reanalyze what works in order to determine how best to teach such students. Chaos theory maintains that "tiny differences in input could become overwhelming differences in output" (Gleick, 1987, p. 8). The frequently used example is known as the *butterfly effect* from the notion that a butterfly flapping its wings in Beijing may affect weather in New York a month later. A small, apparently isolated factor can produce unanticipated results. It is for this reason unfruitful to base a subject as complex as the education of bilingual students on generalizations or stereotypes about students from a particular ethnic group, for example. Social factors do affect such students, but personal characteristics are just as likely to affect their educational outcomes.

This book is addressed to educators working with bilingual students, from teachers who in the confines of their classrooms impart the fundamental skills and hopes for students to administrators and curriculum developers who need to support teachers with their policies and practices. The initial chapter traces the use of languages in U.S. education for two reasons. First, much of the current debate has been foreshadowed by various approaches taken in the past. Second, in education as well as most endeavors, we cannot fully escape the past. In the language of chaos theory, the "sensitive dependence on initial conditions lurks everywhere" (Gleick, 1987, p. 67). Chapter 2 presents major factors affecting students that, although discrete, operate simultaneously on schools and students. No single factor explains what happens to particular students. The interaction among all factors, with each exercising a different force in different contexts, affects each educational situation in each community. In spite of this unpredictability, chaos scientists believe that components influence each other according to determinable patterns. They adhere to the notion that "laws of complexity hold universally, caring not at all for the details of system's constituent atoms" (Gleick, 1987, p. 304). Regardless of the factors that affect particular educational situations, effective practices emerge from research that can guide educators toward the development of quality bilingual programs. In chapters 3, 4, and 5 I analyze useful practices that emerge from numerous bilingual education studies and my own 25 years of working with bilingual teachers of many different languages and observing children in schools. These practices will undoubtedly be explored in future research, particularly if it focuses on different populations and grade levels from our past emphasis on elementary Spanish-speaking students.

The recommendations in this book provide a comprehensive basis for planning, developing, improving, and evaluating bilingual programs. They are dissected into discrete points with respect to the whole school (chap. 3), the curriculum (chap. 4), and the classroom (chap. 5) for clarity, but they need to be applied in a holistic way because they depend on each other. To carry out specific classroom practices (chap. 5), teachers need curricula (chap. 4) that adhere to the same principles and a supportive school environment (chap. 3). The amount of difficulty involved in the implementation of specific recommendations depends on the many factors influencing bilinguals (chap. 2) and the current and historical context of the United States (chap. 1).

My concluding chapter synthesizes the contents of the book to answer the question that led me to write this book: What do we need to do to have quality bilingual education? Education of bilingual students is a complex enterprise impossible to address with simple formulas. It is not, however, an impossible quest. Implementation of the recommendations synthesized in this book needs a flexible approach that considers each individual school situation. Rigor does not always require rigidity. The focus, rather, should be the real-life situation experienced by every teacher. The best educational practices originate from knowing students, their families, and communities. As a guide for teachers and educators, I have chosen to illustrate with real-life examples rather than prescribed formulas. Such examples illustrate that we can create good schools for bilingual students. There is a lot of research and experience to prove it despite claims to the contrary heralded by opponents of bilingual education. The pieces of the educational puzzle exist, but they are scattered. Schools need to study the field and have the political will to put these pieces together freed from restrictive ideologies that reject parts of the puzzle. The major pieces include the research on effective schools, language, and culture; the role of families; and the characteristics of the students themselves.

Although the focus of this book is on improving bilingual education programs in the United States, many of the ideas can be used in schools in the United States where there are bilingual students but no bilingual programs. The framework can also help define policies and practices in other countries. Regardless of how the debate on bilingual education is resolved, bilingual and immigrant students throughout the world require thoughtful and empathetic attention.

ACKNOWLEDGMENTS

Writing in your second language to conform to another culture's written discourse is not an easy job. I could not have produced this book without Bill, my husband, an American native English speaker and good writer. Endless discussions about content and organization and careful review of the drafts rendered the final manuscript. I owe my inspiration to teachers and principals I have worked over the years and bilingual students I have interviewed and observed. You will meet them throughout this book. Sheer numbers and confidentiality preclude me from naming them all. I am also grateful to my own students, who throughout my career have shared their wisdom, particularly Ester deJong, with whom I wrote a paper reflecting the seed of my notions on the conditions necessary for good bilingual education and the reviewers who generously gave advice and encouragement: Christian Faltis, Arizona State University, and Bernard Spolsky, Bar-Ilan University.

I dedicate this book to my mother, who taught me that bilingualism is desirable, and to my daughter, who demonstrated that it is possible to become bilingual, bicultural, and academically successful in the U.S. context.

Introduction

Much of the debate on bilingual education is politically motivated, more suitable for talk shows than for improving schools. The United States can create quality bilingual education for the increasingly diverse student population, but only if we observe what really happens in our schools. If we continue to deal with bilingual education as a label, the sterile debate on how abruptly language minority students should be Americanized and Anglicized will continue to isolate many of our students. This book explores the abundant, although often inconsistent, research on the education of bilingual students. It also provides a personal testament to what I have observed in classrooms, in consulting with schools, and in training teachers for challenging roles in bilingual education.

When I attended a bilingual school in Latin America, bilingual education was viewed as quality education delivered in two languages. The elite eagerly enrolled their children in schools that offered, in addition to the regular curriculum, the opportunity to master at least two languages, the prerequisite many believed, to vocational and social success. These values inhere in a number of bilingual schools throughout the world (Fishman, 1976). Yet in the United States, the term *bilingual education* evokes a different meaning. It refers to the education of children whose home language is not English. Bilingual education is often associated with urban education (where the children of immigrants often find themselves in compensatory programs and where high dropout rates are viewed as the failure of students rather than the failure of the system). Bilingual students are often branded as not only children whose English is inferior, but as students who are themselves inferior.

To educate such students successfully requires educational practices based on understanding how children learn languages and tailored to the talents and needs of language minority students. Their entry into American society requires that they learn English and adjust to the American culture. However, it is not necessary, or wise, that they do so at the costs of their native language and culture that, for many are the foundations for their learning. Strong bilingual schools or programs not only meet the needs of bilingual students but also introduce monolingual students to diverse cultures and languages. Rather than eliminate other languages and cultures in U.S. schools, English-based education has the opportunity to take advantage of the linguistic and cultural diversity of our mixed society.

Certain factors such as family background, socioeconomic status, educational level of the students and their family, and status of the language and ethnic group in the society undeniably affect schooling. But there is a danger that "stressing social and economic disadvantage as a major cause of educational underachievement can seem to absolve educators from their professional duty to educate all pupils effectively" (Tomlinson, 1989, p. 26). The danger increases when teachers and administrators stereotype students on the basis of such factors, limiting expectations and opportunities.

This book attempts to overcome such stereotypes, concentrating on what schools can do for bilingual learners. Careful review of the extensive research bearing on bilingual students indicates how to organize schools to provide good education for such students. However, before addressing the focus of this book—how to achieve quality bilingual education for language minority students—a few definitions are necessary: Who are bilingual and bicultural individuals and what is compensatory and quality education?

BILINGUAL AND BICULTURAL INDIVIDUALS

Bilinguals know more than one language to different degrees and use these languages for a variety of purposes (Mackey, 1968). Traditionally, only full fluency in two languages was accepted as bilingualism (Bloomfield, 1933). This narrow definition has evolved with the study of bilingualism. Grosjean (1989) defined a bilingual as a person who has developed competencies in two or more languages "to the extent required by his or her needs and those of the environment" (p. 6). Individuals are now generally considered bilingual even if their knowledge of a second language is limited.

Personal and social variables, independent of instruction, influence language development and language loss on bilinguals. Language status, attitudes, motivation, size of the ethnic community, and need affect second language acquisition and maintenance of the native language (Dorian, 1982; Gardner, 1982; Schumann, 1978; Spolsky, 1989). In turn, an individual's degree of bilingualism constantly changes given experiences with the languages and the need to develop them. As Mackey (1968) suggested, "bilingualism is not a phenomenon of language; but it is a characteristic of its use" (p. 554). Therefore bilingual students present a variety of profiles, depending on the level of development of each language, whether they are literate in either or both, to what extent they use each language, and for which purpose.

Bilinguals have a unique ability to shift languages. While communicating with monolinguals they partially deactivate their other language. To communicate with similar bilinguals they make use of both languages, alternating and even mixing the languages. This process, called *codeswitching,* is a natural phenomenon and not evidence of poor language skills. On the contrary, bilingual children develop the ability to codeswitch and use it to enrich communication (Genishi, 1981). Bilinguals alternate languages for many reasons. Often a word in the other language comes to mind first or more accurately expresses the meaning. Change in language is prompted by topic, addressee, environment, or the need to call attention to, to give emphasis to, or to express solidarity with an ethnic group (Mackey, 1968; Romaine, 1995).

The definition of culture—as that of bilingualism—has gone through redefinition. The classical view of culture was based on the notion of uniform and static knowledge and behavior transmitted through generations. A more dynamic view sees culture as a process that "changes, expands and adapts to new circumstances" (Wurzel, 1988, p. 3). This dynamic process is nourished by life experiences.

The backgrounds of bilingual students vary greatly and thus do not fit a neatly defined cultural paradigm. Many enter a new cultural environment when they move to the United States. Socialized to a culture in their home country they now enter schools that operate according to different cultural norms. The socialization of children born in the United States to immigrant parents or families that use languages other than English transcends cultural and linguistic boundaries because members of their extended family who interact with the children are cross-cultural individuals transformed by the contact between the ethnic and American cultures. In these homes there is "an intermingling or merging of culturally diverse traditions" (Duranti & Ochs, 1995, p. 6).

Both languages and diverse cultural experiences play a role in performance, behavior, and attitudes of bilinguals. Introduction of a new language and encounter with a new culture shocks the linguistic, cognitive, and affective systems of bilingual students. Understanding bilinguals as unique individuals with more than one language available to them, rather than as the sum of two monolinguals,[1] and influenced by a dynamic cross-cultural experience, rather than rigid cultural stereotypes, is vital for designing school policy, classroom practices, and assessment procedures. Bilingual students are especially successful academically and socially when they value and cultivate their bilingualism and feel adjusted to both their heritage culture and their host culture. Schools and families who promote bilingualism and sociocultural integration ease the adjustment of children to the new social environment.

Often schools attend to the needs of those students who are not fluent in English but do not view as bilinguals those students who also know English. For example, a Korean-American first grader fluent in English and Korean was not making much progress in an English remedial reading class in a suburban school. As soon as the teacher recognized the boy's bilingualism and his cultural heritage and incorporated them as part of the classroom content, his reading ability blossomed and in less than 8 weeks was transferred out of remedial reading. Teachers should encourage the use of both languages as resources for communicating and learning. Language and literacy ability are measured in terms of ability in both languages rather than each one separately, as well as ability to communicate in monolingual situations.

Many schools, curricula, and instructional practices pose as cross-cultural when they introduce songs, dress, and food from different nations. Although, well

---

[1]See Grosjean (1989) for a complete discussion on the contrasting views of a bilingual as two monolinguals versus a distinct individual.

intentioned, such superficialities add to stereotypes. Far more significant are students' life experiences and their families' and communities' body of knowledge and beliefs. For example, a young Puerto Rican student was having difficulty with math tests. Her teacher learned that the student's mother insisted that her child do math in her head, considering the use of pencil and paper an inferior skill. Once the teacher understood this, she was much better equipped to help the student transfer the math skills she already had to the school requirements.

I prefer the term *bilingual student* to other terms used in the literature and legislation such as *limited English speaker* (LES), *limited English proficient* (LEP), *potential English proficient, English language learners, non-English speaker,* or *nonspeaker,* all of which assume that language ability is measured by how much a person knows English and imply that only students who are not fluent in English can be considered bilingual. Most recent arrivals indeed are in the very early stages of bilingualism. Others, however, who have studied English before migrating or are exposed to English at home, know English and the home language. The term bilingual students should be applied not only students being served by a bilingual program but to all students who use two or more languages and live a multicultural experience.

COMPENSATORY VERSUS QUALITY EDUCATION

The prevailing approach that has guided language minority students'[2] education is compensatory, the principal goal of which is to teach students English as quickly as possible. Because English is viewed as the only means for acquisition of knowledge, students' fluency in English is the essential condition to receiving an education. Bilingualism is considered a problem and the source of linguistic and academic failure. The compensatory approach funnels scarce resources (teachers, classrooms, time, and materials) into teaching English. Program outcomes are judged solely on effectiveness to teach and learn English.

The political agenda guiding such view toward education of language minority students maintains that it is not the role of public schools to develop students' home languages. Some supporters of this view even consider the promotion of languages other than English a threat to our national unity and identity. Students emerge from compensatory programs with varying degrees of English ability and academic achievement. Many lose their ties with their families and ethnic communities in their effort to learn English (Child, 1943; Rodriguez, 1982). They see assimilation to American culture as a precondition to acquire English as well as academic and socioeconomic success. Others reject American culture because it threatens their basic values (Gibson, 1993; Suarez-Orozco, 1987). Yet others, most unfortunately,

---

[2]*Language minority* refers to speakers of politically and socially subordinate languages, whereas speakers of the dominant language are called the *language majority.*

reject both cultures and as a consequence often drop out, join gangs, or lead troubled lives (Suarez-Orozco, 1993).

The goal of quality education is to educate students to their highest potential. In the case of language minority students, acquisition of English is only part of this goal. Good education, as described by the effective schools movement and other recent educational improvement proposals,[3] orients educational policy. Bilingual learners access knowledge not only through English but through their native languages. Their cultural experience determines their views and assumptions. Quality education for language minority students combines concerns for language development and cultural awareness in a constant quest for good education. Expected outcomes of quality schools include academic success; individuals who can function within their families, communities, and the larger American society; and a good command of the English language. Native language proficiency will vary depending on the amount of instruction, support for language use in the community, and students' individual characteristics. The key factor is the acceptance by schools, families, and students of bilingualism as a resource.

For too long advocates and educators have focused on finding the ideal way to teach English. The real choice is between compensatory and quality education (see Table 1). This book is dedicated to those who believe in the potential of language minority students and believe that they, as all students, are entitled to quality education. Specific school and curricular policies as well as instructional and assessment practices delineate necessary conditions for quality education. Many factors, however, influence the individual, community, and school environment.

TABLE 1

Compensatory Education Versus Quality Education

	Compensatory Education	*Quality Education*
Policy	Choice of language for instruction	Right to good education
Pedagogy	• Search for the best model to teach English	• Effective schools, advances in education
	• Education is possible only in English	• Language and culture of students are vehicles for education
Expected outcomes	• English proficiency	• Academic achievement
		• English proficiency
		• Varying degrees of native language proficiency
		• Sociocultural integration

---

[3]For a synthesis on the findings of effective schools see Edmonds (1979) and Mace-Matluck (1990). Educational innovations such as whole language (Freeman & Freeman, 1992; Goodman, 1986), process writing (Graves, 1983), cooperative learning (Slavin, 1970), critical pedagogy (Walsh, 1991), curricula based on the multiple intelligences theory (Gardner, 1983), and school reform as advocated by the Coalition of Essential Schools (Sizer, 1984, 1992) are also important.

These conditions must be applied with a thorough understanding of what factors affect each particular situation. Continuous research and experimentation should add to the knowledge we presently have. What must remain constant is our belief that individuals can become bilingual and multicultural and that such qualities are detrimental for neither the individual nor the nation.

1

Bilingual Education Debate

The paradox of bilingual education is that when it is employed in private schools for the children of elites throughout the world it is accepted as educationally valid (Fishman, 1976; Fishman & Markman, 1979; Lewis, 1977). However, when public schools implemented bilingual education for language minority students over the past 50 years, bilingual education became highly controversial.

A pioneering study conducted by the United Nations Educational, Scientific, and Cultural Organization (UNESCO) more than 40 years ago revealed that children educated in their second language (a language acquired in addition to the home language) experienced difficulties in school. The report of experts from around the world sponsored by UNESCO declares that the home language (also called the mother tongue or native language) is the best initial medium of instruction because it is the vehicle through "which a child absorbs the cultural environment" (UNESCO, 1953, p. 47), it facilitates literacy development and learning of different subjects, and it promotes understanding between the home and the school. UNESCO recommended using students' native language for instruction and literacy development for as long as feasible. Acknowledging a number of practical limitations—inadequacy of vocabulary in technical areas, shortage of trained teachers and educational materials, multiplicity of languages in a district, and popular opposition to the use of the native language—the report nevertheless argues that they should not stand in the way of making the greatest effort possible to use the mother tongue. The report also refutes objections that are still used to oppose use of native language in schooling: that some home languages do not have a grammar, that the child already knows the native language, that using native languages impedes national unity, and that emphasizing native languages prevents acquisition of the second language. The report points out that all languages have grammar, written or not; that children still have a lot to learn of their language when they enter school; that "the national interests are best served by optimum advancement of education, and this in turn can be promoted by the use of the local language as a medium of instruction (p. 50), and, most significantly, that "recent experience in many places prove that an equal or better command of the second language can be imparted if school begins with the mother tongue as the medium of instruction" (p. 49). The report also underscores the importance of teaching language minority students their national language ("the language of a political, social and cultural entity," p. 46) as a second language by gradually introducing it in elementary schools to prepare students for further education.

Many educators and linguists today echo UNESCO's recommendations (Cummins, 1984; Ramirez, 1992; Snow, 1990; Wong Fillmore & Valadez, 1986). Yet others, mostly social scientists and journalists, still adamantly oppose instruction through the native languages and believe that in the United States, intense instruction in English is best for students who speak other languages (Epstein, 1977; Porter, 1990; Rossell & Ross, 1986).

This debate over choice of language for instruction is a phenomenon of the 20th century. In the first century after the American Revolution many languages were used in schools. Communities of settlers and immigrants continued to use their home languages for religious, educational, social, and economic purposes as they established themselves in the new continent. It was not until the beginning of the 20th century that "legal, social, and political forces strongly opposed maintenance of languages other than English" (Heath, 1981, p. 7). Thus the United States went from a multilingual society using and accepting the languages of the European colonizers and immigrants to a monolingual society, considering speakers of other languages as language minorities. Language use in education was affected by these changes. Schools went from naturally using the languages of the communities and introducing second languages as needed to using English and considering those students who did not speak English a problem.

Presently, much of the debate centers around which are the best models for educating language minority students. Proponents of bilingual education defend models that use and promote the native language of the students, whereas opponents favor models that only emphasize English language development. This controversy, I believe, emerges from one basic difference. Proponents of bilingual education believe that students learn faster when they are educated through their native languages while studying English. Opponents maintain that language minorities need English as a precondition to becoming educated; thus, the faster these students are incorporated into English instruction the sooner they will reap the benefits of schooling. This book challenges bilingual education's opponents who, in effect, would postpone quality education until students master English. I believe that language minority students are entitled to quality education as soon as they enter schools and to postpone their access to quality education is to accept mediocrity and failure.

This chapter traces the history of language use in education, contrasts the various models of bilingual education and English-only instruction, and discusses the nature and complexity of the present debate on bilingual education. The conclusion addresses the dilemma of advocates of language minority ents.

LANGUAGE MINORITY STUDENTS
IN U.S. SCHOOLS

It was not until the end of the 19th century that the United States adopted English as the national language and the language for education. Therefore, native speakers of other languages were relegated to language minority status regardless of whether they were indigenous, descendants of colonizers, immigrants, colonized populations, refugees, or sojourners. Their children learned English to function because English became the national language used in most circles, and later especially in media and most specifically television. Even in the most remote villages of Alaska, television has been instrumental in introducing English to children. Over the generations, many communities have lost the original language (Veltman, 1983). The flow of new immigrants and efforts to revitalize languages has kept the United States multilingual.

European colonization decimated much of the Native American population and, as a consequence, many languages were lost. After colonization, language loss accelerated through Americanization programs that imposed English on younger generations. Of the existing 155 languages, only 20 are likely to survive with some vitality into the 21st century (Crawford, 1995). Europeans of many different language backgrounds established colonies in the United States. In addition to English, Spanish, French, Dutch, Swedish, German, and Russian were used in communities, churches, and schools (Brisk, 1981a). Some communities have continued to use these languages through the centuries; for example, Spanish in Northern New Mexico or German in what are known as Pennsylvania Dutch villages.

In the 19th and 20th centuries, immigration to the United States was uneven. Peak periods occurred in the first two decades of the 20th century and from 1985 to the present. The place of origin of the immigrants has also changed. During the first half of the 19th century, northern Europeans came to our shores. During the second half of the 19th century through the first decades of the 20th century, large numbers of eastern and southern Europeans joined the flow from Europe. Asians, especially Chinese, were attracted to participate in the development of the American west. The Chinese Exclusion Act of 1882 drastically curtailed the influx of Asian workers. Those in search of laborers looked for help from Latin American countries and the Philippines. Although Europeans constituted about 90% of the immigrants during the 19th and early 20th centuries, better economic conditions in Europe after World War II gradually reduced European immigration. Since the 1960s most of the immigrants to the United States have been Hispanic (47%) and Asian (22.4%; Portes & Zhou, 1993). The 1965 Immigration Act opened the door to Asian immigrants, and political and economic problems have driven large number of Latin Americans to the United States.

Another source of linguistic variety resulted from the incorporation of new lands. In 1867 the United States purchased Alaska from Russia. Several Pacific Islands, the Philippines, and Puerto Rico were annexed to the United States in 1898 as a result of the Spanish-American War. In Alaska there are speakers of several Eskimo and Athapascan languages. In the Pacific Islands, Chamorro, Samoan, Palau, and a number of other local languages are still spoken. In the Philippines over 70 languages are spoken, Tagalog being dominant. Large numbers of Philippines moved to the United States unaffected by laws that blocked other Asian populations. In 1946 the Philippines obtained its independence, curtailing immigration to the United States. In Puerto Rico, Spanish is the dominant language, in spite of early efforts to eliminate it through imposition of English in schools (Von Maltitz, 1975). When Puerto Rico obtained commonwealth status in 1952, migration between the island and the U.S. mainland accelerated. Puerto Rican children have school experiences similar to immigrant children as they move to the mainland, and when they move to Puerto Rico, where the language of instruction is Spanish, they have experiences similar to returning immigrants whose children have largely lost the home language and thus experience difficulties in the local schools. Returning Puerto Rican children are dominant in English, although not always fully literate, with varying ability in Spanish (Vazquez, 1989).

International business and the popularity of U.S. higher education attracts nearly 1 million sojourners. These foreigners who come temporarily to work or study often bring children who enroll in public schools. The number of foreign students in universities has tripled in the past 20 years. Close to half a million students are enrolled in colleges and universities throughout the country. About 20% of them are married and likely to have children (Davis, 1994).

According to a 1989 survey, Spanish was spoken by 58% of all speakers of languages other than English. Other European languages were spoken by 21%, and Asian and Pacific Island languages were spoken by 14%. The remaining 7% speak a variety of languages. Not only the immigrants themselves but their descendants continue to speak their original language. Half of the population who reported a home language other than English were born in the United States (McArthur, 1993).

Language minority students enter schools in the United States at different ages and with different educational and linguistic backgrounds. They may only know their home language, but a good number have some knowledge of English. Many of the Southeast Asian refugees, for example, studied English in camps in Thailand and the Philippines before reaching the United States. Some may be even more advanced academically than students in their same grade level because of differences in curriculum between the United States and their home country. Other students come with little or no schooling at all, as was the case at one Boston high school that suddenly received children from war-torn Salvador and Amerasians from Vietnam in the 1980s. The Salvadoran children were barely literate in Spanish because their schooling had been interrupted by the civil war. The Amerasian children born of Vietnamese women and U.S. soldiers lacked education because as pariahs, they were not allowed into school in Vietnam.

Presently there are bilingual students in schools in all 50 states, Pacific territories, and Puerto Rico. Many of these students have been reported as being limited English proficient (LEP), as measured by English language tests. The number of so-called LEP students increased by 51% in 5 years, from 1985 to 1990, bringing the total number of these students in the United States to about 2.5 million (Olsen, 1993). The actual number of bilingual students in schools, rather than just LEP, is much greater. According to 1989 U.S. Census figures, 5,226,000 children 5 to 17 years old (or 13% of the school-age population) spoke a language other than English at home. Of these, 68.6% were Spanish speakers, 10.2% spoke other European languages, 13.9% were speakers of Asian and Pacific Island languages, and 7.2% spoke other languages (McArthur, 1993). These statistics do not take into account bilingual children who speak English and another language at home and are thus counted in the census data as English speakers. The presence of language minority students is particularly felt in the largest school districts where the language minority enrollment comprises 70% to 96% of the total number of students (Bermudez & Márquez, 1994).

The presence of bilingual students in U.S. schools is significant and the result of internal and external historical factors. Educators and policymakers must consider their needs and potential contribution to our education system. The multiplicity of languages and the complex nature of bilinguals renders a complicated but exciting educational field for research, practice, and educational innovation. Unfortunately, languages become entangled in political battles, dragging the education and the future of innocent children into such conflicts.

LANGUAGE USE IN EDUCATION
SINCE INDEPENDENCE

Indigenous inhabitants, colonizers, and immigrants to the United States have and continue to represent a variety of language backgrounds. Like it or not, the United States is highly multilingual. Fashions in using language in education and attitudes toward bilingualism have undergone many changes since the United States became independent. The changing models of education and research perspective reflect shifting political moods rather than sound educational and linguistic research.

During the initial colonization of the United States, European settlers used the languages of their countries of origin. The Continental Congress considered French and German important for political purposes. It recognized the need to disseminate information among disparate populations to broaden the cause of independence (Heath, 1976). The settlers established schools that educated their children in their own languages, especially French, German, Spanish, and Swedish while teaching English as a second language. Schools that used English as the medium of instruction taught one of the other European languages as a second language (Keller & Van Hooft, 1982).

The presence of many languages in U.S. schools was an accepted reality until the 1870s. "[N]ewspapers, schools, and societies provided instructional support for diverse languages" (Heath 1981, p. 7). There was, however, concern for seeking a common language, especially to conduct government affairs (Heath, 1981). The original colonies and territories incorporated later into the Union comprised local governments that used different languages, such as German in Pennsylvania, French in Louisiana, and Spanish in New Mexico and California. English, nevertheless, always played an important role in the public life of the colonies because from the beginning England colonized the United States. The form of government embraced after the American Revolution reflected English values (Conklin & Lourie, 1983). Economic and historic factors helped solidify the position of English as the language of government.

As immigrants settled during the 19th century, parochial and private schools used the community language for instruction (Brisk, 1981a). When public schools were first established in the 1820s, they often used the language of the population in the area to attract students. Once public schools became more popular than parochial schools, there was less concern for catering to the different linguistic groups (Heath, 1977). Even schools run by Native Americans used their own languages, but their efforts were squelched when the Bureau of Indian Affairs established schools with the purpose of isolating "the Indian children from their families in order to instruct them in western culture and the English language" (Brisk, 1981a, p. 4).

During the first half of the 20th century, English was imposed as the language of instruction in most states. As many as 34 states enacted laws mandating English as the language of instruction. Other languages were forbidden and teachers could be fined or jailed if found using them: "No polyglot empire of the old world has dared be as ruthless in imposing a single language upon its whole population as was the liberal republic 'dedicated to the proposition that all men are created equal'" (Johnson, 1949, pp. 118–119).

A beam of light in these dark times for bilingualism was the Supreme Court ruling in the case *Meyer v. Nebraska* (1923). Authorities prosecuted a teacher for teaching a 10-year-old to read German under Nebraska laws that prohibited teaching in any language other than English before Grade 8 in either public or private schools. The Supreme Court overturned the conviction because the right of a teacher to pursue his or her vocation is guaranteed by the the Fourteenth Amendment. The Court did not object to state requirements for instruction in English but found prohibition of teaching a foreign language unreasonable because "proficiency in a foreign language seldom comes to one not instructed at an early age, and experience shows that this is not injurious to the health, morals or understanding of the ordinary child" (*Meyer v. Nebraska* 262 U.S. 390,91, 1923, p. 403).

Such a dramatic shift from tolerating to rejecting languages other than English has multiple explanations. English was the language of those with greatest political power. German, another powerful language, lost favor during World War I. Industrialization brought to urban centers people who spoke different languages and needed a common language to communicate. Xenophobia, directed at massive immigration at the turn of the century, created fear that citizens might lose out to foreigners. These immigrants were perceived as uneducated people who could only be unified and uplifted by education in English (Kloss, 1977; Leibowitz, 1976, 1980).

Political, social, and economic rationales for denigrating all languages other than English advanced linguistic and cognitive theories that attacked bilingualism. Popular research contended that bilingualism caused mental retardation and failure in school (Goddard, 1917; Pintner & Keller, 1922; Saer, 1923; for critical review see Darcy, 1953). Standardized testing, only in English, became popular in the 1920s, reinforcing the view that intellectual achievement and knowledge of English were synonymous. Ignorance of English was attributed to the inferior intelligence of the immigrant students. Some researchers even blamed the use of foreign languages at home for the children's mental retardation (see Hakuta, 1986, for a summary and analysis of this literature). Those who propagated this vicious circle were increasingly elected to school boards or hired by them as superintendents and principals.

Public schools quickly adopted a "sink or swim" attitude during the first half of the 20th century. Special programs such as English as a Second Language (ESL) served only adults. The assumption was that children learn languages easily and nothing special needed to be done. Most students were merely put back a grade or two and often retained until they knew enough English to manage. Teachers punished students who conversed in languages other than English (Cummins, 1981; Ovando, 1994). This imposition of English created educational difficulties for speakers of other languages in the public schools retarding academic progress. A 1911 survey of 30 U.S. cities found that 28% of American-born students and 27% of foreign-born English speakers were behind grade level but 43% of foreign-born non-English speakers were behind grade level. When broken down by nationality, 51% of German students, 59.9% of Russian Jews, and 76.7% of Italians were behind with respect to age and grade level (Cohen, 1970). Some of those foreign-born students thrived in English-only programs. Henry Kissinger, although he never lost his ethnic accent, is a latter day example. But for many others, the educational "cost" of monolingual instruction in English was very high dropout rates. A 1908 survey of students who reached high school in five major cities illustrates the situation of the children of immigrants whose home language was not English. When compared with children of White English speakers they fared rather poorly. In Boston, nearly 70% of White students overall reached high school, whereas only 38% of the students whose home language was not English achieved that goal. In Chicago the rates were 42% and 18%, in New York 32% and 13%, in Philadelphia 27% and 13%, and in St. Louis 27% for Whites and 10% for speakers of other languages. African American students were not included in these surveys (Pearlman, 1990). Thus when the instruction was all in English, less than half as many students whose home language was not English entered high school when compared with White English speakers.

Despite the lack of public support for bilingual education, there were bilingual programs—mostly dual language programs—in private and parochial schools. These schools extended the required curriculum to include instruction in the cultural, linguistic, and religious heritages of the particular ethnic group. A great number of them were bilingual (Fishman, 1966; Fishman & Markman, 1979).

Massive school failure of students of Spanish-speaking background in the public schools reported in a study of five Southwestern states (U.S. Commission on Civil Rights, 1971b) attested to the failure of "sink or swim" strategies. In isolated communities in Arizona, California, Florida, New Mexico, Texas, and New Jersey, educators and parents created bilingual education programs to improve the education of their children (Brisk, 1981a). Programs such as the Coral Way school in Miami (Mackey & Beebe, 1977), Rock Point in Arizona (Holm & Holm, 1990), the Nye school in Texas (Andersson & Boyer, 1978), P.S. 25 in New York City (Von Maltitz, 1975) and Calexico, California (Andersson & Boyer, 1970) were initiated in the early 1960s. These programs used English and the native language of the students in all grades for language and content area instruction. In most cases these programs included English speakers, and the programs were hailed as examples of educational excellence. Several of them still exist.

National interest in bilingual education spread when Title VII, the Bilingual Education Act (an amendment to the Elementary and Secondary Education Act) was enacted in 1968. This federal legislation provided funds to create bilingual programs in poor school districts. These programs promoted the use of the students' mother tongue to initiate instruction, whereas English was taught as a second language, and later introduced in instruction. The original bill stated as one of its goals the maintenance of bilingualism for students who already knew another language. The legislation that was enacted replaced that goal with another one, making students proficient in English only. The home language was there to facilitate the acquisition of English, but its maintenance was not to be encouraged (Lyons, 1990).

The impact of the federal law, both good and bad, was widely felt. A number of states reversed the laws that permitted English as the only language of instruction by passing bilingual education legislation. Massachusetts was the first state to enact such a law with its Transitional Bilingual Education Act (1971). More than 20 other states followed Massachusetts' example by creating transitional bilingual education programs (August & García, 1988). These programs differed from those that had begun to emerge in the early 1960s in that the native language of the students was only used as a bridge until they knew enough English to be transferred to the mainstream. Bilingual education then became an educational strategy to address the English language needs of the students rather than a full program of instruction in which the native language and English have equal status.

Court cases, some related to desegregation, helped defend the rights of bilingual students to education in their native languages (Brisk, 1978; Center for Law and Education, 1975; Rossell & Ross, 1986; Teitelbaum & Hiller, 1977). Parents sued school districts to force them to provide for bilingual students. In one of these cases, *Lau v. Nichols,* decided by the Supreme Court in 1974, Justice Douglas held that "there is no equality of treatment merely by providing students with the same facilities, textbooks, teachers, and curriculum; for students who do not understand English are effectively foreclosed from any meaningful education" (p. 566).

The suit was initiated in 1971 by 1,800 Chinese students who charged the San Francisco Unified School District with failing to provide programs to meet their linguistic needs. The Court supported the students but did not recommend a specific remedy. Instead the Court ordered the school district "to apply its expertise to the problem and rectify the situation" (*Lau v. Nichols,* 1974, p. 565). The Office of Civil Rights published in 1975 the *Lau Remedies,* a set of guidelines for school districts with language minority students (U.S. Department of Health, Education and Welfare, 1975). The *Lau Remedies* contained instructions for identification, assessment, and mainstreaming of students. It suggested program options and standards for teacher preparation. The *Lau Remedies* recommended bilingual education as the best approach for elementary education, suggesting a number of approaches for the high school level. To reinforce the impact of the *Lau Remedies* the Federal Government published regulations popularly know as the Lau Regulations (HEW, 1975). Unlike *Lau v. Nichols,* other court cases actually mandated bilingual education (*ASPIRA v. Board of Education of the City of New York,* 1974; *Ríos v. Read,* 1977; *Serna v. Portales Municipal Schools,* 1972; *United States v. Texas,* 1971).

Bilingual communities both defensibly and opportunistically entered desegregation suits as secondary parties to defend the needs of bilingual students in desegregation plans. Bilingual students need to be present in critical masses in order to receive instruction in their native language. However, desegregation plans tend to spread students around and bilinguals in many cases might be classified as "White" or "non-White" depending on the school system's need for racial diversity. In a number of key cases the courts required bilingual education to be part of the overall desegregation plan: *Keyes v. Denver School District No. 1* (1973) in Denver, *Morgan v. Kerrigan* (1975) in Boston, *Bradley v. Milliken* (1975) in Detroit, and *Evans v. Buchanan* (1976) in Wilmington, Delaware.

The spread of bilingual education permitted opportunities to evaluate the results of bilingualism. Peal and Lambert's (1962) landmark study demonstrated the cognitive advantages of full bilingualism. Other research expanding on the benefits of high proficiency in two languages lent further support to bilingualism (Ben-Zeev, 1977; Ianco-Worrall, 1972). These studies demonstrated that bilinguals had higher scores in verbal and nonverbal IQ tests and displayed higher verbal and cognitive flexibility and increased ability to analyze syntax than monolingual students of the same age and general intelligence level (Segalowitz, 1977). These studies demonstrated rather convincingly that having to learn and differentiate between two languages can be an educational and linguistic advantage and not an impediment as had been claimed in earlier research.

Mostly English-speaking students benefited from the results of this research on the advantages of bilingualism. Canadian Immersion and two-way bilingual education programs that included English speakers promoted acquisition and development of English and another language. On the other hand, programs exclusively for language minority students emphasized English language acquisition. Home languages were used only as a tool until sufficient proficiency in English was achieved. The criteria for effectiveness of bilingual programs for English speakers included English and second language proficiency as well as academic and intellectual achievement. In contrast, evaluations of bilingual education programs for language minority students focused on English reading, and some also on math achievement (deJong, 1993). Little attention was paid to either overall academic performance—in any language—or the quality of the education afforded to these students. Success of a bilingual education program was simply measured by how fast students learned English or, worse, how quickly they "graduated" to English-only classrooms.

In the 1980s, opposition toward use of languages other than English in education and other services for language minority students swept the country. Criticism extended even to transitional programs that use the native language temporarily and only for the purpose of developing English. The xenophobic intolerance to other languages was partly a reaction to mounting immigration. The National Immigration Act of 1965 rapidly expanded immigration, especially from Asia and Latin America:

> In 1990, the foreign-born population of the United States reached an estimated 21.2 million. In absolute terms, this is the highest number in the history of the nation ever, although relative to the native-born population the figure is lower than that at the turn of the century. [In the 1890s], immigrants represented 14.8 percent of the total population or almost double today's figure of 8.6 percent. (Portes & Zhou, 1993, p. 77)

This new wave of immigration was felt in the school systems throughout the country. Although the student population in Grades K through 12 increased by only 4.5% between the years 1985 and 1991, the enrollment of bilingual students increased by 51.3% during the same period (Olsen, 1993).

A national organization, U.S. English, was founded in 1983 to defend against the perceived threats to the English language produced by massive immigration. U.S. English led the national effort at the federal and state level to pass legislation making English the country's official language. Although the organization did not succeed in amending the federal Constitution, several states passed such legislation. For example, California's bilingual education law was not reauthorized after voters passed Proposition 63, which made English the official language of the state (Crawford, 1989). Support for English was perceived as a license to attack other languages not only in schools but in the workplace, the streets, and other public places (Crawford, 1992). Despite the hysterical view of U.S. English, the demise of English is purely fictitious. Nearly 95% of the population in the United States speaks English, and 85% are native speakers (Fishman, 1988). Most immigrants shift to English within one generation. Spanish speakers, who are perceived as the least likely to switch to English, still do so within two generations (Veltman, 1983).

Not surprisingly, the federal bureaucrats joined the opposition during the Reagan years. U.S. Secretary of Education Terrel H. Bell withdrew the Lau Regulations and even the Lau Remedies. The Office of Civil Rights relaxed its monitoring of school districts to assess their compliance with *Lau v. Nichols* (San Miguel, 1988). The reauthorization of Title VII in 1984 included program options that did not require the native language. In 1984, 4% of the funds could be used for English-only models, and in 1988 this level was raised to 25%. Secretary of Education William Bennett adamantly opposed bilingual education (Fitzgerald, 1993) despite a government report that reiterated the value of such programs (U.S. General Accounting Office, 1987). These efforts greatly weakened the implementation of bilingual education programs and created divisions where harmony once existed among ethnic and English-speaking communities. Even in Florida, antagonism between Cuban and Jewish populations, which in the 1960s had joined to create one of the model bilingual schools in Coral Way, threatened the program (Crawford, 1992). Many bilingual religious schools, once the mainstay in ethnic language maintenance, were converted to monolingual schools, especially in large urban centers, where the largest numbers of language minority students live (Fishman, 1966).

Court decisions reflected this erosion of support for bilingual education as a solution. Instead, in *Castañeda v. Pickard* (1981), the Court imposed a broad framework based on three criteria: programs must be based on educational theory (any theory adequately supported by some experts), appropriate implementation of this theory, and evaluation of programs. This framework has been used in several cases since. In *Teresa P. v. Berkeley Unified School District* (1989) for example, the Court accepted programs that use only English as valid alternatives because they were supported by the theory accepted as sound by the Court.[1] In *Castañeda v. Pickard,* the Court decided that emphasis on English language ability over curriculum taught in the native language did not violate appropriate implementation. Bilingual education, an appropriate remedy for the 1970s, was no longer found appropriate in the 1980s, even if the circumstances were comparable. The *Lau* decision claimed that only educators could recommend specific remedies. History, however, has shown that educational decisions are ruled by sociopolitical moods.

Bilingual education is being viciously criticized as the cause for immigrant children not being able to learn English, but ESL and structured immersion are hailed as models for educating language minority students (Porter, 1990; Rossell, 1990). These programs are systematically promoted through legislation and litigation (Fitzgerald, 1993). Despite opposition, advocates for language minority students advance their agenda through research and legislation. Willig's (1985) meta-analysis of bilingual education studies pointed at the effectiveness of bilingual education as measured by tests in English of reading, language skills, mathematics, and total achievement and tests in other languages of reading, language, mathematics, writing, social studies, listening comprehension, and attitudes toward self and school. The research by Ramírez and his colleagues—which was silenced for a while by the Reagan administration—con-

---

[1]The expert who testified against the plaintiffs in the *Teresa P. v. Berkeley* case was neither a linguist nor an educator. She admitted ignorance with respect to issues of language and second language acquisition and acknowledged that she had visited only one Berkeley classroom for 3 minutes. Yet her opinion with respect to the adequacy of English-only programs to educate language minority students was accepted.

trasted bilingual education programs with programs that use mostly or only English. In all of the programs the students learned English and made steady progress. Students who remained in bilingual education programs through sixth grade, however, progressed faster after fourth grade, reaching or surpassing national norms in English and math tests, whereas those in the other programs continued to test below the national norm (Ramirez, 1992).

The reauthorization of Title VII in 1994 continued federal support for bilingual programs. Bilingual students are also taught in their native languages through Title I programs, designed to improve academic achievement among poor children (Lyons, 1994). Inspired by the effective school movement, bilingual educators are identifying successful programs and analyzing all their features in an effort to understand in a more global way what program characteristics allow language minority students to succeed in school (Mace-Matluck, 1990).

Paradoxically, opponents of bilingual education for language minority students do not oppose programs for English speakers. These programs are regarded as crucial in educating students for a global economy. Bilingual education programs that include English speakers proliferated throughout the country, many supported by Title VII funds (Christian, 1994). As Title VII weakened its support for bilingual programs for language minorities, it funded developmental or two-way programs that included English speakers. Unlike the models exclusively for language minority students, these programs have as a goal fluency in two languages. Even general educational policy evinces the importance of bilingualism for educated English-speaking students. The most prominent legislation of the 1990s includes as an objective that "[t]he percentage of all students who are competent in more than one language will substantially increase" (National Education Goals Panel, 1994, p. 9). Arizona, New York, North Carolina, and Massachusetts have enacted laws mandating foreign language education programs or proficiency in a foreign language as a requirement for graduation (Massachusetts General Laws, Ch. 71, 1993; Met & Galloway, 1992).

During the past two centuries, use of languages in education has been increasingly politicized. History has repeated itself but in modified ways. The acceptance of languages in education observed in the early part of the 19th century was apparent again in the 1970s but languages other than English appeared in schools with a much lower status with respect to English than they had a century earlier. The imposition of English only at the turn of the century reappeared in the 1980s, although this time some minority students were served by special English language programs rather than leaving all to sink or swim.

Efforts to make English speakers fluent in other languages have also seen ups and downs. Suspicion toward foreigners in the early part of the century discouraged second language learning. Interest in foreign language learning following World War II wavered in the 1970s. The pendulum is swinging again in favor of bilingualism for English speakers. Foreign language programs are starting earlier in elementary schools and bilingual education programs that promote bilingualism are becoming increasingly popular (Met & Galloway, 1992).

Current xenophobia is quite complex. It rejects the use of languages other than English by those who speak them as their home language, but not by English speakers. Some legislation eliminates the use of ethnic languages in education and other legislation mandates foreign languages. To a great extent these are one and the same, because Spanish is the most widely taught foreign language according to Met and Galloway (1992), and Spanish speakers are the largest ethnic group in the country. In other words, English speakers are encouraged to learn Spanish and Spanish speakers are forced to forget it.

DEFINING BILINGUAL EDUCATION

Underlying the lack of communication in discourse on bilingual education are different perceptions of bilingual education. Bilingual education broadly defined is any "educational program that involves the use of two languages of instruction at some point in a student's school career" (Nieto, 1992, p. 156). This simple definition is not what most people have in mind when they think of bilingual education. Many people in the United States, especially its critics, think that bilingual education is giving "instruction in the native language most of the school day for several years" (Porter, 1994, p. 44). Some proponents define bilingual education as "dual language programs" that "consist of instruction in two languages equally distributed across the school day" (Casanova & Arias, 1993, p. 17).

Schooling generally defined as bilingual education actually comprises a variety of approaches. Some programs have as a goal bilingualism, whereas others seek development of proficiency in English only. Programs are designed to serve different types of students: English speakers, international sojourners, or language minority students. Some models integrate these students. Models vary in how much and for how many years they use each language for instruction. The initial language of literacy and content instruction varies across models. Some use mostly the native language initially, others deliver instruction in both, and still others commence instruction in the second language, adding the home language after a few years.

There are special programs for language minority students in which all the teaching is done in English with a second language approach. The distinction between bilingual education and English-only instruction models is important. Bilingual education assumes use of English and another language for instruction. Submersion, structured immersion, and ESL models work with bilingual learners but are not bilingual because they rely on only one language—English—for instruction. Some educators would object to some of the models I have included in the bilingual education list (see Table 1.1): "Programs that do not provide significant amounts of instruction in the non-English language should not, in fact, be included under the rubric of bilingual education" (Milk, 1993, p. 102). I have included within bilingual education all models that use two languages for instruction regardless of the amount of native language instruction, but I have not included those that only use English even if they serve bilingual students.

BILINGUAL EDUCATION MODELS

Bilingual education models are described broadly according to their goals, type of students served, languages in which literacy is developed, and languages of subject matter instruction. Bilingual education models are divided between those that have as a major goal fluency in two languages and those that strive for fluency in the second language, English. The first type has no limitations in the number of years a student can attend and it can include a program within a school or the whole school is bilingual. Dual language schools, Canadian immersion education, two-way bilingual education, two-way immersion education, and maintenance bilingual education are included in this category. The second type, which includes transitional bilingual education, submersion with native language and ESL support, bilingual immersion, and integrated bilingual education, shares the goal of preparing students to function in monolingual classes. Therefore students attend such programs for a limited number of years. Integrated bilingual education also mainstreams students. Because mainstreaming takes place unbeknownst to students within an integrated cluster, there is no stigma attached to bilingual education or use of home languages. Students continue to use their native language even after reaching proficiency in English, and English speakers learn to respect different languages and cultures (Brisk, 1991c, 1994b).

Dual Language Schools

In dual language schools, also called mainstream bilingual education (Baker, 1993), the curriculum is delivered in two languages, conventionally half of the day in one language and half in the other. A full range of courses is offered. The particular language of instruction for each discipline may vary. These schools tend to be private (Mackey, 1972), often attracting international sojourners as well as children whose parents want them to become bilingual. These schools can include native speakers of both languages, native speakers of English only, or native speakers of other languages. Dual language schools differ from the two-way programs in that they are not purposely created to serve language minority students, although some language minority students may take advantage of them. L'Ecole Bilingue in Arlington, Massachusetts attracts European speakers of French and native English-speaking Americans. From kindergarten through Grade 6, teaching time is equally divided between English and French. Two teachers are assigned to each grade, each teaching in one language. ESL is offered to students who enter the school after kindergarten and need help catching up with English. Most English speakers start at the preschool level, which is completely in French. The French curriculum follows strict requirements as in France, whereas the English curriculum has the flexible characteristic of a U.S. school (Coady, 1994).

Some dual language schools serve English-speaking students only. Over 1,500 all-day schools, many with religious affiliations, representing over 20 different languages, are located throughout the country. The English curriculum is comparable to any U.S. school. The ethnic language curriculum usually includes language, culture, and religion. Two thirds of these schools teach in Hebrew or Pennsylvania German (Fishman, Gertner, Lowy, & Milán, 1985).

Throughout the world, dual language schools were created to serve the children of the international community whose parents work in international organizations, embassies, and businesses. These schools serve students who come from different language backgrounds. They usually instruct in two languages and often offer tutoring in the native language of the students. For example, the United Nations International School in New York City serves the children of United Nations delegates, other international students, and English-speaking U.S. students. The languages of instruction are English and French.

Canadian Immersion Education[2]

In the 1960s a movement developed in Canadian public schools to make English speakers fluent in French. A group of parents and linguists frustrated with the poor results of French foreign language education looked for an alternate approach to teaching French. This new approach immerses the students in the second language for the first 2 years of school. Language, reading, and all subjects are taught in French. Beginning in the third year, English—the native language of the students—is introduced for a small portion of the day. With each grade the amount of English instruction increases until in the upper grades (7–12) most of the instruction is in English and French is only in a few courses. Because all the students are English speakers, teachers use second language strategies when teaching in French to facilitate comprehension and learning (Lambert & Tucker, 1972).

A late immersion variation introduces intensive instruction in French in the fifth, sixth, or seventh grade. For 1 or 2 years all subjects are taught in French except for English language arts. Before being totally immersed in French, students study French as a second language for 2 or more years. Following the French immersion years, students continue to receive French language and another subject in French. Double immersion programs are yet another variation of the initial model. It is called *double immersion* because students receive instruction in two second languages, French and Hebrew, through second grade. The French curriculum includes language arts, science, mathematics, and social studies. The Hebrew curriculum includes language arts, history, and religious and cultural studies. English is gradually introduced beginning in either third or fourth grade (Genesee, 1984).

Canadian immersion education, especially the early immersion variation, has been replicated for English-speaking students in the United States using French,

---

[2]This model was originally called *immersion education.* To avoid confusion with other models also called *immersion,* I have chosen to call it Canadian immersion whether it is implemented in Canada or the United States. Canadian programs are solely in French, but this is not so in the United States.

Spanish, or German as the immersion language (Campbell, 1984; Cohen, 1976). Careful evaluations have found immersion education to achieve high fluency in a second language for speakers of English. Students score at or above the norm of English speakers who have attended monolingual English schools in tests of reading, mathematics, and intelligence (Cohen, 1976; Genesee, 1987; Lambert & Tucker, 1972; Swain & Barik, 1976).

Two-Way Bilingual Education

Two-way programs (also called developmental programs or dual language programs) are similar to dual language programs, except that they were established to serve simultaneously children of language minorities and English speakers. Their goal is to develop fluency in two languages for both sets of students and, also, to instill respect for each other and for their cultural backgrounds. The advantage of these programs over Canadian immersion is that students learn languages and acquire positive attitudes toward cultures not only from instruction but from each other, because in two-way programs there are native speakers of both languages studying together. Programs vary in the amount each language is used, the subjects taught in each language, and the distribution of language use within the day (Lindholm, 1990; Massachusetts State Department of Education, 1990). The majority of such programs in the United States are in Spanish and English, but programs also exist in Cantonese, Korean, Navajo, Japanese, Russian, Portuguese, and French (Christian, 1994). Most two-way programs are in elementary schools, many started in the 1960s in response to the needs of language minority students. For example, the Coral Way School in Miami created in 1963 pioneered this approach for Spanish- and English-speaking students. For the first three grades, all students receive instruction either in the native language or in the second language in groups segregated by native language. Groups are mixed for physical education, art, music, and lunch. At these times both languages are used and allowed. After third grade about half of the day is spent in mixed groups, where instruction in all subjects is done in English for 3 weeks and in Spanish for 3 weeks. Spanish- and English-speaking teachers meet daily to plan together (Mackey & Beebe, 1977).

The Amigos program in Cambridge, Massachusetts has consistently divided instruction equally between English and Spanish, but since it was initiated in 1986, the timing of language use has evolved. At first, Amigos adopted the traditional approach of splitting each school day between the two languages. Later, it devoted alternate days to one language and then the other. More recently, students in this program spend 3 to 5 consecutive days in each language. The advantages of such an arrangement are that students do not have to constantly switch languages and it gives more time to teachers to complete units (Cazabon, Lambert, & Hall, 1993). Other bilingual programs experiment with a variety of structures, depending on students' and teachers' language ability, resources, and parental pressures (Christian, 1994; Mackey & Beebe, 1977; Massachusetts State Department of Education, 1990).

Two-Way Bilingual Immersion

Two-way bilingual immersion programs drawing on the Canadian immersion and the two-way models were designed to serve English-speaking and language minority students simultaneously. Initial instruction is done in the language of the minority students with minimal or no English language instruction. Instruction in English is increased with each grade but both languages are used for a number of years. Thus language minority students begin with immersion in their native language, whereas for English speakers, as in the case of Canadian immersion, the immersion is in the second language. In a San Diego school, two-way immersion program students are instructed in Spanish in all subject areas from first through third grade. They also have English language arts classes. From fourth through sixth grade Spanish instruction is divided equally with English (Krashen & Biber, 1988; Lindholm & Aclan, 1991).

Maintenance Bilingual Education

Maintenance programs also called developmental serve exclusively language minority students but compare in many other ways to dual language and two-way programs. Maintenance programs seek to develop and maintain the native language of the students and develop a positive attitude toward the native culture while also achieving proficiency in English. Literacy and subject matter instruction in both the native language and in English are vital to achieving these goals. The specific courses taught in each language vary over the grades and across programs. For example, Rough Rock School in Arizona uses Navajo and English as the languages of instruction. Students learn to read first in Navajo. Mathematics and all other subjects are taught in both Navajo and English through second grade. In third to sixth grade, students not only study Arizona's required curriculum in English but also take courses in literacy, social studies, and science taught in Navajo. In junior high school, a year-long science course in Navajo is required. Navajo History, Navajo Social Problems, Navajo Government, and Navajo Economic Development prepare senior high school students for leadership in their community. In Rough Rock High School, students take a Navajo Research course that requires an original research project (Holm & Holm, 1990).

Also in Arizona, Spanish elementary maintenance programs use the native language for initial literacy. Mathematics and other subjects are taught in Spanish and English. Some programs may offer mathematics in English and social studies in Spanish, whereas others alternate the languages within each subject by day, week, or unit. Art, music, and physical education are taught in Spanish, English, or both depending on the language ability of the personnel (Medina & Escamilla, 1992b).

In a longitudinal study Ramirez (1992) defined such programs as "late-exit transitional bilingual education" (p. 3). Because these programs required students to take at least 40% of their instruction in Spanish through sixth grade regardless fluency in English, this description adheres more to the maintenance model than to the traditional transitional model (described later) in which English instruction is continuously increased and students are exited as soon as they are fluent in English.

The process of desegregation has, in most areas of the United States, made it virtually impossible to sustain maintenance bilingual schools. To do so would require, in effect, segregating a school by ethnic group. José Cárdenas' plan in Denver's desegregation case observed that Mexican American children had problems because schools were an alien environment whether integrated or segregated. He proposed two maintenance bilingual schools for Chicano students but only one pilot project with a large number of—but not solely—Mexican American students was allowed (*Keyes v. Denver School District No. 1,* 1973). The Rafael Hernández School, a Spanish maintenance bilingual school with 98% Hispanic students, was dismantled during Boston's desegregation suit (*Morgan v. Kerrigan,* 1975). The school was ordered to admit Black and White students. To satisfy both the desegregation requirements and the pressure from the Hispanic community to keep the bilingual nature of the school, the Rafael Hernández School was transformed into a two-way school (Brisk, 1978).

Transitional Bilingual Education

In transitional bilingual education (TBE) the native language of language minority students is used while the students are learning English. Once students are proficient in English, they are transferred to the mainstream. The goal of these programs is to develop English skills without sacrificing or delaying learning of content courses. Gradually students take more subjects in English until they can be totally mainstreamed. Literacy in the native language serves as a foundation for English reading and writing. Although TBE programs are supposed to be a "full-time program of instruction" (Transitional Bilingual Education, 1971, p. 270), most emphasize language development. TBE programs vary with respect to the amount of native language instruction, the courses offered, and how soon students are mainstreamed. In early-exit TBE programs evaluated by Ramirez (1992), students received only literacy instruction in the native language and the rest of the subjects were in English. At the end of first or second grade most students were mainstreamed. In Massachusetts by law, all bilingual students with limited English proficiency can participate in transitional programs, yet among school systems and even within schools, substantial differences abound with respect to language distribution and exiting of students. Some programs use native language for literacy, math, social studies, and science. Students start learning English in ESL classes. As they become more proficient in English, teachers start using English in the content areas. Other programs teach subjects bilingually, using mostly English texts as the teacher explains concepts in the students' home language and in English. Yet others team English-speaking teachers with native language instructors to cover the curriculum in both languages. The variation depends on specific language, availability of materials and certified teachers, and parental pressures (Brisk, 1990, 1991b; Brisk, David, Martínez, Rodriguez, & Solá, 1982).

Transition to the mainstream in Massachusetts varies from student to student although most students are mainstreamed within 3 years. Some students attend the program for only 1 year, but others remain longer than the 3 years prescribed by law. Readiness, school transfer, and parental and students' wishes determine when students are mainstreamed (Brisk, 1994a). Bilingual students take nonacademic subjects such as art, music, and physical education with mainstream teachers in English. In some schools bilingual students are integrated with the English-speaking students. In elementary schools, because classrooms are self-contained, TBE students tend to be more segregated, working mostly with bilingual and ESL teachers for instruction in the native language and in English. Team teaching allows teachers who are native speakers of English to teach mainly in English, whereas native speakers of the language of the children teach literacy and subjects in that language. Once fluent in English, students are mainstreamed with little or no support from the bilingual program. At the middle school and high school levels, there is more flexibility. Students enroll in bilingual and mainstream courses depending on their level of language proficiency. In South Boston High School, the headmaster hired bilingual teachers for the mainstream program. Bilingual students could take courses in the mainstream program regardless of language ability because the teachers taught bilingually (Brisk et al., 1982).

TBE programs are mostly the result of legislative compromise that requires mainstreaming when English language proficiency is considered adequate to pursue studies in English. Because success of TBE is perceived by the speed at which students are mainstreamed, there is a lot of pressure to exit students. When the goal is mainstreaming rather than learning, teachers, students, administrators, and even parents focus on English language acquisition, often at the expense of content-area learning. A recent survey on parental attitudes toward TBE showed parents support TBE but for two different reasons. Some feel it is the only way their children will learn English, and others want their children to remain bilingual to be able to continue family communication and to take advantage of job opportunities (Stergis, 1995).

Submersion With Native Language and ESL Support

A modified version of TBE for schools with few students in each grade level places students in the mainstream classroom and pulls them out daily for native language and ESL instruction. The purpose is mainly to help students with their work in the mainstream classes. The bilingual teacher tutors small groups of students from the same grade level by reviewing in their home language particular lessons covered in their mainstream classes. The same bilingual teacher or an ESL teacher may reinforce English language and literacy development using the native language. Bilingual teachers occasionally assist bilingual students after they develop full fluency in English. Bilingual teachers also assist the mainstream teachers in communication with the families. The actual implementation of these programs varies depending on the number of students and availability of teachers (Brisk, 1991b).

A school in metropolitan Boston has 65 Japanese students from kindergarten through eighth grade assigned to mainstream classes according to grade level. A Japanese-speaking teacher and two English-speaking aides who know some Japanese help the students in three ways. For the younger students, one of the instructors spends time with them in their mainstream classes. Older students drop in for tutoring and assistance with homework. Newcomers are pulled out daily for tutoring in English and other subjects. Sometimes students do their assignments in Japanese, which the staff helps them translate. The bilingual staff works closely with the mainstream teachers and the students' families (Brisk, 1991b).

Bilingual Immersion Education

Bilingual immersion programs place students of the same language background in segregated classes. Most of the instruction is in English except for the first hour of the day, when teachers teach native language literacy and explain concepts in the students' language. Classes in English focus on those concepts already introduced through the native language (Gersten, Woodward, & Schneider, 1992). Unlike the Canadian immersion model, this is a transitional program. Students remain in it for between 2 to 4 years before transferring to mainstream classes. In McAllen, Texas students started the program in kindergarten (Baker & de Kanter, 1981), whereas in El Paso they entered in first grade after attending kindergarten in Spanish with some ESL instruction (Schneider, 1990). Teachers are bilingual and allow students to use their native language even when they are instructed in English. The teachers also receive training in second language methodology and teaching content in a second language. In McAllen, kindergarten students in the bilingual immersion program performed better in tests of English reading than those in TBE. Schneider (1990) compared students in Grades 1 through 5 in bilingual immersion with TBE students in tests of math, reading, and language arts. The results were mixed except for language arts, where bilingual immersion students scored slightly better than TBE students. All students obtained comparable grades once mainstreamed into English-only classes.

Integrated Bilingual Education

The inherent segregation of TBE programs has prompted the development of integration strategies to bring TBE and mainstream classes together. Integration of students with different language backgrounds varies with respect to organization, relative use of different languages, and the role of the bilingual teacher. Integrated bilingual programs preserve instruction in the native languages and allow native language use when students are in the mainstream classroom (Brisk, 1991c, 1994b).

Although the overall goals of these programs are similar to TBE, they also aim to integrate bilingual students with mainstream students by increasing academic and social contact, expose English-speaking students to other languages and cultures, support bilingual students who have already been mainstreamed, and sensitize mainstream teachers to the educational needs of bilingual students.

In many schools bilingual students and their teachers occasionally attend mainstream classrooms where instruction is exclusively in English. While the mainstream teacher conducts the class, the bilingual teacher helps bilingual students to comprehend and participate. Such a practice, which schools claim is integration, resembles submersion with native language support more than it does bilingual integration because the teachers and their classes do not have equal status and the native language of the bilingual students is not for general classroom instruction. Such deviations from the true integration model have been opposed by bilingual education advocates as excusing forfeiture of native languages.

For integration to be truly bilingual teaching is done in both the native language of the bilingual students and in English. Mainstream and bilingual teachers and students equally share their classrooms. A fifth-grade integrated cluster developed in Chelsea, Massachusetts brought bilingual, mainstream, and chapter 1 teachers together with their 50 students (Brisk, 1991a). Together these teachers developed the curriculum, assigned responsibilities, planned individual student assignments, dealt with student problems, and communicated with parents. The bilingual teacher taught in Spanish or bilingually. The other two teachers taught in English but allowed use of other languages in their classroom. Bilingual students often helped when there were communication difficulties.

There are many ways to implement bilingual integration depending on the number of classes involved, grade level, extent of the integration, and degree to which English speakers develop a second language. In several elementary schools in Springfield, Massachusetts bilingual and monolingual teachers team teach. Bilingual students receive instruction in both languages. In other districts three or more bilingual and mainstream classes of the same grade level work together. Some clusters integrate around a specific discipline or meet together just once a week. English speakers acquire the second language from contact with bilinguals or from some systematic teaching (Brisk, 1994b).

Integration programs at the secondary level are easier to schedule because students regularly travel from one classroom to another. It is harder, however, for mainstream teachers because the content of their classes is more difficult to understand for bilingual students (Brisk, 1994b; Faltis, 1994). June, a mainstream social studies teacher, developed strategies and used assistance to help her communicate with her students and facilitate their learning. She secured materials in Spanish for her classes, prepared bilingual lists with the basic vocabulary that she presented at the start of the class, and read aloud difficult material and tests in English. The bilingual aide and bilingual college student volunteers assisted June during small group discussions (Brisk, 1991c).

ENGLISH-ONLY INSTRUCTION MODELS

"[Fifty]% of all students who have been labeled limited-English-proficient are in classrooms where no special services are provided for them (not even a minimal pull-out ESL)" (Escamilla, 1994a, p. 3). They attend school with English-speaking peers in what has been characterized as sink-or-swim or submersion education. Teachers in such classrooms rarely have any special preparation for teaching bilinguals (Macías, 1994; Waggoner & O'Malley, 1985). Other schools, although they do not offer any instruction in the native language, provide some kind of specialized English language program. These programs can be full-time, part-time, or simply pull-out classes where students are temporarily taken from their home-rooms for special instruction. The students can be from the same language group or from a variety of language groups working together. The most common English-only instruction programs are ESL and structured immersion.

ESL

ESL provides special classes in the English language for students who are not proficient in the language. Students spend most of the school day in mainstream classrooms but attend daily ESL classes. In some cases students are pulled out from their classes to take ESL with a special teacher. In others, labeled *pull-in ESL,* ESL instructors assist mainstream teachers in their classrooms with students who are not proficient in English. One program for bilinguals devoted half of the school day to ESL learning language and subject content and the other half to mainstream homerooms (Flanagan, 1984). In high school, ESL is usually offered as a subject. Classes are offered at various levels of English language proficiency. Typically students attend beginning, intermediate, or advanced ESL classes.

Another type of ESL program is called high-intensity language training (HILT). Students concentrate on English for a particular period, which may last a summer, a semester, or even a year studying only English with other language minority students before they are integrated into the school. I visited such a program in California that served over 500 students in Grade 4 through high school. The program was housed in its own school building and the students attended English language classes all day. They took separate courses in oral language, reading, and writing. Most students were transferred to a regular school within 1 year. By focusing solely on English language rather than academic content and without English-speaking peers to practice the newly learned language in informal situations, students in such programs had no occasion to naturally practice the language or acquire the language they needed for school.

Typically ESL classes concentrated on teaching English from purely an oral language perspective. Under the influence of the general modern language field, the need for proficiency in a second language for everyday interaction transformed some ESL curricula. The type of second language that English speakers need when they go abroad is not the same as what students who do not speak English need when attending school in the United States. Practitioners have realized that students need English to function socially as well as academically, thus oral practice is not enough for an ESL curriculum. Well-educated students must be able to understand content area texts; write reports, book reviews, and essays; and interact in class around mathematics, science, social studies, and literature. Present emphasis is on literacy as well as language through content area. This latter form, known as *content-based ESL,* adheres to the notion that language can be learned while learning something else (Crandall, 1987). This new trend of teaching English through content affects student groupings. Traditionally, regardless of grade level, students were assigned to beginning, intermediate, or advanced classes. Although easier for the purpose of teaching language, grouping by proficiency poses a problem for academic content courses. It is difficult to organize the ESL curriculum around grade-appropriate content instruction if several grade levels are included in a class. Grouping of students for ESL instruction by grade level also facilitates coordination with homeroom teachers at the elementary level and content teachers at the secondary level.

Structured Immersion

Structured immersion stands for two different kinds of programs. The most common type places language minority students of the same language group in segregated classrooms for instruction in English. Content area courses are taught using the sheltered English approach. Teachers simplify language, develop highly structured lessons, and use nonlinguistic support, such as pictures, objects, films, and hands-on activities to present lessons (Northcutt & Watson, 1986). The teachers are supposed to have training in ESL and sheltered English techniques. A second type of structured immersion shares all characteristics with the first but teachers have some knowledge of the students' home language so that they can understand students and occasionally use the students' home language for clarification (Ramirez, 1992).

Much confusion surrounds structured immersion. Proponents of structured immersion include this model as one of the options of bilingual education when in effect it reimposes sink-or-swim methods in language-segregated classrooms. Added confusion comes from the so-called supporting research. Advocates of structured immersion misuse the results of research on Canadian immersion education as proof that structured immersion works (Gersten, 1985; Rossell & Ross, 1986). Because Canadian immersion and structured immersion are two different models, it is ludicrous to use the success of Canadian immersion to prove the potential effectiveness of structured immersion. More credible are the results of Ramirez (1992), who evaluated structured immersion programs of the second type as compared with early-exit and late-exit TBE. Students in structured immersion programs scored on English reading and math tests at comparable levels to students in early-exit TBE, but were actually outperformed on standard English tests by students who had studied in late-exit TBE.

Added confusion comes when the results of bilingual immersion programs are used to support the claim that students will learn English faster than in TBE programs. In the first place, the results of bilingual immersion are mixed. Bilingual immersion students do better than TBE students in language arts but not in reading (Schneider, 1990). Second, bilingual immersion develops literacy in the native language, a fact that supporters of bilingual education have always maintained helps English language learning. Structured immersion does not develop literacy in the native language, so there is no guarantee that the results on English tests will be comparable.

These three models—Canadian immersion, bilingual immersion, and structured immersion—only share the term *immersion* and the approach to teaching in the second language. Supporters of structured immersion who use the results of evaluations on the other two models to convince policymakers of the virtues of structured immersion are being devious and doing a real disservice to language minority students. Fifty years of instruction in only English have already demonstrated the devastating effects of such policy on the educational success of considerable numbers of students.

COMPARISON OF MODELS

Models share characteristics across three criteria: linguistic goal, target population, and language distribution in literacy and subject matter instruction (see Table 1.1).

ESL, structured immersion, TBE, submersion with native language and ESL support, and bilingual immersion education share the goal of making students proficient in English as quickly as possible so that they can eventually be educated in the mainstream. Such programs are *subtractive* because the development of the second language is done at the expense of the native language. Dual language, two-way, two-way immersion, Canadian immersion, and maintenance bilingual education programs aim at full education with development of a second language in order to function academically. In other words, these approaches are *additive* because they foster development of both the second and native languages (Lambert, 1977). Subtractive models emphasize English language development and success is measured by how quickly the students exit the program. Additive models focus on dual language development as well as academic preparation. They last a number of years and success is measured by the students' general achievement in school as well as their proficiency in both languages.

The integrated bilingual education model lies somewhere between the two categories. It shares characteristics of subtractive models in that there is not an overt purpose to fully develop the native language of the students. Mainstreamed bilingual students, however, continue to use and value their bilingualism by maintaining continuous contact with the bilingual program and because they serve as interpret-

TABLE 1.1

Models

Models	Goals	Target Population	Language Literacy	Distribution Subject Matter
English-only Instruction Models				
ESL	ELD	Minority	In English	Content-based ESL (some programs)
Structured immersion	ELD	Minority	In English (some limited L1)	Sheltered English for all subjects
Bilingual Education Models				
Dual language	Bilingualism	Majority, international	L1 and L2 or L2 and L3	All in L1 and L2; or all in one, and some in the other
Canadian immersion	Bilingualism	Majority	L2 first, English later (early)	All subjects in L2 for 2 years; in English and L2 remainder of schooling
Two-way	Bilingualism	Majority, minority	L1 first for each group or L1 and L2 for both	All subjects in L1 and L2 distributed equally over the grades
Two-way Immersion	Bilingualism	Majority, minority	First in minority's L1 then in English	All subjects in minority's L1 first, increasing use of English over the grades until it reaches 50%
Maintenance	Bilingualism	Minority	L1 literacy first, then in English	All subjects either in both languages or some subjects in native language others in English
Transitional	ELD	Minority	L1 literacy first, then in English	Most subjects in L1 with ESL instruction; gradually to all subjects in English
Submersion with L1 support	ELD	Minority	English literacy, limited L1 literacy	All subjects in English with tutoring in L1
Bilingual immersion	ELD	Minority	L1 and English literacy from the beginning	Concept development in L1; sheltered English for all subjects
Integrated TBE	Partial bilingualism, ELD	Minority with majority participation	L1 literacy first, exposure to English from the beginning	All subjects in L1 and in English, but assignment by student suited to language needs, and particular program structure

Note. E.L.D. English language development L1 = native language; L2 = second language; L3 = third language.

25

ers within mainstream classes between dominant speakers of English and the other language. Ideally, in integration programs native English speakers develop communication skills and interest in the language and culture of the language minority students (Brisk, 1991c).

Models group three ways with respect to the population they target: language minority, language majority, or both groups of students. Additive models serve language majority students or both groups, whereas subtractive models serve only language minority students. Bilingual programs for English speakers or for both groups are enrichment programs. Bilingualism is seen as a resource that enhances education. These students profit from the academic and cognitive benefits of bilingualism. Students educated bilingually substantially improve their scores in achievement tests and IQ examinations, but only after 5 or 6 years of bilingual instruction (Baker, 1993; Cummins, 1980). Programs for language minorities only are compensatory. Bilingualism is perceived as a problem that schools need to resolve by making students monolingual in English. Thus the models with the least educational advantages serve the most needy students.

Models serving both English speakers and speakers of another language have the added advantage of promoting interaction between students who are learning a second language and native speakers of that language. Thus, two-way, integrated bilingual, and some dual language programs provide ideal settings for students studying English or another language. These models allow students to not only interact with a teacher who knows the language, but with other students their age who are native speakers. Although students acquire a high level of proficiency in the second language, research on Canadian immersion models has shown that learners experience language fossilization.[3] In these programs—as in structured immersion, bilingual immersion, and TBE—the teacher provides the only opportunity for interaction with fluent speakers of the target language.

Bilingual education models take three different routes when choosing language for initial instruction: the native language, the second language, or both simultaneously. All three approaches show positive results in reading achievement. However, initiating students to schooling in the second language has often resulted in failure (see Lombardo, 1979, for a review of this literature). These mixed results have puzzled practitioners and provide fuel for the controversy over language choice for education of language minorities. Opponents of bilingual education claim that research proves that initiating students in the second language is not detrimental, whereas proponents signal the research that proves otherwise. An analysis of the factors affecting the programs studied partially explains these seemingly contradictory results. Students succeed in programs that start in the second language when the students are members of language majority, have a strong basis in their native language and positive attitudes toward it, hear and see their language constantly used in their environment, and eventually take courses in it in school. Programs fail

---

[3]*Fossilization* is the phenomenon observed in second language learners by which certain errors become permanent features of their language (Selinker, 1972).

when students belong to language minorities with a weak literacy background in their native language, limited use of the language in the larger environment, and poor attitudes toward their own language. These programs never make an effort to teach it in school (Brisk, 1981b). The concern is not the choice of language but the characteristics of the population served.

In addition to these broad distinctions among models, actual implementation of a specific model greatly varies from school to school. Community support, school leadership, teacher beliefs, parental pressures, and student needs contribute to the creation of very different programs. Careful examination of studies comparing implementation of models shows that there can be as much difference between what happens within schools using the same model as between schools using different models (Baker, 1993). Specific characteristics of a school, rather than the model they employed, made a program more or less effective. For example, Ramirez (1992) noted that students who had attended one of the late-exit model schools performed significantly better than other late-exit schools because their kindergarten emphasized thinking skills in the native language. Schneider (1990) admitted to great differences in instructional practices between the lower and upper grades of the models she compared, resulting in more differences between grade levels than between models. Lower grades used what are presently considered better teaching approaches, whereas upper grades used approaches that are not considered as good for literacy development. Reading scores declined for both models in the upper grades. The Amigos Program, a two-way bilingual education program in Cambridge, Massachusetts, has been hailed as the best model for both language minority and English-speaking students. Important positive outcomes of this program are academic achievement and language proficiency in both languages and positive attitudes toward the languages (Cazabon et al., 1993). A two-way middle school in the Southwest failed the test on language attitudes. Spanish was highly devalued and Spanish-speaking students who were not fluent in English were ostracized in English language arts classes (McCollum, 1993).

What I have chosen to call submersion with TBE support is known in Massachusetts as TBE and in Berkeley, California as the individual learning program. Ramírez (1992) use late-exit TBE for programs that fit the definition of maintenance bilingual education. Integration is more frequently used to define mainstreaming than bilingual integration.

These labels have little meaning in educational practice. Models present contrasts and commonalties that highlight the greater importance of specific factors in implementation that often escape the definition proper. Moreover, these labels are manipulated for political reasons. For example, the use of the word *immersion* for programs that are actually segregated ESL coincided with the release of evaluations of Canadian immersion programs showing excellent results. Proponents of structured immersion launched a campaign for their program profiting from the prestige of the Canadian immersion programs. They disregarded the fundamental differences, focusing on the fact that instruction was initiated in the second language (Gersten, 1985; Rossell & Ross, 1986). Ramírez (1992), on the other hand, chose to use *late-exit TBE* rather than *maintenance* because the transitional concept is the only one accepted in the present political climate. Therefore it is preferable to promote the need for extended TBE rather than maintenance bilingual education.

UNDERSTANDING THE PRESENT DEBATE

The only consensus in the United States between proponents and opponents of bilingual education is that it can benefit English speakers who want to become proficient in another language. Otherwise, contending views diverge radically from the very definition of bilingual education to the types of programs appropriate for language minority students, and whether public schools should promote bilingualism among language minority students. The debate even concerns how to measure academic achievement among such students.

Proponents define bilingual education not only by the use of two languages, but by the relative proportion of time spent in each language. They dismiss programs with limited use of the students' native languages. Opponents have persuaded political and school authorities to redefine bilingual education not in terms of how students can be taught in two languages, but rather how quickly students can attain proficiency in English. Such a redefinition focuses on programs that use only English. For example, in Title VII, The Bilingual Education Act, a program option is labeled "Special Alternative Programs," which use only English for instruction. Legislation proposed in 1995 in Massachusetts would redefine bilingual education as a "program of instruction for children of limited English-speaking ability" (House No. 1447, 1995) and promote structured immersion as a form of bilingual education even if this model uses only one language—English—for instruction.

Proponents of true bilingual education prefer long-term programs in which both languages are used extensively and in which English-speakers and language minority students learn together. TBE has been a mixed blessing. Such programs have recruited motivated bilingual teachers and created a supportive bilingual environment in schools (Brisk, 1994a). However, much research demonstrates that TBE fails to match achievements possible with long-term bilingual instruction. Students who attend bilingual programs for more than 3 years show better academic performance, mastery of English, and diminished dropout rates (Curiel, Rosenthal, & Richek, 1986; Otheguy, 1994; Ramirez, 1992; Thomas & Collier, 1996). The fear of segregating students has led proponents to support two-way and bilingual integrated models—partly to build a larger constituency for such programs. Ironically, bilingual education's opponents favor programs, such as structured immersion, that actually segregate language minority students until they can be mainstreamed.

Defenders of bilingual education point to the economic and political advantages of supporting existing linguistic and cultural resources in a global economy (Secada & Lightfoot, 1993), the positive effects of bilingualism on cognitive and linguistic development (Snow, 1990), the effects of using the native language in enhancing

English language development and academic achievement (Cummins, 1984), enhanced self-esteem and identity formation (Secada & Lightfoot, 1993), the need for equity (*Lau v. Nichols,* 1974), and role-model benefits that occur when students study with teachers of their own ethnic group (Engle, 1975; Snow, 1990).

Opponents claim, however, that native language instruction diverts precious time from learning English (Rossell & Ross, 1986), bilingual education segregates bilingual students and does not provide equal education opportunity (Porter, 1994), preservation of native languages and cultures should not be financed by public schools (Epstein, 1977), English language instruction prepares students better to function in school in English (Rossell & Ross, 1986), English is of paramount value in forging national unity and for transmitting American democratic values, the variety of languages makes it impractical to develop programs (Glazer & Cummins, 1985), and bilingual programs add to the already strained budgets of school systems. Glazer (1993) pointed out that often the opponents refer to their own personal history, claiming that they or their ancestors managed without it. Therefore they see no reason why recent immigrants deserve, would benefit from, or even need such a program. Many opponents argue that, to the extent that federal and state bureaucrats compel local schools to provide bilingual education, this is an intrusion on what should be the prerogatives of local governments (Glazer, 1993).

The intensity of the debate often becomes personal. Opponents claim that bilingual education is defended by activists who are inflexible and do not care about students (Imhoff, 1990). Proponents believe that the opposition derives support from xenophobic organizations that fear and scorn immigrants, particularly Hispanics[4] (Crawford, 1992).

The arguments of proponents focus on the national and personal benefits of bilingualism. They see bilingualism as a resource that bilingual education fosters. Opponents only see benefits in developing and strengthening English. They consider bilingualism as a problem aggravated by bilingual education and the use of students' native languages. Only when they cease to see bilingualism as a problem does their attitude toward bilingual education change. For example, Glazer (1975), who considered using languages other than English for instruction unnecessary and a "quixotic enterprise" (p. 184), changed his mind once he reflected on the benefits of bilingualism. He now writes about the intrinsic value of maintaining native languages and cultures. Glazer (1993) no longer thinks that knowing Spanish is a problem, but instead finds it an advantage because "our most populous neighbor is a Spanish-speaking nation," and "Spanish is one of the major languages of the world" (p. 322). He concluded that bilingual education can encourage bilingualism, which in turn can be used to all students' advantage.

Views are so divergent that they make dialogue difficult and color the interpretation of program evaluations. For example, Zappert and Cruz (1977) and Rossell and Ross (1986) came to different conclusions when reviewing bilingual education

---

[4]Although Puerto Ricans are not immigrants, they are perceived and treated as such by the general U.S. public.

evaluations. Both reviews classified outcomes from bilingual education programs based on students' performance: where students performed better than, worse than, or comparable to students in mainstream classes. Zappert and Cruz (1977) considered bilingual programs inherently advantageous because students were learning two languages "without impeding their educational progress" (p. 39) when they performed at the same level on standardized tests as their mainstream cohorts. By contrast, Rossell and Ross (1986) concluded that bilingual programs that offered comparable results to monolingual programs were "doing nothing" for their students. For Zappert and Cruz, having an extra language was educationally superior. For Rossel and Ross, learning two languages was a waste of time and money. Zappert and Cruz valued bilingualism for language minority students, whereas Rossell and Ross did not.

Proponents of bilingual education contend that bilingualism is good for all students. They feel that the presence of students of other languages and the existence of bilingual programs can only assist the goal of bilingualism for English speakers. Opponents see the promotion of bilingualism among English speakers as a separate agenda from making language minority students English speakers. They accept as a goal of all schools teaching foreign languages. However, for some reason this appreciation for language learning does not extend to native speakers in bilingual education programs.

CONCLUSIONS

The debate on bilingual education is not about education but about language and models. It is not even a general debate on bilingual education. Bilingual education is actually thriving for English speakers in public schools. That such programs grow as attacks on bilingual education for language minority students intensify reinforces the impression that for many in the educational establishment, bilingualism is a luxury best afforded by those who already speak English. ESL, structure immersion, and TBE are usually promoted for language minority students as a means of accelerating their acquisition of English, the highest educational priority. This contrasts with Canadian immersion and dual language models, the goal of which is full bilingualism for English speakers. Even support for two-way programs, serving both English speakers and language minority students, emerges from the ideal setting these programs provide for second language learning among English speakers.

The choice of which language to use in the instruction of language minority students dominates discourse. Proponents of bilingual education favor the use the native languages in addition to the national language, English. Opponents see no advantage in using native languages. Models have been developed and compared on the basis of language of instruction. This sterile debate is of very little relevance to the 6 million children and their parents whose home language is not English. For them it is an educational rather than an ideological question. Unfortunately, educational principles have not prevailed in choice of language for instruction. Political and economic forces have always influenced the use of languages in public education in the United States, but especially so during the 20th century. Our society seems to be unable to differentiate between choice of a national language and choice of language for education. All countries need at least one national language to conduct government; yet during its heyday as a colonial power, Great Britain resisted the promotion of a national language policy for either the British Isles or for its colonies (Heath, 1976). In the United States, national language policies responded to economic and political concerns. Toward the end of the 19th century, English emerged as the country's national language and as the mandated language of instruction in public education. Although educators then as much as now thought that native languages were a natural medium for schooling, political forces prevailed.

Despite educational research that proves that using the native language of the students enhances education and eventually improves basic language skills, educators are unable to persuade politicians and bureaucrats. Indeed, many of the objections to using the native language of the students addressed in the UNESCO report over 40 years ago still appear in attacks on bilingual education.

The debate on language is neither reaching a resolution nor helping language minority students' education. English language instruction is a necessary condition for good bilingual education, but it alone is not sufficient to overcome the failure of our schools. Teaching in the native languages of the students solves the home–school language mismatch, but this is only one of the problems faced by language minority students. In the early 1970s, the U.S. Commission on Civil Rights (1971a, 1971b, 1972a, 1972b, 1973, 1974) reported that in addition to lack of use of the native language, isolation of students, disregard for their cultural heritage, exclusion of parents and communities from participation in school affairs, poverty, poor financing of schools, and quality of classroom interaction contributed to lack of academic progress and student dropout. Because language is not the only problem, language should not be the only focus of solutions.

The discourse on education of students who come to school with a language and cultural background other than English has been fixed on the issue of language choice. Arguments in favor of bilingual education stress the advantages of using the native language of the students. Those against bilingual education list the benefits of English-only instruction. Models are hailed or attacked depending on the languages of instruction. Many concerned educators realize that in order to improve the education of bilingual students, we need to go beyond the debate on language choice and support for particular models. Evaluations of programs based on models are unreliable because models do not teach and rarely learn. Issues of pedagogy need to be addressed. Besides, implementation of models is not consistent and such inconsistencies are not related to language or model characteristics but to educational factors. For example, a recent study in New York City comparing TBE with ESL models provided controversial results. The chancellor for the public schools recognized that the study did not provide useful guidance for reforming schools. He appointed a committee to look at more educational factors such as:

what is being taught in bilingual and ESL programs, whether bilingual programs follow an appropriate core curriculum in the native languages, how well prepared the teachers are in these programs and what modifications might be needed to respond to the city's changing demographics. (Dillon, 1995, p. B4)

The relentless attacks, mostly by noneducators, on the use of native languages force supporters of bilingual education to channel most of their energies to the political battle in defense of allowing native languages to be used in the the schools. Although careful research points more and more toward the benefits of long-term bilingual education, opponents dismiss all forms of bilingual education including TBE for language minority children leaving proponents defending a weaker form of TBE as a compromise solution for keeping some native language use in education (Secada & Lightfoot, 1993).

Political struggles in defense of bilingual education are needed because without political support public education cannot succeed. Lack of public support for programs affects the quality of any program. This was true even back in the 19th century when the first public bilingual schools were started (Keller & Van Hooft, 1982). However, the focus needs to switch from languages to schools: Schools, not languages, educate students. The question that needs to be asked is what conditions create successful learning environments for language minority students.

As a linguist, I cannot deny the importance of the languages of the students, or the necessity to learn to function in English. There is much to learn from the work on bilingualism and second language acquisition that can benefit educational policy. However, it needs to be separated from language as a political and ideological symbol. In addition, there is much to learn from the work of educational anthropologists. They argue that differences "between majority and minority cultures in interaction, linguistic, and cognitive styles can lead to conflicts between school and child that interfere with effective education" (Jacob & Jordan, 1993, p. 8). Languages and cultures need to be regarded as facilitators and not as the only goal of education. Switching the perspective brings attention to education itself. Success rests not only in choosing languages and considering culture but paying attention to advances in education.

2

External and Internal Influences on Bilingual Students' Education

While the political and ideological debate over language choice for instruction rages, the number of bilingual students in the United States steadily increases. Bilingual programs only serve a small percentage of bilingual students.[1] Many more attend ESL classes, and a majority of bilinguals with low proficiency in English are enrolled in mainstream classes (Escamilla, 1994a). Some students experience success in school, but many do not (Trueba, 1987). Educators, linguists, and social scientists have over the years offered explanations and possible solutions. Blame has been attributed to the students themselves, their homes, schools, or even society. At first students who failed were labeled *alingual* or *nonspeakers* because they lacked fluency in English. Later studies attributed failure to the mismatch between the children's language at home and English as the predominant language of instruction (Cárdenas & Cárdenas, 1972). By the late 1960s, introduction of the home language in school was considered the solution giving rise to bilingual programs (Andersson & Boyer, 1970).

Presumptions about the students' culture were also offered to explain students' failures. From claims of "cultural deprivation," which branded differences as deficits, researchers moved on to explore discontinuities between students' home and school environments. The way students were enculturated to learning at home markedly differed with schools' expectations (Philips, 1972). The hope was that by incorporating students' culture in the curriculum and methods of teaching, educational performance would be enhanced (Saravia-Shore & Arvizu, 1992). A first-grade Spanish-speaking teacher engaged the students in playing a language game as part of the language arts lesson. She allowed for student collaboration, talk, and even maintaining discipline. Although the game assumed competition, the students

---

[1]For the remainder of the book I use the term *bilingual* instead of language minority student. Although many students enter school monolingual in their home language, they are at the onset of bilingualism.

helped each other without regard for their own chances to win. Language use in this classroom and the nature of the interaction among participants (including the teacher) "seems to match the general language use of the community surrounding the school" (Carrasco, Acosta, & de la Torre-Spencer, 1992, p. 424). In contrast, the same students working with a teacher unfamiliar with the students' language and culture became quickly bored playing a comparable game. The lesson was rigid and limited to the teacher giving directives and asking questions. Efforts from students to help each other and maintain discipline were misinterpreted, resulting in reprimands and lack of participation from a student who knew no English.

Ogbu and Matute-Bianchi (1986), Gibson (1993), and Suarez-Orozco (1993) observed students who succeeded academically in spite of the fact that schools ignored their language and culture. These students were recent immigrants from China, India, and Central America. These families moved to offer their children a better education and better socioeconomic opportunities. Motivated by their hope for the future and a sense of duty to their parents, who sacrificed so much, these students performed admirably in school. Language minority students who are not immigrants and who have seen the doors of success and upward mobility closed to their community generation after generation have no basis for hope in the future. For groups that have been traditionally neglected, the incorporation of their language and culture shows a sense of respect, which in turn breeds trust between school and community. Trust for the intentions of the schools to educate is an important variable (Erickson, 1993). Students can succeed in schools that do not consider their language and culture if parents and students trust that these schools are sincerely interested in providing a good education. Erickson gave Catholic and Muslim schools as examples.

For Cummins (1989), neglect of home language and culture may be significant, but more significant are inadequate teaching methodology, unfair assessment, and lack of communication with the community, "result[ing] in the personal and/or academic disabling of minority students" (p. 60). Zanger (1987) demonstrated in her research with bilingual high school students that structural and interpersonal barriers block students' integration into mainstream America. This isolation limits students' chances to develop English and progress academically. Spolsky's (1978) extensive study of Native American communities in the Southwest concluded that linguistic, cultural, economic, political, social, and psychological factors need to be considered to understand educational situations and make decisions on educational policy. Configuration of the languages, strength of religion and culture, employment, government policy, national ideology, socioeconomic status, and attitudes toward languages all need to be taken into account when planning a bilingual program.

Collectively, the research on variables influencing the education of language minority students indicates that multiple situational and individual factors affect students' school performance. Situational factors—including linguistic, cultural, economic, political, and social—influence how students of a particular ethnic group are viewed by educators and peers, which in turn determines students' and their families' expectations of schools and how much schools provide for them. Personal characteristics—especially language, culture, and educational background—influence how bilingual students function in school. Bilinguals' families play a pivotal role in language development, identity formation, and achievement motivation. Educators need to understand how situational factors, personal characteristics, and families affect individual students' education (see Fig. 2.1). The type of education schools provide ultimately determines the educational success of bilingual students, but knowledge of such external and internal factors can help school staff better support bilingual learners and their families and understand how these factors are influencing school policy and practice.

SITUATIONAL FACTORS

Linguistic, cultural, economic, political, and social factors within the society at large influence how students—especially how bilingual students—perform (see Table 2.1). Use of the languages in the curriculum, congruency of cultural content and teaching strategies, adequacy of education to demands of the world of work, and attitudes toward bilingual students reflect the influence of these social factors on schools. Bilingual students' motivation to learn, their performance, and the social integration of schools are affected by how schools approach education of their bilingual students.

Linguistic Factors

The particular characteristics of languages make a difference in the extent and willingness to use them in education. World languages that are standardized and written are perceived as more worthy of use in education or simply more practical

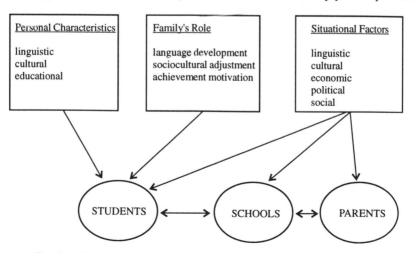

Fig. 2.1. External and internal influences on bilingual students' education.

TABLE 2.1

Effects of Situational Factors on Schools and Students

Factors	Effects	
	Schools/Teachers	Families
Linguistic		**Students**
• Nature of languages: world/regional and standardized/nonstandardized and writing systems	• Willingness to teach languages and use them for education	• Level of language proficiency • Motivation to learn and use the languages
• Amount of language use in community, media, technology, home	• Availability of personnel, materials, etc. • Amount of language use	**Parents** • Promotion and use of languages
Cultural		**Students**
• Curriculum content	• Content choices	• Familiarity with content
• Assumptions on background knowledge	• Amount of clarification	• Comprehension level
• Attitudes toward knowledge	• Teaching strategies	• Learning strategies
• Ways of communicating and disciplining	• Classroom interaction and management	• Classroom behavior
• School routines	• Student evaluation	• Performance
• Expected parent participation in education	• Perception of behavior	• Students' attitude toward parents
	• Perceptions of parents' involvement in education	**Parents**
		• Participation in school
		• Understanding of and attitude toward school practices
		• Relationship with children

Economic

- Economic viability of languages
- Differential social mobility, career opportunities
- Changing educational demands
- Educational costs and requirements

- Inclusion of languages in curriculum
- Appropriate education
- Perception of parents' and students' motivation
- Level of education provided
- Bilingual staff and resources for the program
- Threat to jobs and budgets

Students
- Motivation to learn
- School achievement
- Level of education received
- Adequacy of services

Parents
- Perceived economic advantage of knowing English and/or home language
- Attitude toward the role of education on economic activity

Political

- Laissez-faire language policy
- Treatment of immigrants
- Language diversity and political

- Choice of instructional language subject to ideologies rather than to students' needs
- Treatment of students
- Acceptance of home languages

Students
- Learning subject to ideology
- Educational disenfranchisement
- Social integration
- School achievement

Parents
- Formation of ethnic strongholds

Social

- Attitudes toward languages and ethnic groups
- Socioeconomic level
- Race, gender
- Reasons for being in the United States
- Size and cohesiveness of community
- Proximity to country of origin
- Extent of stay

- Attitudes toward students
- Students' expectations
- Motivation to teach

Students
- Academic achievement
- Language proficiency
- Level of bilingualism
- Social integration

Parents
- Attitude toward home language and culture
- Adjustment to new social environment
- Ties to homeland
- Motivation to promote English and maintain home language

because their application is more widespread. It is usually relatively easy to recruit personnel who can teach in these languages and to obtain commercially distributed learning materials. Regional languages and languages that are not written or standardized present more of a challenge and their practicality is questioned. Such is the case of Native American languages that are used by small communities, and, for the most part, have not developed a writing system. Linguists have helped communities develop writing systems in order to produce educational materials, but some question whether such efforts are worthwhile. There is more interest and financial support in the United States for saving the spotted owl than for preserving indigenous languages.

Characteristics of the writing system and similarities or differences compared with English play a role in decisions and attitudes toward teaching writing in two languages. Languages with Latin orthography, such as English and other European languages, are considered easier to learn to read and write than languages that use the Arabic orthography or the logographic system of Chinese. In Arabic the shape of each letter changes depending on its position in a word. To read and write in Arabic, students need a greater amount of information than students using a Latin alphabet. Level of difficulty of an alphabet is related to how much accumulated knowledge is necessary to be able to decode (Gilson, 1986). Another dimension of difficulty relates to whether the system is alphabetic, syllabic, or logographic. In alphabetic systems, relatively few symbols are needed (26 in English). Syllabic systems (employed in Korean, Japanese Katakana, and Cherokee) are easy to learn to decode but present difficulties with respect to how the syllables combine to render different meanings (Tzeng, 1983).[2] Logographic systems require a large number of symbols because each character represents a word or morpheme. Characters combine to represent additional words.[3] Chinese requires learning between 3,500 and 4,000 characters for basic reading. Newspapers use between 4,000 and 8,000 different characters (Leong, 1978). In spite of the amount of learning the Chinese writing system requires, Liu (1978) claimed that it has a system that can be taught to students for more efficient instruction. Traditionally, Chinese writing has been taught by rote, taking much longer to learn. A child learning Chinese or Arabic needs to learn many more symbols than a child learning to read in Spanish or English. If a writing system is too difficult, learning to decode becomes an end in itself, whereas to be literate the learner needs to focus on the meaning of the message.

Bilinguals can learn more than one writing system, but depending on the nature of the system and the similarities and differences, they pose different challenges. Similar systems such as English and Spanish use comparable symbols but they represent different sounds, causing some confusion. Different systems such as English and Chinese do not cause confusion but the learner needs to learn a whole new set of symbols. Tzeng (1983) theorized that "readers of different scripts learn

---

[2]An English equivalent would be *together* versus *to get her.*
[3]For a complete explanation of the Chinese writing system see Liu (1978).

to organize the visual world in radically different ways" (p. 81). Therefore, different cognitive strategies are needed for languages with very different scripts. Decisions to teach literacy in home languages is influenced by level—or perception—of difficulty of a particular writing system as well as possible confusion between alphabets of the two languages involved. Schools may start both languages simultaneously, begin with home language first and then introduce the other language, or decide not to teach literacy in the home language but limit its use to oral interaction. In these monoliterate bilingual programs, literacy is achieved only in English.

The extent to which the languages are used in the community and nation is important. Opportunities to use such languages stimulates motivation to learn and to practice them. In the United States, many languages are commonly spoken and used. English is the language of the government, education, business, and the world of work in general. English is the predominant language of the media. It is the language of signs, directions, and most written expression in the environment. English is also the international language of computer communication. Other languages are spoken mostly in small communities, usually in addition to English. They are used in the home, ethnic neighborhoods, and religious institutions. A few languages are also used by media catering to local communities. There is, however, little public use of these languages outside the immediate ethnic community (Ferguson & Heath, 1981). Therefore, daily use of the native language at home is a major factor in supporting the development of that language (Hernández-Chavez, 1978). Parents often switch to using English at home, believing that it will accelerate their children's acquisition of English. This pressure to use English results in language death or language shift. Indigenous languages are disappearing because young Native Americans no longer speak them (Spolsky, 1972). European languages from the times of colonization and languages of the immigrants are still spoken, but mostly by new waves of immigrants; those who have been in this country for one or two generations no longer speak them (Veltman, 1983).

The nature of languages and extent to which these languages are used outside the school influence school policies and practices as well as the language proficiency of students. It is much easier, for example, to convince school officials to start a Spanish program rather than a Khmer bilingual program. There are many qualified teachers fluent in Spanish—either as their native or second language—and abundant learning materials for any grade level. Because Spanish is a world language, these bilingual programs often receive support from English-speaking parents who want their own children to learn Spanish. Khmer, on the other hand, is only spoken in Cambodia, and there is a dearth of qualified teachers and appropriate materials. Unlike Spanish, Khmer's writing system is very different from English. To many, the notion of a Khmer bilingual program sounds impractical and frivolous. These people feel that the only use of the language is around the home; therefore home language use will provide sufficient development to fulfill the needs for Khmer. Outside the home, these students will only need English; thus, the school should worry about developing English. Families' motivation to promote home languages can also be affected by such "pragmatic" views of languages. Home language is often deemed unnecessary and even an impediment to learning English. As parents acquire fluency in English, they may also lack fluency or the habit of using the native language. Often the continuous use of the home language depends on the presence of monolingual speakers, usually older family members or recent immigrants.

School and family efforts to develop English language skills are supported by the extensive use of the language outside the school. The same is not true with home languages. Therefore, the burden of native language development falls more heavily in schools and homes. Schools need to become microsocieties in which the home languages are visible and necessary for daily functioning. In the age of technology, connections with schools abroad where those languages are the primary language may provide external support and motivation to use Spanish, Chinese, Japanese, and other languages.

Linguistic factors influence the ability and willingness of schools to create bilingual programs regardless of the merits of developing home languages and using them in bilingual programs. Schools are supported and often influenced by parents' views with respect to the need for using the home languages in schools. Students' development of their home languages and English will be affected by how widely and how well both languages are employed, both in school and outside of school.

Cultural Factors

The dominant American culture shapes nearly all public schools in the United States. School culture determines curriculum content, assumptions about background knowledge, learning philosophies, teaching approaches, classroom interaction and management, school routines, and parental participation. Differences in culture between the school and the students influences the teachers' perception of students and their families, the students' behavior and performance in school, and parents' interactions with school and their children.

Decisions about what to teach are based on what society considers necessary and valuable to learn. World history courses that concentrate mostly on European history reflect the historical background that, implicitly, U.S. schools consider important. Students from other parts of the world are often deracinated because the curriculum lacks their own historical content. Their American classmates and even their teachers may be ignorant about the bilingual students' own historical background.

When teachers introduce a topic, they usually make assumptions about what their students know. When students have a very different background knowledge from that expected from U.S. students, curriculum content becomes difficult to comprehend. For example, a Japanese adolescent was totally confused during a class discussion on school desegregation. She had none of the historical and social background to help her comprehend the concept of desegregation.

Assumptions about background knowledge also influence assessment of students. A student may appear to know a lot or not enough depending on the match between teacher and students' background knowledge. For example, the scores given by an Arabic and an American teacher differed when grading compositions on the topic of Ramadan. The Arabic teacher's scores on breadth of content were for the most part lower than those given by the American teacher because she expected Arabic students to know more about Ramadan. The American teacher who knew little about Ramadan was quite impressed with what the students had written.

Whether learning means memorizing or doing a critical analysis of what is taught depends on teaching philosophies and attitudes toward students. Ballard and Clanchy (1991) suggested that there are "culturally divergent attitudes to knowledge" (p. 21) that define teaching and learning philosophies. For example, Asian cultures equate knowledge with wisdom handed down from teachers to students. The duty of the teacher is to impart this knowledge well and the duty of students is to learn it without questioning. Australian schools, on the other hand, favor a perspective that sees "students as independent learners, with the competence to analyze, to question, to criticize, to evaluate" (Ballard & Clanchy, 1991, p. 23). Thus, Australian teachers merely present material; students look at it critically and transform it before assimilating it. Although American culture also favors such an analytical approach to learning, our education of poor children as well as language minority students is often ironically characterized by rote learning and memorization due to the notion that these students are not capable of an analytic approach to learning that requires higher order thinking skills (Cummins, 1984; Moll, 1988). It is possible that the success of Asian children in school is partly due to the match between Asian learning philosophy and school strategies used with bilingual students in schools. Even if successful in their early years, such bilingual students may be at a disadvantage when tests or high school and college courses require them to critique knowledge.

Children are socialized by their parents and communities to ways of communicating and relating to others. Cultures differ in their assumptions of what are proper ways to use language, engage in written discourse, and relate to adults. Ways of interacting and using language, as well as disciplining and motivating students, vary from culture to culture (Conklin & Lourie, 1983; Saravia-Shore & Arvizu, 1992). Cultures differ in the verbal and nonverbal behavior of interactions. Of significance in school situations are the rules between adults and children. The way children are supposed to act and respond to an adult addressing them differs among cultures. Looking at an adult means either paying attention or disrespect, depending on the culture. In some cultures, adults ask many questions of children as a strategy for teaching them, assessing their knowledge, and making them think. In other cultural groups, adults ask questions only when they do not know the answer (Conklin & Lourie, 1983). In the typical U.S. classroom, where teachers constantly question students mostly for the purpose of evaluating, children of other cultures may become confused as to the intent of the teacher when asking questions for which she has the answers (Heath, 1983).

Different cultures produce contrasting discourse and text structures. In the American culture, speeches are an opportunity to present the speakers' point of view and persuade the audience with their ideas. Among Native Americans, such a structure would be considered dishonest. Speakers are supposed to present facts in order to allow the audience to come to its own conclusions (Conklin & Lourie, 1983). Text organization also differs among cultures. Stories, letters, academic papers, and newspaper editorials follow specific rules of content and organization in different cultures.[4] For example, in Latin America a business letter starts with a salutation of respect, whereas in the United States it goes directly to the business at hand.

Disciplining strategies are cause for major miscommunication. Disciplinary strategies unknown to students often yield poor results. When a teacher was hit by a Haitian student, a discussion of the reasons why the student had hit her and a polite suggestion not to hit again was an invitation to continued poor behavior. More successful would have been an appeal to respect teachers and not bring shame to the family, as commonly practiced by Haitian teachers (Ballenger, 1992).

In addition to the academic and behavioral differences, the workings of the school such as schedules, organization of the day, and classroom etiquette differ in other cultures. Immigrant students found different from their own school experience the absence of recess, long days, snack time, informality at the start of the day, and calling the teacher by name rather than title (Clayton, 1993). In Pakistan, students are required to stand up when responding to a teacher. In an American classroom, this would be considered unnecessary and even disruptive behavior.

Teachers' perceptions of students and their families are biased by their own cultural norms and the lack of familiarity with the culture of bilingual students. Students are labeled as timid, uninterested, or disruptive and parents are often judged as disinterested in education. Such biases affect teachers' relations with students and their families, evaluation of students' performance, and the quality of the teaching. In turn, families and students have difficulty trusting, respecting, and learning from such teachers. Cultural congruence, or the degree to which cultures are similar, fosters understanding and communication between cultural groups (Schumann, 1978). The more different the culture of a group is from American culture, the more difficult the interaction between bilingual students and the American teachers and peers will be.

Students' performance in school is sensitive to cultural incongruencies. Unfamiliarity with curriculum content and rules of behavior make learning and interacting difficult and awkward. Students' performance and behavior are considered inadequate and inappropriate in the American school context. Often such students are labeled as having learning disorders, or being "timid" or "silly," as having "tuned out," or other misinterpretations of their reaction to the new cultural environment.

Parent participation in education is defined differently in U.S. schools than in

---

[4]See Grabe and Kaplan (1989) for a synthesis on the theory and practical implication on this topic.

schools in other parts of the world. U.S. schools expect parents to do volunteer work, participate in school governance, and engage in other activities. Many parents come from countries where they are not expected to go to the schools or participate in organizations. They see their role as supporting and monitoring their children at home by making sure they do their homework and instilling in them a sense of duty to the family to do well in school (Nieto, 1992). In cases in which parents are used to participating in schools, language difficulty and the nature of interactions in school activities inhibit parents from participation.

Families feel the effects of American culture in the clash of values with respect to rearing practices. Such practices may surprise school staff and upset their children, especially those who have lived in the United States for a while. Children adopt cultural traits of the host society, often causing conflicts with the home. They often consider their parents too strict and old fashioned.

Economic Factors

Economic factors influence the need to learn languages and motivation to do well in school. Knowing English and having educational credentials open job and career opportunities. Knowing the native language may also be economically beneficial, especially if it is one of the languages used for business or services. For example, knowing Japanese or Spanish can be useful given present trade relations with Japan and Latin America. In communities where there are large numbers of speakers of a particular language, hospitals, government offices, and businesses hire speakers of that language to service their customers. In some cases the home language may even be more crucial than English if there are well-established ethnic communities with plenty of opportunities for employment. Portes and Zhou (1993) and Gibson (1993) found that certain ethnic communities offer better career opportunities and social mobility for their members than mainstream America. Thus Cubans in Southern Florida and Punjabis in Valleyside, California succeed within their communities where they do not encounter artificial barriers created by prejudice.

Career opportunities and social mobility motivate achievement in school. Suarez-Orozco (1987), for example, reported on Central American high school students who learn English at fast rates and succeed in school and even college. They are driven by a determination to improve their families' economic situations. Their parents strongly believe that education holds the key to their children's future. Suarez-Orozco (1987) observed that "such values and anticipation may immunize students against the poisons of degradation they nevertheless encounter in the inner-city schools" (p. 167).

For many ethnic minorities, however, the "American dream" of hard work translating to economic prosperity is a myth. Ogbu and Matute-Bianchi (1986) believed that groups that have been historically marginalized by society, such as Mexican Americans, Native Americans, and Puerto Ricans doubt that education makes a difference to their economic conditions. These groups have statistics and experience to disprove the theory that correlates economic prosperity and educational achievement. Mexican Americans with a college education earn only 10% more than those with just a high school education (Goho & Smith, 1973). Hispanics with doctorates earn less than their non-Hispanic colleagues (Veltman, 1983). Society creates "glass ceilings," limiting career mobility or career stereotypes (Chinese work in restaurants, migrant workers are Hispanic, policemen are Irish), limiting choice. Bilingual students perceive that prejudices toward their ethnic group create "assigned" careers and this diminishes their motivation to succeed in school. The families of these students question whether schools make a real effort to educate their children. They get discouraged when, even with an education, their children's situation is not better than their own (Richards, 1987). Such parents cynically believe that the purpose of education is to widen the economic gap between groups rather than help their children have a brighter future. Teachers, on the other hand, perceive only that these students and their families are not interested in education or in pursuing socioeconomic mobility. They compare these students with those who succeed and conclude that students' and families' apathy causes the failure rather than sociohistorical factors.

The opportunities for economic and social mobility that existed earlier in the century have greatly diminished. Education was less crucial for economic success. Well-paid blue collar positions that do not require high levels of education are quickly disappearing. A high school education is now a minimum requirement for most productive work. Students need to acquire sufficient education to move from entry-level jobs to professional jobs if they hope for socioeconomic mobility (Portes & Zhou, 1993).

Economic factors motivate some students and their families, but others are discouraged. Demands on literacy and education levels required to climb the economic ladder increase constantly. Past experience on how the country absorbed immigrants is no longer applicable. Schools face the double duty of graduating students with educational skills demanded by today's market and breaking the psychological barriers that historic marginalization has raised in the minds of students and their families. In the present global economy, schools also need to question educational practices that erase languages that could be economically advantageous for those who speak them.

Launching programs proposed by advocates of bilingual education apparently threatens some teachers and administrators. To recruit qualified personnel to serve the increasing numbers of bilingual students may, in a level-funded school district, reduce the job opportunities for current personnel unfamiliar with the languages and cultures of the students. In addition, school committees claim that providing education in the home languages increases the costs of education beyond their school systems' budgets. Because of the dramatic increase in bilingual students, many school districts find themselves with a large percentage of bilingual students and a small percentage of bilingual teachers. Therefore, either new teachers need to be hired or existing teachers may have to retool to work with the bilingual students. Any efforts to serve bilingual students with prepared personnel are blocked because it would come at the cost of existing personnel. In California, where bilingual students with limited English proficiency represent a quarter of the student body, the teachers' union has adamantly opposed a new certification system proposed by the State Commission on Teacher Credentialing. The proposed certification would require all teachers working with bilingual students to undergo training in cross-cultural, language, and academic development (CLAD) (Schnalberg, 1995). Failure to obtain such certification would force teachers to transfer. For many teachers, this would mean losing their jobs because new job opportunities are for teaching the increasing number of bilingual students.

Bilingual education is perceived by opponents as just a job program for members of ethnic communities. Bilingual education has indeed opened career opportunities to adults from ethnic communities because of their language skills. However, only 15% of bilingual teachers come from the same ethnic groups as the students. The beneficiaries are those English speakers with skills in other languages, particularly Spanish.

School districts claim that bilingual education costs more, but this claim is hard to prove and much debated. Although materials in the native language and the cost of busing children to schools that offer programs in their language add to costs, bilingual teachers, as teachers with less seniority, actually command lower salaries. School accountings make it difficult to determine exact expenses just for the bilingual program. In Massachusetts, a law requires that the state provide school districts with students in bilingual programs with additional funding for each bilingual student. Because the money awarded is not earmarked for bilingual education, districts are free to spend the additional funds anyway they choose. Although bilingual education adds to the state budget, it does not mean that the added expense actually funds bilingual education.

Whether the added cost of bilingual education is real or only perceived, the negative effects on students are the same. School personnel and school boards lament the presence of these students and begrudgingly serve them. This unwelcoming school climate creates substantial barriers for bilingual students. In a community in Massachusetts with 80% Spanish-speaking students, the school committee chair saw her role as a guardian of the school budget to avoid tax increases; education took a back seat. Proposals to improve services for bilingual students were judged for their costs rather than their educational merits. Demoralized bilingual administrators and teachers abandoned the school system, curtailing the already limited services for bilingual students.

Economic factors determine whether schools provide bilingual students with an appropriate education or not. Schools that believe in the economic advantages of knowing more than one language and of adequately preparing all students for the demands of the future will see fit to meet the needs of bilingual students. On the other hand, schools that perceive bilingual students as an economic burden unconsciously or consciously renege on their commitment to these students. No consideration is given to the negative social and economic consequences of limited education.

Political Factors

Politics influence schools' willingness to use bilingual students' native languages and to foster their cultures. School policies are related to social and governmental policies on language and immigrants, and on views with respect to the role of language on national unity. Language means power; therefore, groups press governments to place their language in a position of power. The United States was founded as a multilingual nation where a variety of languages were used for daily life, government, and education. Toward the end of the 19th century, several states enacted legislation requiring knowledge of English to vote, cementing the political power of English speakers. Unassimilated groups including Native Americans and Hispanics whose ancestors preceded English speakers in North America were effectively disenfranchised. Neither their linguistic and cultural rights nor those of the immigrants that followed have ever been clearly established or respected.

Except for provisions for Native Americans within their reservations, language policy in the United States has been one of laissez faire. Any policy giving rights to linguistic minorities is the result of political pressure from ethnic groups as in the case of the *Lau* Supreme Court decision or the passing of the Bilingual Education Act (Title VII). The former was the work of Chinese immigrants, the latter of Spanish speakers in the Southwest. Organizations such as U.S. English also lobby to curtail the use of languages other than English. Language policy in the United States is not the result of carefully planned programs, but the aftermath of countervailing political activities or legislation.

Political pressures also influence the treatment of immigrants. Over the years, U.S. history has witnessed rejection and acceptance of different groups. Depending on social and historical circumstances certain groups were welcomed and others were considered undesirable. For example, in Lowell, Massachusetts in the early part of the 20th century, Swedish and other northern European immigrants occupied a place of privilege whereas Greeks were shunned. In the same city today, Greeks exercise considerable political power and Cambodians and Spanish speakers bear the brunt of rejection (Crawford, 1992).

Government policy is presently quite inconsistent toward various immigrant groups. It is either receptive, indifferent, or hostile depending on the group (Portes & Zhou, 1993). For example, the U.S. government in the 1980s and 1990s welcomed and assisted Vietnamese refugees escaping the Communist regimes, was indifferent to most legal immigrants from Latin America, and was hostile to Haitian boat people. These policies change at different points in history. For example, Cubans fleeing Castro's regime in the 1960s were able to establish themselves and succeed in this country thanks to generous help from the government. Twenty years later, Cubans who came to the United States during the Mariel boat lift were thrown into jail. Early Cuban refugees were seen as heroes because they were denouncing a Communist regime. Mariel Cubans' reasons for leaving were perceived as social and economic rather than political opposition to a government repudiated by the United States.

The type of political regime that refugees escape and the political relations with the country of origin influence treatment of refugees and immigrants. For example, Russian Jews were welcomed in the 1980s because they were escaping the communist regime of the former Soviet Union. Salvadorans, on the other hand, escaping a U.S.-supported rightist regime, were considered illegal immigrants and even those who applied for asylum were ignored by most government programs. Attitudes toward Japanese immigrants have changed dramatically from mortal enemies to economic partners.

Government policies toward language and immigrants influence schools' willingness to use the languages of immigrant children as well as how they treat specific groups of students. The federal government plays a limited but critical and symbolic role in bilingual education. For example, when the Bilingual Education Act (Title VII) was passed in 1967, the immediate impact was minimal, because limited appropriations funded only 69 projects. However, the message to the nation was favorable for the use of home languages in education. Within 5 years, more than 20 states had passed legislation supporting bilingual education. The Commission on Civil Rights vigorously monitored compliance of the *Lau* decision, which required school districts to provide adequate education for bilingual students.

In the 1980s the federal government funds were rerouted to support English-only programs. The Department of Education's Office of Bilingual Education and Minority Language Affairs allotted up to 20% of school grants for programs of intensive English language education that did not use the students' native language. A new federal government mandate defined English language development as the main goal of bilingual education. Native language was discouraged or allowed only on a transitional basis. States followed suit mandating English as their official language and mounting attacks on bilingual education (Stein, 1986).

The present increasingly negative attitude toward bilingual education is closely tied to the perceived threat of increasing immigration. In the first 4 years of the 1990s, 4.5 million immigrants arrived in the United States, increasing the percentage of foreign-born population to 8.7%, the highest since the turn of the century. Along with proposals to curtail immigration have come legislative initiatives that may alter the access of bilinguals to good schooling. Immigrant phobia led California's government to pass Proposition 187, which denies services, including education, to illegal immigrants. It also resulted in proposals to declare English as the country's official language. In this climate, attacks on bilingual education and the use of ethnic languages continue to increase.

A common argument against support of languages and cultural diversity is the belief that diversity brings divisiveness. But "[u]nity and diversity are not necessarily incompatible. Tolerance and cooperation between groups may be as possible *with* linguistic diversity as they would be *unlikely* when such linguistic diversity is repressed" (Baker, 1993, p. 253).

Those who believe that a single language brings unity naturally support policies to assimilate immigrants to English and mainstream American culture. Yet the imposition of English and prejudice toward cultural groups is a sure recipe for formation of ethnic enclaves, exactly the opposite of what is sought. Child (1943), in his study of Italian American second-generation immigrants, found that although some of the Italian Americans assimilated, others formed self-sufficient "in-groups." They rejected everything American, associated only with the Italian community, and felt that all their needs were taken care of by this community. More recently, Portes and Zhou (1993) observed that well-established ethnic communities remain within themselves, because they can enjoy social and economic mobility ("the American dream") without having to face intense prejudice. Crawford (1992), studying the effects of U.S. English efforts to impose English, concluded that it heightened divisions in communities in which ethnically diverse groups had previously managed to get along with each other.

The concept that a single language in a country ensures unity is a myth. Switzerland, a country with four official languages, is a model of unity, whereas Spain launched into a fierce civil war at a time when Spanish was the country's sole official language. Even U.S. history proves the contrary. Linguistically diverse European settlers rebelled against the British crown to form the *United* States of America. Their desire to be freed from British rule, not language, united them. Political, social, religious, and economic factors cause division far more than differences in language.

The quest for language unity pressures schools to impose English and view as American people who only use English in their public lives. Opponents of bilingual education view even temporary use of home languages as inciting separatism. Among some bilingual students, imposition of English and White middle-class American culture backfires. They feel schools want to destroy their identity and ties with their home and community. Students reject White American values, including success in school, and drop out of school. Concerned families redouble their efforts to impose the ethnic language and culture as the only avenue to save their children from gangs, drugs, sex, crime, and other features of American society they greatly fear (Brisk, 1994a; Gibson, 1993; Suarez-Orozco, 1993). The imposition of English creates ethnic enclaves and divisiveness rather than unity. When the native languages of students have been accepted, relationships between English speakers and language minorities blossom. For example, in two-way bilingual programs, the language of bilingual students is welcomed and learned by English speakers. These programs have fostered cooperative relationships between English-speaking and language minority parents as well as friendships between their children (Cazabon et al., 1993).

Politics plays a major role in how ethnic groups are treated, what the government believes their rights are, and how much government is willing to support their causes, including use of home language in education. The unfounded fear that use of languages other than English in education undermines national unity jeopardizes support for use of ethnic languages in schools. Regardless of the strength of educational and social arguments in support of use of home languages in education, politics sets the tone for the general lack of support for use of home languages in the education of bilingual students.

Social Factors

Status of languages and their speakers, status of dialects and subgroups within ethnic groups, socioeconomic level, race, gender, and reasons for being in the United States shape attitudes and expectations of teachers toward bilingual students. Size and cohesiveness of the community assist families' adjustment and impact language proficiency and social integration. Ties to the homeland and expected length of stay influence motivation to learn English and maintain the home language.

Some languages and their speakers are held in higher regard than others. These attitudes change with time and place. Often the most recent immigrants occupy the lowest social strata. Historical circumstances change the status of particular immigrant groups. For example, the status and perceptions toward Chinese immigrants are very different today from what they were in the 19th century. Chinese presently enjoy a high status and are perceived as high achievers. In the 19th century, prejudice against the Chinese, who were mostly poor, uneducated farmers, culminated with the passing of the 1882 Chinese Exclusion Act prohibiting migration of Chinese laborers. The only Chinese allowed entrance were officials, teachers, students, merchants, and visitors (McKay & Wong, 1988). These well-educated immigrants established themselves and changed the reputation of Chinese from "undesirables" to that of a "model minority" capable of educational and professional accomplishments (Siu, 1992).

Social status varies for ethnic groups in different regions of the country and often coincides with numbers. When immigrants arrive in large numbers they are seen as an economic threat to the local labor force. For example, Puerto Ricans fare better in San Francisco than in New York. Franco-Americans experience better status in California than in New England. The children of a Mexican family enjoyed the curious attention of teachers and students in South Carolina but suffered rejection when they moved to Connecticut where large numbers of Spanish speakers have sought employment. Whereas in South Carolina they were expected to teach their classmates Spanish, in Connecticut they were promptly told to forget their Spanish.

Compounding the status of a language is the status of dialects and different groups within a linguistic group. Portuguese-speaking Brazilians, Cape Verdeans, continental Portuguese, and Azoreans regard each other and themselves as having different status within their society. Brazilians are regarded and regard themselves and their dialect as having the highest status (Macedo, 1981). The different status of Puerto Ricans, Mexican Americans, Cubans and other Latin American groups in the United States is well documented, corresponding with their level of success in school performance (Fernandez & Nielsen, 1986; Portes & Zhou, 1993; Suarez-Orozco, 1993).

Socioeconomic level (based on parents' wealth and education) correlates with students' performance in schools. Students who come from families with higher income and higher levels of education tend to do better in school. Fernandez and Nielsen (1986) found that although socioeconomic level correlated with students' attainment in school, it was more significant for White than Hispanic students. Lower class immigrants' problems are exacerbated when they move from rural to urban communities because their lifestyle changes dramatically. Aldo, a Guatemalan high school student, felt like a prisoner in Boston's inner city. For safety reasons, his parents only allowed him to go out of the house for school and work. In Guatemala he lived in a rural community where he roamed freely with his friends. Yet another problem brought about by low socioeconomic level is that poor immigrants share neighborhoods with poor English speakers whose language also commands poor attitudes. Consequently, the English that bilingual students learn may, in fact, impede later social mobility.

Value orientations in the United States with respect to race and gender further shape attitudes. Negative attitudes toward native-born minorities due to race are extended to immigrants who are not White and who settle in depressed economic areas (Portes & Zhou, 1993). In Florida, for example, early Cuban refugees who tended to be White have fared better than Haitian refugees who are Black. Issues of gender affect female students in U.S. schools with respect to abilities and interests inherent to the gender. Compounded with even stronger attitudes in the culture of bilingual students, female students' chances for academic and social success in the greater society are weakened.

Attitudes toward an ethnic group as well as attitude of the ethnic group toward the host society are influenced by the reasons that placed a particular group in the United States. Ethnic groups have become incorporated in the society through conquest, wars, immigration, and flight from political persecution. These historical and political events mold society's views of these groups. Native Americans are viewed with a mixture of the superiority and guilt of the conqueror and early Cuban and Russian refugees are seen as heroes escaping Communist regimes, whereas Mexican immigrants are rejected as an economic burden. Negative attitudes toward these ethnic groups breed negative attitudes among ethnic groups toward Americans. In the early part of the 20th century, Greeks in Lowell, Massachusetts were highly discriminated against. As a consequence, they organized their own social structure and did not encourage socialization with Americans among their children (Crawford, 1992). Historical reasons are also to blame for negative attitudes toward Americans. Groups such as Puerto Ricans that became part of the United States as a result of war rather than free will have a love–hate relationship toward Americans and English.

Attitudes toward languages, dialects, and ethnic groups open opportunities for success for some but not for others. Disparagement by teachers and other students contributes to bilingual students' poor performance in school (Ramirez, 1985). Differential attitudes within an ethnic group also affect students' performance. McCollum (1993) observed that a Spanish-speaking teacher's negative attitude toward the Spanish dialect of Chicano students curtailed these students' desire to learn Spanish. When the status of a group changes, so does students' performance. Although Japanese Americans currently do well in school, they performed poorly when Japan was the enemy of the United States.

In addition to academic and linguistic success, attitudes affect the chances for social integration. In the United States assimilation is seen as a precondition for social, political, and economic participation. Although most immigrant groups aspire to social and economic incorporation, they do not all have the same options. Some succeed in assimilating into mainstream middle-class America, others are socialized with poor native-born Americans, and still others choose to incorporate into an established ethnic community. Portes and Zhou (1993) distinguished between prejudicial and nonprejudicial reception of different ethnic groups as a variable that hinders or favors societal incorporation. Many Spanish speakers and Asian immigrants experience prejudice but most European immigrants do not. Most vulnerable are the children who may join the "adversarial subculture developed by marginalized native youth to cope with their own difficult situation" (Portes & Zhou, 1993, p. 12). Members of this subculture reject what they see as White-American values such as educational aspirations and social adjustment (Ogbu, 1993).

Additional social factors surround the families' adjustment to the new society, their desire to learn English, and their desire to maintain the home language. When families leave their countries, they also abandon a familiar and supportive network. As they settle in this new foreign environment, some seek established communities of their own ethnic group where they feel welcomed. Large, cohesive communities provide much help as well as support for native language maintenance. However, living in an ethnic community diminishes the need to use and learn English (Schumann, 1978) and hinders social integration with English-speaking Americans. The dilemma for families is in choosing between seeking support or enhancing their children's chances for social integration. Mei, a high school student from Hong Kong, commented on how miserable her parents were when they moved away from their Chinese neighborhood to an upscale suburb. The move to the suburb provided social mobility and the opportunity to develop English and make American friends for the children, but it took away the supportive network for the parents. Living in a neighborhood surrounded by English speakers does not guarantee social integration. Rodriguez (1982) recollected how his family lived in their own island with little contact with the neighbors. It was not until he was in third grade, when he became fluent in English and avoided Spanish, that he made some friends in the neighborhood.

Motivation to learn English and maintain the home language relates to a certain degree with ability to return or visit the homeland and the expected length of stay. Puerto Rican and Latin American families expose their children to the home language and culture with frequent trips or visits from relatives. Such is not the case with Southeast Asian refugees, for whom travel is practically impossible due to distance and visa problems. Time and distance reduce home language ability among younger generations who tend to favor English.

Extent of stay influences motivation to learn English and maintain the native language. Many immigrants come with the intention of staying permanently or for a long time. Others expect to be in the United States for a few years while studying or representing their company. Schumann (1978) believed that laborers who plan on a temporary stay have little motivation to learn the language, whereas professionals have high motivation. These professionals want their children not only to learn as much English as possible but to maintain their home language so that they can continue their schooling without problems when they return. Schools often feel imposed on when the have to serve children of sojourners. The expectations are limited and teachers feel they have fulfilled their obligations as long as students are not terribly unhappy or disruptive.

Social factors affect the interactions between schools and students and ultimately students' performance. Unfortunately most bilingual individuals suffer social prejudices that thwart their aspirations. Societal pressures force immigrants to make difficult choices between home language and English as well as ethnic and American culture. Individuals with many of these social characteristics that predict failure can still succeed without abandoning home language and culture thanks to personal, family, and school resources that support them in their struggle (Brisk, 1994a). For example, Patricia, a Dominican student, succeeded in high school and went on to college and a business career. She later married a middle-class American and is raising five bilingual children. Her mother, although a cleaning woman without much education, was determined that her daughter would do well as a student and professional while keeping her home language ability and cultural ties. Bilingual and ESL teachers helped and encouraged her to enroll in a college preparatory program and to take extra courses and summer programs to enhance her chances for a better future. Patricia herself had a good educational background from her country and strong determination to get ahead.

Parents have a difficult time in the new society. Those who settle in ethnic communities enjoy the support of a familiar network and are able to better support their children in adjusting to school and the American environment. Influenced by prevalent attitudes toward languages and people of different culture and race, parents either become ambivalent toward their own language and culture or react against American culture. They encourage English language learning for pragmatic reasons, such as job opportunities and school success, but not in the hopes that their children will integrate into the American culture.

Even if insensitive attitudes cannot be eradicated from society, the concerted effort of family, school, and student can clear the road blocked by social barriers. Students can achieve academic and linguistic success as well social integration and mobility. The school, as the first American institution immigrants encounter, has the opportunity to buffer the impact of negative social factors during bilingual students' formative years.

Personal Characteristics of Students

Focus on situational factors alone leads to stereotyping students of the same ethnic background. Asians do well in mathematics, Hispanics do not want to learn English, and Vietnamese are overachievers: These are some of the sweeping statements made about whole ethnic groups. Students' performance in school also depends on individual students' linguistic, cultural, and educational factors. Linguistic factors include language proficiency, literacy level, level of bilingualism, attitude toward the native and second language, motivation to learn the second language and maintain the first, language learning style, and age. Level of cultural adjustment and social integration, knowledge of host culture, and ability to deal with cultural conflict comprise the cultural factors. Important educational factors encompass educational background, learning styles, achievement motivation, aptitude, and attitude toward school. All these factors bring about different levels of performance by bilingual students who apparently encounter comparable circumstances and who, as members of the same ethnic group, are affected equally by situational factors.

Linguistic Factors

Students' linguistic abilities vary with respect to the number of languages they know, the skills they master for each language, and how proficient they are in each skill. Language proficiency is influenced by attitudes, motivation, learning style, and age (see Table 2.2). Although we often think of bilinguals as knowing one home language and English, there are students who are familiar with more than two languages. To develop the linguistic profile of individual students, teachers must determine what language or languages the students know, what skills within each language they master, how well they master each skill, and how other variables influence the process.

There is great variation in the possible language and literacy ability of bilingual children. Saville-Troike (1984), in a study of 19 children from seven different language backgrounds with different levels of English proficiency, found great variety across and within linguistic groups. The one generalization that she could make was that "[t]he lowest academic achievers in our sample were among the most successful at interpersonal communication, especially with other children" (p. 216). Other research has demonstrated that literacy in the native language and biliteracy correlate with academic success (Cummins, 1984; Duncan & DeAvila, 1979). Thus, knowledge of English is a social advantage, but literacy is an educational advantage.

TABLE 2.2

Linguistic Characteristics

- Oral and literacy skills in home language
- Oral and literacy skills in English
- Oral and literacy skills in other languages
- Attitude toward languages
- Motivation to learn and maintain home language and English
- Language learning style
- Age

Students with only oral ability in their home language are either preschoolers or children who have not had a chance to go to school in their home countries for social or political reasons. The latter have a very difficult time in school. For example Jaime, a 12-year-old from war-torn El Salvador, could not write his own name when he arrived in Massachusetts, yet he had cared for his mother since his father had been killed. He was mature and became the best fund-raiser for the annual school trip, keeping accurate account of his earnings. Feeling humiliated around literate students who were less mature than he, he dropped out of school soon after starting.

Monolingual literate students tend to do well in school. Language proficiency in academic language provides a strong basis for acquisition of English and functioning in school. Roberto, a youngster from the Dominican Republic, called "el cerebrito" (the brainy one), blossomed in a bilingual program and eventually obtained a medical degree from an Ivy League school.

Children born in the United States often acquire the home language and English before entering school. These children have different degrees of ability in their languages. Place in the family is an important variable, with older children more fluent in the home language and younger ones more fluent in English. These children are accustomed to a bilingual environment and function best with bilingual teachers. In a bilingual Spanish first-grade class the teacher allowed for free language choice during writing workshop. Students freely chose the language of writing and discussing. Their literacy acquisition was not constrained by forced language choices (Homza, 1995). In cases where there are no bilingual teachers, recognition of the students' home language and culture also helps. Joseph, on the other hand, ran into problems reading English. He was fluent in English but the school did not acknowledge his Korean language and cultural background. Joseph overcame his reading problems after the reading specialist had him write a book on his Korean background and share this knowledge with his classmates.

Bilingual students with low literacy ability have either a limited ability to read and write in both or only one language. Trix-Haddad (1981) studied Sabah and Husein, two Arabic students who spoke fluent English but showed great problems reading English. These students had been raised in Detroit. They never had the opportunity to learn to read and write in their native language and their English literacy skills were extremely limited. This tends to be the case among bilingual students who are raised in the United States. Their parents do not teach them reading and writing in the native language because they deem it unnecessary. Teachers ignore the fact that these students are bilingual because they speak English and do not work with them as bilingual individuals. Even when giving instruction in English only, teachers cannot ignore the bilingual and cross-cultural background of these students. These students are sometimes referred to as *semilinguals*[5] (Skutnabb-Kangas, 1979).

Students who are orally limited in English but are able to read and write it feel

---

[5]This term has been criticized by Edelsky (1991) because the students can actually function in two languages so they are bilingual, but they do not pass reading and writing tests.

comfortable doing academic work in English but not in face-to-face interaction. They usually prefer to talk in their home language. These students may or may not be literate in their native language. Alice, a first-grade Haitian student, would only speak Haitian Creole yet she tested at grade level in English reading. Tang, a Thai kindergarten girl, never talked to her teacher in English but could write books with greater proficiency than her English-speaking peers.

There are some students who are bilingual and biliterate because they have gone to bilingual schools in their home country or have parents who have taught them to read and write in both languages. Mei, for example, had gone to school in Hong Kong, where teaching is done in English and Chinese. She felt comfortable in classes taught in English. She benefited, however, from taking a college preparatory course offered by an ESL teacher in order to make a cultural adjustment. Bilingual and biliterate students have the greatest advantage because proficiency in two languages enhances academic achievement and language proficiency. It also benefits possible long-term needs of learning additional languages. High levels of bilingualism are correlated with higher achievement in a variety of areas: educational expectations, reading, vocabulary, and math (Fernandez & Nielsen, 1986); ability to formulate scientific hypotheses (Valdesolo, 1983); cognitive flexibility (Cummins, 1979; Peal & Lambert, 1962); deductive reasoning skills in mathematics (Dawe, 1983); metalinguistic awareness, or ability to think about language and analyze linguistic input (Ben-Zeev, 1977; Hakuta & Diaz, 1985; Ianco-Worrall, 1972); and better scores on reading tests (Fernandez & Nielsen, 1986; Lindholm, 1991). Bilingualism in childhood affects the ability to learn additional languages later in life (Penfield & Roberts, 1959).

Attitudes toward the languages, motivation to learn and maintain them, language learning style, and age accelerate or slow down the process of acquiring languages. Attitudes toward the languages affect language development and language loss. Gardner and Lambert (1972) found four types of bilingual individuals with respect to attitudes toward the home language (French) and the second language (English): positive attitudes toward both, the home language only, the second language only, or neither. Positive attitude toward a language correlated with higher levels of proficiency. Those individuals who had positive attitudes toward both languages achieved high levels of bilingualism. Positive attitude toward either English or French correlated with competence in either English or French but not in the other language. Ambivalent students did not reach high levels of competence in either language.

Improving attitudes becomes an important aspect of language development. Promoting a positive attitude toward the home language affects proficiency in the second language as well. Mexican American students who believed that losing Spanish was a precondition to learning English averaged poorly in English proficiency tests (Hakuta & D'Andrea, 1992).

Motivation to learn a new language and maintain the first is considered an important factor in language proficiency and language loss. There is disagreement as to whether motivation is an individual choice or is restricted by social circumstances. Gardner and Lambert (1972) distinguished between integrative and instrumental motivation. Individuals with integrative motivation want to learn the language to socialize and share in the culture of the speakers of that language. Learners with instrumental motivation have practical reasons for learning the language; for example, to pass a college entrance exam in order to attend an American university. Gardner and Lambert believed that an integrative motivation gives a greater chance at higher levels of proficiency. Tollefson (1991) and Peirce (1995) contended that individuals' motivation is restricted by social agendas. For example, individuals want to learn English to attain professional status similar to what they held in their own country, but English classes teach survival skills suitable only for menial jobs. In order to learn a language, motivation is not enough; learners need to practice with native speakers. If native speakers are unavailable or unwilling to practice English with them, progress becomes almost negligible. Peirce (1995) found in her research that immigrant workers felt inadequate in front of native speakers and remained silent. Zanger (1987) interviewed bilingual high school students who, except for their ESL teacher, had no contact with speakers of standard English in their neighborhoods, schools, or workplace. Individuals may be motivated to learn a second language but a positive reaction from the host society is also necessary.

Motivation to maintain and develop the native language also needs to be supported. Opportunities to use the language, pragmatism, and cultural disposition influence the learners' motivation. Hernández-Chavez (1978) concluded that using the language in school was not sufficient for adequate development. Intensive use within the home and community was essential. The amount of native language use within the home depends on the birthplace of the parents, their English language ability, and connection with family in the country of origin (Hakuta & D'Andrea, 1992). Loyalty to the home language wanes when the social and economic value of English is paramount. It is simply more practical to know English. Some families feel that the home language is essential in maintaining the culture. They will help their children develop their native languages. Others feel that they can preserve their culture even if they give up the home language (Dorian, 1982).

Different students approach learning a second language differently. Some are daring and others are cautious (Wong Fillmore, 1979). Daring learners try the language without fear of making errors. They seek speakers of the language and practice it. This approach greatly benefits the acquisition of language for social interaction and sometimes also of literacy. For example, a Guatemalan middle school student made great efforts to communicate with her American classmates using any English she had. When communication stalled, she asked a bilingual person to write down in English the sentence she gave in Spanish. Paper in hand she ran to her American friend and repeated it. Within 6 months of being in the country, she needed little assistance to interact with her American friends. A Chilean girl, about the same age, when given a choice of the language to use for writing, used Spanish. After several weeks of working individually with a bilingual college student, she started plugging in a few English sentences. Eventually either type of learning can succeed, depending on the initial reaction by teachers. Too often daring learners are further stimulated and timid ones tend to be forgotten. Daring types must be reminded that they need to polish their language even if their initial inaccurate language served its purpose of getting native speakers' attention. The timid types need to be delicately encouraged to avoid complete silence. One teacher in Hawaii, working in small groups, required timid learners to be prepared to tell something at least once a week. Eventually all actively participated in her class.

The relation between age and second language acquisition has been the subject of various studies (Hatch, 1983; Krashen, Scarcella, & Long, 1982; McLaughlin, 1984; Singleton, 1992). Acquiring a language before the age of 10 gives the students a greater chance to reach nativelike pronunciation. Younger learners also have the advantage that their message is less complicated and often they can communicate without much language. Older learners have more abstract concepts to convey for which language is essential. Children who learn a second language in infancy develop nativelike intuition that allows them to judge what is correct or incorrect (Hatch, 1983).

For school-age children it is important to distinguish between language for social interaction and language for academic performance (Cummins, 1984). Given the appropriate context, proficiency in language for social interaction can be developed with relative speed. Age, however, makes a difference with respect to proficiency in the language needed to succeed in school if full proficiency must be achieved by the time students complete high school. Younger students have the disadvantage of less of a background in the native language, which provides a good foundation for the second language, but they have more time to learn the second language in school. For older students, who have attended school in their countries, the reverse is true. Collier (1989) reviewed the results of math, language arts, reading, and science in English taken by second language learners. She found that achieving comparable scores to native speakers of English in mathematics and language arts tests took between 2 and 4 years, whereas achievement in reading and science tests took between 4 to 7 years. Therefore a student entering elementary school has time to develop English proficiency, whereas a high school student has less time and a more difficult task because high school subjects have greater language demands than elementary school activities.

Cultural Factors

Bilingual students' school performance and sociocultural integration are influenced by their cultural norms of behavior and their reaction to living in two cultures. Cultural norms are established through home and school socialization. The patterns of home socialization establish the values, behavior, and ways of interacting and using language. Previous school experience determines students' expectations of teachers and of themselves in schools. When students are faced with two conflicting cultures they may adjust to live within both, reject one of them, or feel ambivalent about both. The interaction of all of these cultural factors influences school performance.

Children are socialized by their parents and communities to ways of communicating and relating to others. Students grow accustomed to specific ways in which adults and children are supposed to communicate, behave, and relate. Students carry these ways to school but "schools are alien institutions for many of these children. In schools, the rules that govern behavior, the goals of the actors, and the messages that are conveyed are often mysterious" (Snow, 1990, p. 63). For example, Spanish-background students are used to paying attention to more than one person at time. Their teacher may consider them inattentive when they simultaneously listen to the teacher and a classmate. These students get admonished and punished. Vietnamese students are not supposed to contradict their teachers. When a teacher directly asks them if they understood an explanation, they respond affirmatively even if they have not comprehended. Unless the teacher knows that "yes" is a sign of respect rather than understanding, the opportunity to teach them is lost. Warm Spring Native American children are used to testing privately what they have learned. Only when they are sure of their competency will they demonstrate publicly to others. In the typical U.S. school where the teacher asks them questions to evaluate their comprehension, they will not respond. Teachers interpret their behavior as lack of knowledge or interest (Philips, 1972).

While attending school in other countries, students learn ways of interacting with teachers established by the rules of behavior in those schools. Students become confused when American teachers behave differently from teachers in their home countries. Chinese students are not used to being questioned by teachers and they become embarrassed when a teacher addresses them.

Expectations of what and how to learn also differ in different cultures. Although all individuals have the capacity to adopt an analytic approach to learning and employ the strategies of critical thinking, bilingual students may come from educational systems that favor memorization and rote learning. These students will easily adapt to academic achievement defined as acquisition of facts, but will have difficulties if academic competence is perceived as the ability to analyze, question, criticize, and evaluate (Ballard & Clanchy, 1991). A belief about learning everything the teacher or the books say causes students to want to take down every word uttered by the teacher or to comprehend every word in a reading assignment. In some countries teachers will actually write on the board everything they say or speak very slowly to give the students a chance to copy everything down. In a U.S. classroom, these students become overwhelmed because the teacher speaks too fast and rarely writes things on the board. The emphasis on understanding word by word leads students to read slowly and make frequent use of the dictionary. Tang, a Vietnamese high school student, admitted to spending 1 or 2 hours a day looking up words in the dictionary. This approach is very time consuming and does not allow time for global comprehension or making inferences about the reading material.

Students confronted with two cultures make different identity choices. Four types of patterns emerge depending on the languages and cultures individuals choose to embrace (see Table 2.3): integration (both dominant and ethnic), assimilation (dominant only), segregation (ethnic only), and deculturation (ambivalent to both; Berry 1983; Taylor, 1987).

Integrated students accept both worlds with ease. For example, a group of Italian immigrant students in Canada freely used English or French at school (depending on the language of the school) but switched to Italian within the family and community. Neither teachers nor parents had to coerce them to use either the language of school or home (Bhatnagar, 1980).

Assimilated students embrace American culture at the expense of their home culture. Rodriguez' (1982) autobiography is an account of the benefits and sufferings of assimilation. His complete switch to English endeared him to his teachers and classmates and led to a successful career. Dropping Spanish, however, eroded communication within his family. Dinner table conversations with his father that had been intense and animated when Spanish was used slowly lapsed into silence when Rodriguez switched to English, a language his father barely spoke. Although content with his achievements, he was riddled with guilt.

Students who abandon their language and culture may become deculturated because in addition to losing connection with their own ethnic group, they fail to connect with English speakers. Marta, a fifth-grade Mexican American girl, rejected Spanish and was ashamed of being Mexican. She insisted on speaking English only even with monolingual Spanish speakers and in spite of low proficiency. Nevertheless she did not socialize with English speakers (Commins, 1989). Having lost their identity and unable to feel part of the host culture, deculturated individuals develop feelings of anomie, a lack of belonging, and marginality (Taylor, 1987). Some of these students join gangs as a way of achieving a sense of community (M. M. Suarez-Orozco & C. E. Suarez-Orozco, 1993).

Rejection of the host culture results in cultural segregation. Intense prejudice from teachers and American peers or rejection of American values by families drives students to socialize within their ethnic group. Punjabi students in Valleyfield, California learned English but did not achieve social integration with Americans. Mostly poor farmers, their families had a tight-knit community where children were pressed to study, succeed academically, and learn English but maintain their language and culture. Any social relation with Americans was frowned on because they associated American teenagers with drugs, gangs, and school apathy (Gibson, 1993). There are other cases in which the segregation is not initiated by the ethnic group but rather by the host culture. Haitians are segregated because of race by a

TABLE 2.3

Patterns of Sociocultural Affiliation

Type/Culture	Home	American
Integration	+	+
Assimilation	–	+
Deculturation	–	–
Segregation	+	–

Note. + = cultural affiliation; – = lack of cultural affiliation society that still does not integrate Black people well (Portes & Zhou, 1993).

Language proficiency in both languages, sociocultural integration with home and the larger society, and school achievement are most evident among those students who become acculturated (Bhatnagar, 1980; Gardner & Lambert, 1972). Students who accept their bicultural identity when compared to assimilated, deculturated, or segregated students perform better in tests of language proficiency and academic achievement. They become socially integrated with Americans without losing ties with family and community. They become productive leaders in their community because they can deal with both worlds (Kleinfeld, 1979).

Cultural affiliation is not fixed and can change with age and experiences. David went through a full cycle of changes. He came from Puerto Rico as a teenager, quickly embraced English and American culture. However, assimilation did not enhance his social standing. Disillusioned, David dropped out of school for a while. Later, encouraged by parents and teachers, he accepted his bicultural identity and entered college. His success in mathematics courses resulted in a scholarship to complete a masters degree in mathematics education.

Cultural factors affect students' behavior in school and relationships with teachers and peers. Understanding of behavioral patterns facilitates communication between teachers and students. Schools, working together with families, should strive to develop a bicultural identity among bilingual students rather than pressure students to take sides because sociocultural integration brings the greatest benefits to the individual, the school, and the community.

Educational Factors

Bilingual learners are susceptible to educational variables that affect all learners, such as learning style, level of maturation, and specific skills and talents. In addition, bilingual students are uniquely affected by their educational background, achievement motivation, educational aspirations, and life goals. Successful schools recognize the students' individuality and meet their educational needs.

The amount and quality of prior schooling greatly varies among bilingual learners, from equal or superior to their monolingual colleagues, to limited and unstable, to no previous schooling. Students with several years of stable education in their home country are prime candidates for a better transition to schooling in the United States. In some cases they may have even studied English before coming. Some of these students find the American curriculum easy. Patricia, who came at the ninth-grade level from the Dominican Republic, had no problem excelling in school. She was grateful that the curriculum in Boston was less demanding because learning English caused enough stress for her.

Other students have moved from one school district to another, from a mainstream to a bilingual program, or in the case of Puerto Rican children, from a system that uses mainly Spanish to one that uses mainly English. These moves often cause substantial gaps in their school attendance. Some children come to the bilingual program after being in an English-taught program. For example, Linh entered the

Vietnamese bilingual program in Boston after spending first and second grade in a mainstream school in Houston. His oral English was good but his literacy and academic skills were behind grade level. A fifth-grade bilingual teacher complained that several of her students were behind grade level in both languages because the parents had enrolled them in the mainstream program, anxious for their children to learn English. Slow progress in that program had motivated them to switch their children to the bilingual program after a few years. Without schooling in the home language, the children fell behind in general academic skills.

Because Puerto Ricans are U.S. citizens, they can easily move between the mainland and the island, taking their children along. José, a seventh grader with problems in reading in English, was born in New Jersey where he attended first grade in a monolingual English program. He went to Puerto Rico for second grade, where his teacher was visibly unhappy with his inability to read Spanish. After a few years, the family moved to Massachusetts where he enrolled in a monolingual English program again. Although proficient in oral English, he encountered problems with reading academic texts.

Some students do not attend school at all during these family moves. For example, when Cape Verdeans were allowed in the United States within the Portuguese quota,[6] families would go to Portugal to apply and wait for a visa. Often they did not enroll their children in school, speculating that they would leave soon, although the waits were as long as 2 years. In other cases, interruptions in school come as a result of wars or political disruptions in the country of origin. Therefore bilingual students enter the bilingual program with a variety of degrees of academic preparation and language ability.

Students, young and old, may be in school for the first time. Some first graders have not attended preschool or kindergarten either because there were no public programs or because parents do not believe in sending such young children to school. Depending on what happens at home, these students may feel at a disadvantage to those classmates who can handle the alphabet, scissors, pencils, paper, and other materials typically used in school. A Dominican child in a first-grade mainstream class kept getting scolded by the teacher because she spent most of the day going around the room touching everything. A Dominican who served as a teacher aide in the same school pointed out to the teacher that this child had never been in school and was fascinated by all the objects in the classroom. Older students can also come to school with no previous schooling. Many of the Vietnamese students of ethnic Chinese background arrive with no school experience. The principal of a Chinese bilingual elementary school assigned them a buddy who would teach them basic classroom etiquette. Teachers devised special literacy and mathematics programs to accelerate their progress.

Achievement motivation and educational aspiration generally run high among first generation immigrant students (Brisk, 1994a; Gibson, 1993; Suarez-Orozco,

---

[6]Since 1975, when Cape Verde declared independence from Portugal, Cape Verdeans can apply directly for a visa.

1993) and among native-born bilingual students whose families, teachers, or school programs foster such motivation and aspirations.

Ogbu (1993) believed that students of certain ethnic groups (Blacks, Puerto Ricans, and Mexican Americans in the United States) are not motivated because they have witnessed schools failing their own ethnic group for generations. Mexican Americans view and *experience* the schooling system as a tool of the majority population to maintain the inequality of the status quo (Suarez-Orozco, 1987). Schools that make a special effort to demonstrate to these students that they care can overcome such cynicism. Alva (1991), in a study of high school Mexican American students, concluded that school programs that provide college preparatory programs instill in students the belief that they can go on with their education. Students feel motivated to succeed in high school because there is a reason for it. In general, high expectations correlate with achievement motivation. Students become motivated when they realize that their teachers trust their potential.

Educational aspirations and life goals are closely related to achievement motivation and school performance. Even elementary school students differ in life goal aspirations and their differences correspond to school performance. Rodriguez (1983) found that third- and fourth-grade Puerto Rican students with clear career goals performed better in school than those who did not know what they wanted to be when they grew up. In a Boston high school, a number of the Hispanic students taking courses just to fulfill the basic requirements had as a goal going to the U.S. army. Lack of any school or family career orientation led them to choose the one option they had seen in TV advertisements. Those who wanted a specific career took higher level courses as prerequisites for their career aspirations.

Schools must view bilingual learners as individuals with individual needs. The ability of schools to recognize the differences between the students, to understand the forces behind what their students are, and to provide appropriate education greatly influences the future of these students. Paramount should be the goal to help all bilingual students regardless of language ability and educational background to achieve academically, to develop their language skills, and to achieve sociocultural integration.

ROLE OF FAMILIES

Home and community play important roles in students' sociocultural adjustment, bilingualism, and school performance. Parents' characteristics and views govern childrearing practices as well as perceptions and relations with schools (see Table 2.4).

Parents play a crucial role in the linguistic development of their children and they should do so in their own native language. Strong development of the native language is an essential foundation of acquisition of the second language and for academic achievement (Cummins, 1984). Soto (1993) demonstrated that families of high-achieving Puerto Rican children used Spanish more extensively at home

TABLE 2.4

Language, Culture, and Educational Characteristics of Parents

- Language development: native and English
- Attitudes toward native language and culture
- Motivation to maintain native language and culture
- Attitude toward English and American culture
- Promotion of English language and American culture acquisition
- Level of cultural adjustment
- Patterns of socialization of children
- Participation in education
- Level of language(s) proficiency and education
- Views on education and educational expectations

than parents of lower achieving students who were raised in a mostly mixed language environment. The parents of the high achievers strongly believed in developing a foundation in Spanish (at home and school), while slowly introducing English. Their strong support for Spanish did not deter their interest in their children learning English. The parents of the lower achievers were more ambivalent about Spanish. They valued Spanish but supported English instruction at school. Therefore, families of successful bilingual students encourage the development of both the home language and English. Chang recalled how his father, who always spoke in Vietnamese to him, often tested his children's English skills "he'd ask, 'what does this word in Vietnamese mean in English?' and we would tell him, and if not, we'd go up and look in the dictionary. He pushed us a lot" (Brisk, 1994a, p. 8).

Not all immigrant families support native language development because they do not feel it is important. Affective, linguistic, and cognitive development become vulnerable to neglect because parents dismiss interaction in the native language as irrelevant but cannot provide rich interaction in English.

Families of successful students make great efforts to maintain the home culture, including strong values toward work and study habits (Brisk, 1994a; Gibson, 1993; Suarez-Orozco, 1987). To contribute to the development of bicultural individuals, parents need to support cultural traits that will contribute to their children's adaptation to the American social system. Kleinfeld (1979) found that successful Eskimo leaders came from families of mixed cultural backgrounds in which the Eskimo and White cultures had fused. Many parents find the acceptance of American culture difficult because they associate it with poor work and study habits, crime, and gangs (Gibson, 1993).

Parents facilitate their children's adjustment when they can adjust themselves. Parents often settle ahead of their children. Once they are established, have found work and learned some English, they send for their children. Having undergone their own cultural adjustment, they can facilitate that of their children. Other parents seek supportive communities with established ethnic families and churches ready to provide support for the whole family (Brisk, 1994a).

Culture influences the way families socialize their children and relate to school. Values and behaviors of the students to a large extent reflect family values, especially with young children or newly arrived adolescents. Language acquisition, literacy, attitude toward disabilities, discipline practices, and sex roles influence parents' interaction with children, demands imposed on them, educational expectations, and perceptions of school role. For example, female students are at a disadvantage because often their education is a lower priority both at home and school. Punjabi high school girls' performance was not as high as that of boys because they had no hope of going away to 4-year colleges as there were none in the vicinity of their homes. Their families would not allow them to move in order to attend college (Gibson, 1993).

Parents' participation in education—whether it includes participation in the school or not—is a powerful influence (Brisk, 1994a; Nieto, 1992). Home–school collaboration promotes personal relationships that reinforce the roles of schools and homes (Carter & Chatfield, 1986; Garcia, 1988, 1991; Lindholm, 1990; Lucas, Henze, & Donato, 1990). Parents often support education at home, avoiding school involvement.

To a certain extent, education level of the parents correlates with success of students. Educated parents can help their children with homework. They also have an easier time communicating with school personnel. Parents without much education have difficulty helping students with their homework, especially at the high school level (Stergis, 1995). All parents can help students with achievement motivation. They encourage their children to do homework and take advantage of after-school tutoring or summer academic programs. They often forbid work, socializing, or television on school nights (Brisk, 1994a, 1996; Suarez-Orozco, 1993). For example, a successful high school bilingual student reports how seeing her mother working two cleaning jobs so that she could study rather than work during high school motivated her to work hard in school and do well (Brisk, 1994a). Suarez-Orozco (1993) found a similar sense of duty to the family among Salvadoran high school students. Doing well in school is seen by these students as the best reward for their parents' sacrifices.

When children experience poor schools, some parents lose interest and stop supporting their children's education. Figueiredo (1985) studied successful Portuguese adults who had dropped out of school. Families believed their children were learning little in school and pulled them out as soon as was legally possible. They wanted them to work and contribute to the welfare of the family. Getting a degree with little learning was of no value to them. Mexican Americans have experienced many generations of poor schooling. Many families lose faith in education and find that their children can be of more help at the home or farm (Suarez-Orozco, 1987, 1993).

Families want the best for their children. Sometimes they have a clear idea of how to achieve the best, but other times they are not sure. Schools can play a role in assisting families in support of their children. For this, schools also need to know what is best for bilingual students. High and reasonable expectations for academic achievement, support for native language development as well as English, and assistance in cultural adjustment so that students do not reject either culture should be included among the goals on which schools and families need to share and collaborate.

CONCLUSION

Situational, individual, and family factors out of the school's control mold bilingual students and their performance. Schools need to recognize that situational factors influence—often inaccurately—their judgment of students and families. Schools should work with families to tap valuable knowledge and resources with the common goal of helping students succeed. This collaboration is essential because children forging their social and cultural identity are very susceptible to outside influences coming from school and home (Sung, 1987). They can find themselves trapped in cultural conflict when the priorities of school and home conflict. Schools should also recognize and learn characteristics of individual students and their varying needs in order to adjust their efforts to educate bilingual students rather than to justify why they do not succeed. Understanding factors that affect students helps schools build on the positive while compensating for those that are negative.

Students also need to understand these factors, especially the situational ones. The realization that linguistic, cultural, economic, political, and social variables are at work frees students from personal blame. Often bilingual learners attribute problems to personal shortcomings rather than to particular circumstances of the society in which they live.

The education of bilingual students is complicated by the multiplicity of factors influencing the chances for success. Drawing from existing knowledge and moti- vated by successful examples, schools should be encouraged to try. Of paramount importance is to treat and view students as bilingual individuals who have a cultural background that, although different and often in conflict with mainstream America, is still the basis of the students' knowledge. Students cannot be treated as empty vessels to be filled, but as containers rich with knowledge to be added and expanded.

3

Creating a Good School

Individual factors in interaction with situational factors as well as family influence shape bilingual students, making each one a very different learner. For most of this century schools have failed these bilingual students. The research on effective bilingual programs demonstrates that there are specific things that schools can do to provide the kind of education that will give most students, regardless of personal or situational factors, a chance to succeed.

The effective school movement was a reaction to the Coleman et al. (1966) report, which came to the conclusion that the role of the schools was minimal compared to the influence of family characteristics on school achievement. The movement identified the characteristics of effective schools and it showed that these schools can make a difference in students' achievement (Purkey & Smith, 1983). Effective schools' features included instructional leadership, focus on instruction, orderly and safe climate, high expectations, and monitoring student performance (Edmonds, 1979; Weber, 1971). Within this research tradition, effective schools for bilingual students have been identified with similar characteristics with respect to school climate, organization and composition, staff, curriculum, and instructional and assessment practices. In addition, these schools take advantage of the languages known by the students and recognize their cultural background.

As bilingual students' first intense encounter with the English language and with American culture and society, schools must overcome social attitudes opposed to the social and academic development of bilingual learners. Successful schools create a productive academic environment and an accepting community. Although schools cannot change the social reality, they can create a different society within their walls. Getting to know the students and their families as well as welcoming their languages and cultures can build a coherent community where the bilingual program becomes an integral part of the school.

Improvement of bilingual programs necessitates fundamental changes within the whole school because the overall quality of the school will affect the bilingual program. For the most part, good bilingual programs exist within good schools (Carter & Chatfield, 1986; Tomlinson, 1989). To create a sound context for bilingual learners schools should:

- Set clear goals.
- Create a bilingual bicultural society.
- Integrate the bilingual program into the school community.
- Know the bilingual students.
- Provide leadership and support for the bilingual program.
- Set high expectations for bilingual students.
- Hire quality personnel willing and prepared to work with bilingual students.
- Establish productive partnerships with parents and communities of the bilingual students.

GOALS FOR THE SCHOOL

Administrators need to collaborate with faculty to clarify goals for all their students, including bilinguals. This enables schools to develop coherent curricula and consistent language policies, motivate and assess teachers, and stimulate the involvement of their communities in providing constructive criticism and support. School goals for bilingual students must be understood and shared by all faculty, students, and their families.

A strong mission statement shared by the staff and support structures that are created by the principal and other teachers and staff were among the characteristics found in effective bilingual programs (Carter & Chatfield, 1986; Carter & Maestas, 1982; Garcia, 1988; Lindholm, 1990; Lucas, 1993a; Moll, 1988). In Lauderbach, an elementary school in California, the mission of the school benefited all students, English speakers and bilinguals. The mission of the school became very concrete and real, evolving through the staff and community's collaborative work on objectives and strategies. Lauderbach is considered a model effective school (Carter & Chatfield, 1986).

Schools that include a bilingual program must ensure that the whole school embraces three essential goals for bilingual learners:

- Language proficiency to academic grade level.
- Sociocultural integration to their ethnic community and the society at large.
- Academic achievement as defined by school for all students.

Development of language proficiency includes ability in English to perform in school and later in the world of work as well as the English needed to socialize with English-speaking peers. To the extent possible, schools should foster the development of the home language because strong home language proficiency (including ability to read and write) positively affects second language acquisition and academic achievement (Cummins, 1984). Home language proficiency assists sociocultural integration. Students' ties with family and community depend on home language fluency; without it family relations often collapse (Wong-Fillmore, 1991

Ability to use native language at home with adults who are not proficient in English not only helps adult–child interactions, but also helps English language development in an indirect way. When adults who can barely speak English find themselves forced to use English as the only means of communication, they provide a very inappropriate model of the language. A distraught Vietnamese mother recounted how she was forced to speak English with her youngest child who had all but forgotten Vietnamese. In her own words "S'e sound ena ena ol' Vietnam. S'e s'e fo'got" (Wong-Fillmore, 1991, p. 339). The language development of this child would be better served if she could speak Vietnamese with the mother and English with fluent English speakers.

Language proficiency, in oral and written language, implies four areas of competence: grammatical, sociolinguistic, discourse, and strategic (Swain, 1984). A person develops these independently and to different levels for oral and written language. Grammatical competence includes knowledge of vocabulary, pronunciation, spelling, and word and sentence formation. Sociolinguistic competence requires knowledge to appropriately understand and produce language given the topic, status of participants, purposes of the interaction, and other contextual factors. Discourse competence is the ability to form oral or written texts in different genres that are well constructed and make sense. Strategic competence involves the ability to communicate or cope when there is insufficient competence in any of the other areas. Language learners need to develop an awareness of the right to use the language as an additional language competence (Peirce, 1995). A social context that invites language learners to take risks is essential. Often feelings of inadequacy emerge in particular social contexts, interfering with the learner's motivation to use the language. Such feelings emanate from self-perceptions relative to native or proficient speakers of the language. Overcoming these inhibitions, Peirce believed, is critical for language proficiency.

Different contexts place different demands on language proficiency. Language needed during classroom instruction is demanding and decontextualized (Wong Fillmore, 1982). Meaning is not evident from the context as it is on the playground where gestures and actions facilitate comprehension. Students also need language to socialize with their English-speaking peers. Although the latter kind of language is less demanding and often supported by context, it is ruled by cultural norms often unfamiliar to bilingual learners. Whereas conversational skills for social interaction can be achieved within 2 years of exposure to English, the language needed for academic work can take between 4 and 9 years (Collier, 1989; Cummins, 1981).

Language development is supported by use. Schools need to complement the use of the languages—both oral and written—in the home, community, and society at large. Those aspects of the languages most neglected outside the schools need to be reinforced in school. Home language literacy must be emphasized when students only experience oral use of the language. Social interaction in English is needed for students who rarely leave the ethnic neighborhood where all interactions are in the home language. The overall experience of the students at school and outside school should include rich encounters with both languages.

Achieving sociocultural integration allows one to function within the cultural norms of the home as well as the culture of the school and the society at large. Good bilingual education enables bilingual students to function in American society without rejecting their home culture. In St. Mary's, a high school in Alaska for Eskimos, "the school strengthened students' primary identity framework and extended values learned in a village childhood to the contexts of modern life" (Kleinfeld, 1979, p. 133). For bilinguals, schools usually represent their major encounter with American culture. Attitudes and behaviors of teachers and American peers and the role of the ESL and bilingual program impact these students' acculturation process. To achieve the goal of sociocultural integration, schools must know the students, provide a bicultural climate, and assist the students with understanding and functioning in the new culture without rejecting their own ethnic culture.

Academic goals for the school extend to bilingual students as well. Consistent with the current research in education, academic achievement for bilingual students should include developing good thinkers and problem solvers. Students must be expected to learn a body of knowledge not for its own sake alone, but also to practice and develop thinking skills. Sizer (1992), in his seminal work on high school education, proposed that rather than having students memorize facts, their minds have to be developed so that they can deal thoughtfully with the unexpected. This requires the formation of habits. Sizer included among these habits perspective, analysis, imagination, empathy, communication, commitment, humility, and joy. Exhibitions, rather than standardized tests, demonstrate achievement. Through authentic projects, students learn to organize and analyze arguments using tools from various disciplines, separate fact from opinion, develop personal views, respect different views, explain clearly, listen carefully, persevere as required by the task, recognize personal limitations, acquire necessary knowledge, and enjoy the learning process.

The use of home language and culture facilitates academic achievement of bilingual learners. Facts and habits acquired in their home language become part of the bilinguals' reservoir of knowledge that can be used when functioning in either language (Cummins, 1984).

Schools must make clear to bilingual and English-speaking students alike as well as their parents the type of curriculum and instructional practices needed to achieve these goals. It is critical to explain how the use of languages serves the purpose of educating both bilingual and English-speaking students.

All three outcomes are important because they closely relate to each other. Ability in both languages shows positive effects on academic achievement and linguistic development. Knowledge of home language affects knowledge of English. Level of proficiency in the language of instruction affects subject matter achievement. High levels of social integration and good attitudes toward languages and cultures often correlate with language learning and academic achie ment. Schools must work to achieve all three outcomes in order to educate bilinguals.

BILINGUAL AND BICULTURAL SOCIETY

Effective schools establish an orderly and safe climate. In schools where there are students of other cultures an essential ingredient for a safe school climate is respect for languages and cultures. In addition, language acquisition is enhanced when both languages have equal status, are spoken by individuals important to the students, and are necessary for communication in a variety of social environments (Escamilla, 1994b).

When Americans show respect for other people's cultures they gain respect toward their own language and culture. Schools must create an environment of mutual respect where not only English-speaking staff and students value other languages and cultures, but bilingual faculty and students show an appreciation for English and American culture as well as their own.

Respect for languages implies not only the standard varieties of English, Chinese, Italian, Spanish, or other languages but also the dialects that students actually use in their homes. Respect for cultures connotes not only those of immigrant students but the variety of cultural roots represented by American students. In schools that have a bilingual program as a component, home languages and cultures must transcend the boundaries of the bilingual program.

To create a bicultural society the school community must:

- Foster positive attitudes toward bilingual students' home languages.
- Encourage positive attitudes toward English and English speakers.
- Nurture positive attitudes toward the cultural background of students and staff.
- Face linguistic and cultural conflicts.

Attitude Toward Bilingual Students' Home Languages

Schools that value the language of the bilingual students treat knowledge of the language as an advantage, allow use of the language of the students on an equal basis as English, make resources available in the bilingual students' languages, and encourage English-speaking personnel to learn these languages and use them.

There are a number of ways to demonstrate genuine respect for languages. Allowing students to use their home language anywhere in the school, offering courses in that language (including advanced courses at the high school level), providing tests in both languages, and featuring students' languages in signs, ~jects, and other written work all enhance respect. In high schools in California, bilingual students were able to take Advanced Placement courses in Spanish to gain college credit (Lucas et al., 1990). In some high schools that require students to study a second language, courses for native speakers who know the language orally but have never had formal instruction and second language courses for nonnative speakers are offered (Brisk, 1996; Lucas et al., 1990).

Bilingual teachers should feel free to use the bilingual students' home language outside instruction and, ideally, bilingual school staff should use their language with each other. Tests and students' products in the home language should be given as much importance as those in English. Good results in either language should be equally celebrated. Featuring the language around the school does not mean translating everything. Indeed, translation defeats the purpose of developing bilingualism: If everything is translated there is no need to know both languages. A better policy is to have some things posted in English and some things posted in the native language of the students. Balancing the status of both the home language and English in the whole school—rather than just the bilingual class-room—greatly influences the development of language proficiency among bilingual students.

Classrooms and libraries must include material in the bilingual students' languages. Having a multilingual, multicultural library does not mean having a few old books in one corner. Libraries should feature books in the language of the students for the different disciplines as well as literature for different ages filed within those areas. In this way, English-speaking students, while looking for a history book for example, encounter a book on history in another language. In a subtle way, it tells the students that other languages are legitimate for study. A school library in southern California provided bilingual aides to assist the students in their home language (Fulton-Scott & Calvin, 1983). Bilingual parents participating in a family literacy program in Massachusetts took turns at the school library to assist students and read stories in their native languages.

Although materials in the native language are vital, bilingual books also serve various purposes, especially for beginners. Understanding the content by reading in the stronger language helps when deciphering the second language. These books can also be useful for English speakers who show interest in the native language of bilingual students.

Great value is given to the language of students when personnel studies it. A number of the English-speaking teachers and counselors learned Spanish in the effective schools studied by Lucas and her colleagues (Lucas et al., 1990). With the collaboration of a local university, an elementary school in Boston offered after-school Spanish classes in which teachers, the principal, and even the janitor enrolled.

Bilingual students' language should be promoted among all students. The level of teaching and learning varies from complete immersion in the language to simply a specific activity related to the culture of the students. All students are schooled in Spanish and English in the Oyster School in Washington, DC, where about half of the students are Spanish speakers. In a high school in Boston that has a studer body that is about 50% Spanish speakers, English speakers are expected to develop some level of fluency in Spanish. A Korean bilingual teacher in San Francisco, with the assistance of bilingual and English-speaking children, planted a Korean vegetable garden learning the Korean names of the vegetables. This legitimized use of Korean in the school. Regardless of the extent, the commitment to bilingual students' language in these different situations became an integral part of the goals of the school.

Depending on the level of education of the families and students, bilingual students may speak an informal variety of the language. Those born and raised in an ethnic community in the United States may speak a dialect heavily influenced by English. Teachers must distinguish between the home and formal variety in an objective way and must accept the students' variety as a valid form of communication. The use of the different varieties can be contrasted. Students become language detectives, noticing that most books and tests use the more standard variety of the language, whereas plays, movies, oral discourse, and even dialogue in a work of fiction exhibit more informal forms of the language. Teachers must point out that one variety is not better than the other but that one is more appropriate than the other depending on the circumstances. An elementary teacher in the Chicago area, whose students came from different Spanish-speaking regions, developed with her students a glossary of terms for each reading book. One column had the term used in the book (standard Spanish), another contained the equivalent in Chicano Spanish, and the third in Puerto Rican Spanish. The students learned that there were different rather than better forms of the language.

Positive attitudes toward home language must be promoted among bilingual students themselves because they often reject the use of their native language in favor of English as a result of what they perceive to be acceptable in the larger society (Commins, 1989). This is particularly true of students who were born or have resided in the United States for a few years. When they witness respect from teachers and peers they slowly change their own attitudes. Julio, a Spanish-speaking mainstreamed student, was very upset when his mainstream class formed a cluster with a bilingual class. Initially he did not want to use Spanish or work with students in the bilingual class because he saw it as a step backward. Both the mainstream and bilingual teachers patiently discussed his concerns with him. It took several weeks before he cooperated and used his bilingual ability to facilitate communication in working groups of mainstream and bilingual students.

Attitudes Toward English and English Speakers

Positive attitudes toward English and English speakers are vital for the acquisition of that language (Schumann, 1978). Often schools assume that students, by virtue of being in the United States, will develop a positive attitude. Well-planned activities are a precondition for success. Constructive experiences with English-speaking peers can help bilingual students and teachers develop positive attitudes. For example, in a bilingual integrated seventh grade cluster in which English- and

Spanish-speaking students functioned as a unit and all languages and cultures were respected, acceptance of English and English speakers developed naturally. Spanish-speaking students were motivated to learn English because they wanted to communicate with students and teachers they liked. Edgar, one of the bilingual students, felt proud of his efforts to communicate with English speakers: "I feel good relating to American kids who do not speak Spanish and the teacher doesn't know it either. This way I have to make an effort in English to try to understand. Every day I learn new things and have more friends" (Brisk, 1991c, p. 122).

Edgar's experience is far from universal. Historical factors and pressure to assimilate contribute to the development of negative attitudes toward English. Students from ethnic groups colonized or conquered by English speakers either in the United States (Native Americans, Mexican Americans, and Puerto Ricans) or abroad may have developed unfavorable attitudes. For example Ahmed, a sixth grade Pakistani student, refused to learn English because he felt he was betraying Urdu, his mother tongue. His country was under British rule for many years and English dominated that society. Schools must help bilingual students draw the distinction between English as a symbol of conquest and domination and English as the language of peers, teachers, shopkeepers, and other people they encounter in their daily life, as well as poets and writers whose work they can learn to enjoy. Teachers need to show Ahmed how through history different groups have conquered others and their languages became the symbol of domination.

Pressure to assimilate and learn English can backfire. Rather than submit to the pressures of learning English at the expense of their home language, some students reject English and American culture: "Pressure for assimilation at the expense of one's home culture forces young children to make painful personal choices which often affect their self-esteem and, in some cases, their ability to learn English and other academic skills" (Secada & Lightfoot, 1993, p. 51). English can be promoted without losing respect for the students' native languages.

Respect for English extends to English speakers from other cultures. English speakers from Caribbean countries encounter difficulties because they speak a different dialect of English and have a different cultural background. Rather than considering the English of a Jamaican girl incorrect, I suggested to a third-grade teacher that she see it as a different language. In turn, she needed to teach American English as a second—rather than better—language to this student making her see the differences.

Attitudes Toward Cultures

Nieto (1992) identified four levels of attitudes toward culture as manifested in education: "tolerance, acceptance, respect, and affirmation, solidarity and critique" (p. 276). To tolerate means to accept but not to embrace. Schools merely recognize the culture through isolated celebrations such as Puerto Rican week or multicultural festivals. Acceptance includes acknowledging the students' language and culture to a limited degree; for example, in TBE programs in which the language and cultur are recognized as long as the students are in the program, but they are not embraced by the whole school. When there is respect for the culture of the students it is evident throughout the school and curriculum. Affirmation, solidarity, and critique represent the highest level of multicultural education. Culture of the students and families is accepted as legitimate, is considered active, and is subject to conflict when in contact with other cultures. Conflict necessitates analysis, or critique, because without it "cultural understanding remains at the romantic or exotic state" (Nieto, 1992, p. 277).

Schools should aspire to the higher levels of attitude toward culture of all students, bilingual as well as English speakers. A positive attitude toward the culture of the bilingual students develops trust in the educational system. When the school—an institution representing the dominant society—respects their culture and background, students are more willing to advance within the system. If that trust is lacking, these students are more likely to abandon traditional forms of advancement—especially education (Ruiz, 1993).

Functioning in a new cultural context is a difficult experience. Cultural adjustment is greatly assisted by acceptance on the part of English speakers. Bilingual students will be more willing to share in the American culture if they feel that Americans have a positive attitude toward them and their culture (Schumann, 1978). Incorporation of the students' language and culture enhances self-esteem (Garcia, 1991; Pease-Alvarez, Garcia, & Espinosa, 1991). Acceptance of the students' culture helps them establish an identity that is rooted in their cultural group but extends beyond it into the new social group.

Kleinfeld (1979) studied a high school for Eskimo children that successfully prepared students to function effectively in American society as well as in their own communities. These students had developed a bicultural identity because the

> significant reference groups in the majority culture (such as teachers, majority-group classmates, media) hold the minority culture in esteem and significant reference groups in the local minority culture (such as parents, peers, older youth who are trend-setters) hold the majority culture in esteem [and because] central socialization settings (home, school, religious groups, ethnic organizations) fuse elements from both cultures rather than separate them. (p. 137)

Evidence of respect and interest in the students' culture is found in school values, curriculum, social relationships, and preparation of personnel. The presence of the students' cultures should be natural and constant and it should transcend all corners of the school. For example, at St Mary's, a high school in Alaska for Eskimo students, leadership was defined reflecting Eskimo values "not as putting ones self above others but as working hard for the benefit of the group" (Kleinfeld, 1979, p. 132). Elements of Eskimo culture were integrated into all courses and extracurricular activities. The social structure of the school reflected the highly personalized style of an Eskimo village but comportment in the classroom followed the more formal rules of interaction between teacher and students typical of U.S. high schools. Eskimo ways "were the scaffolding through which students acquired the behavioral structure of the majority culture" (p. 131). Even where there are a variety of cultures, cultural integration is possible. For example in a high school in Boston in which there were students of 10 different language backgrounds, the various cultures of the program were nourished by accepting students' ideas in class, by inclusion of their culture in the curriculum, by inviting speakers from those cultures to address the students, and by having mixed ethnic groups working cooperatively in class (Brisk, 1996).

Personnel sensitive to cultural varieties sets the tone for positive attitudes. Schools need to hire or provide professional development for existing personnel. For example, in several California high schools the counselors studied cross-cultural counseling (Lucas et al., 1990). A new English-speaking principal of an elementary school in Boston with a large percentage of Puerto Rican students arranged to visit the town in Puerto Rico that most of his students came from. This visit gave him an understanding of the educational system and social environment familiar to his students and their families.

Schools need to help bilingual students gain respect for American culture. Fomenting positive attitudes toward American culture means dealing with a cultural mosaic with internal conflicts due to race, ethnicity, religion, and class. In order to instill positive attitudes among bilingual students, Americans themselves need to define their culture and become more inclusive with respect to all citizens. In a democracy, people group and regroup themselves across regional, ethnic, religious, racial, and other boundaries. These boundaries are flexible and constantly change cultural characteristics. What defines American identity is the coexistence constantly reshaped by immigration (Lerner, 1957). Developing a positive attitude toward Americans and their culture must encompass all members of the American mosaic and their contributions to American language and culture.

A school environment that respects languages and cultures incorporates students and their families with their own characteristics and life experiences into the life of the school rather than waiting until they have assimilated into American culture and developed English proficiency. Their presence is seen as a way of enriching the knowledge the school offers to all. Language and culture is the starting point for growth rather than something to be hidden and forgotten.

Creating a bicultural society is essential for achieving the goals of language proficiency, sociocultural integration, and academic achievement. Bilingual students who feel respected rather than threatened will want to learn English, commute between two cultural worlds, and dedicate their energies to their academic work. Valuing the language and culture of the students impacts on their self-esteem and students "with high self-esteem work harder, learn better, and achieve more" (Snow, 1990, p. 64).

Programs that bring bilingual and English-speaking students and faculty together for academic and social activities in an environment of respect for all languages and cultures can be instrumental in developing good attitudes toward each other's languages and cultures. Luis, an elementary student in a bilingual integrated program in which all cultures and languages were highly respected, illustrated the value of a bicultural environment by his comments: "I like to speak Spanish and English. I can practice Spanish and practice English and I don't feel strange and scared and different" (Brisk, 1991c, p. 122).

THE BILINGUAL PROGRAM AS AN INTEGRAL PART OF THE SCHOOL

An important educational dilemma is how to handle differences: Segregate students who have the same needs to provide specifically for those needs, or integrate them to avoid the social stigma of segregation (Minow, 1990). School desegregation and the current effort to integrate special education students into the mainstream reflects the conviction that different types of students will benefit from studying together. On the other hand, single-sex schools, alternative programs for children with emotional needs, and some types of bilingual education programs have provided for specific educational needs by catering to a specific population. Effective school research adheres to the integration of the bilingual program to the school as a whole (Carter & Chatfield, 1986).

There is a continuum of possibilities to implement integration. The most complete integration of bilingual education comes when the whole school is bilingual and the students come from English-speaking and other language backgrounds. For example, the Oyster School in Washington, DC is a public bilingual school in which all the students learn and study in English and Spanish. The school is composed of roughly half Spanish and half English speakers. The time devoted to instruction is equally divided between the two languages (Fern, 1995).

Two-way bilingual programs accomplish integration of students within the program, but the program itself needs to be integrated into the school. The Amigos program, a two-way bilingual program in Cambridge, Massachusetts, enrolls English and Spanish speakers in a bilingual elementary school program. There is an equal percentage of students of each language group. Students take all their classes in English and in Spanish in mixed native language groups. Each group alternates the language of instruction by week. Students are encouraged to use the language of instruction and language mixing is discouraged (Cazabon et al., 1993). Students become fluent in two languages, form friendships within their own and the other cultural group, and prefer being schooled in this integrated setting (Lambert & Cazabon, 1994).

Bilingual schools and two-way programs are more the exception than the norm. Usually schools offer a bilingual program within the school directed only to language minority students. In this case, schools must integrate bilingual and mainstream classes and teachers preserving bilingual education for bilingual students. In bilingual integrated programs, bilingual and mainstream students and teachers come together on an equal basis, sharing skills and facilities. The main language of the classroom shifts depending on the class and the teacher but both languages preserve equal status (Brisk, 1991a, 1994b). This type of program is different from the more common "inclusion" approach in which bilingual students and teachers participate in a mainstream classroom with the bilingual or ESL teacher acting as a secondary teacher, the main language of the classroom is English, and students are viewed as outsiders.

Bilinguals benefit from interaction with native speakers of English who accept them regardless of level of language proficiency. When English-speaking friends trust the bilingual students' ability to communicate, they include them in their activities and conversations, allowing them an opportunity to acquire the language (Wong Fillmore, 1979). However, when bilingual learners feel like outsiders or do not want to reveal their lack of proficiency, they become silent (Peirce, 1995).

In the integrated programs, bilingual classes are clustered with at least one mainstream class. These clusters operate as a unit in separate but adjacent classrooms or bilingual and mainstream students and teachers share the same class. These clusters interlace completely for all curricular areas or just for certain activities. These clusters should have at least an equal number of bilingual and mainstream students even if this means that other mainstream students will not participate. Distributing bilingual students throughout the school can diffuse the support for these students (Miramontes, 1994).

Integration can be complete or just for a certain curricular area or activities. In grade-level fully integrated clusters, bilingual and mainstream teachers plan together to define curriculum, language of instruction, student assignments, and contact with families. At the start of the year students and teachers in the clusters formed in the Chelsea schools met together to convey to the students the notion that they were all part of a team. The bilingual teachers taught in Spanish or bilingually and the English-speaking teachers taught in English but allowed the native language of the students in their classes. The students received a full curriculum and were assigned to classes depending on their language needs (Brisk, 1991a, 1994b).

In clusters that integrate only for certain activities, bilingual and mainstream teachers plan together, convey to students and parents that they are an integrated cluster, bring students together at least once a week, and plan special programs for the whole cluster, such as field trips or a special final project. In an elementary school in Chelsea, teachers met weekly to plan activities in their own classrooms that led to bringing the bilingual and mainstream students together once a week. Some chose reading and others chose math as their focus of integration (Brisk, 1994b). In the Carpinteria, Unified School District in California's early childhood program, bilingual and monolingual children were naturally integrated through play activities and field trips and most cognitive activities were conducted in the students' native language in separate groups (Campos & Keatinge, 1988; Krashen & Biber, 1988).

Certain elements are essential to accomplish any kind of integration:

- Equality of status for bilingual and mainstream teachers and students.
- Clear understanding of the program by students and parents.
- Freedom of language use.
- Classroom methodologies that encourage student interaction and initiative.
- A coordinated curriculum.
- Flexibility to meet individual students' needs.
- Emphasis on bilingual and mainstream teachers' strengths.
- Physical proximity of classrooms in the cluster.

These elements were present in bilingual program integration carried out in Chelsea, Massachusetts at the elementary and middle school (Brisk, 1994b). All students and teachers in each cluster had equal status. Teachers were responsible for all students. In turn, students felt equally comfortable relating to all teachers. Each teacher preserved his or her own classroom, but all students and teachers in the cluster felt free to go in and out of all the classrooms. For example, a bilingual first-grade teacher had a cocoon for students to observe a live caterpillar in the process of metamorphosis to a butterfly. All first graders in that cluster came to her room first thing in the morning to check on the cocoon and note any changes in their science notebooks. Mainstream students would then go on to their own room to start the morning session.

The concept of the program was introduced to students and parents of the various clusters at the beginning of the year. Special activities helped the initial encounter among students. For example, one first-grade teacher explained to the students that they were going to work with a partner from the other class. They gave half of a picture to each student in the bilingual class and the other half to each student in the mainstream class. The two students whose halves matched worked as partners for the rest of the period. In looking for the other half of the puzzle, students had to interact with each other, thus quickly breaking barriers between the groups. Teachers and administrators must reassure parents that their children will be learning in this new social structure. For example, one evening the parents of the fifth-grade cluster attended an abbreviated version of a day in school. Teachers staged 10-minute renditions of their classes. Parents followed their own child from class to class to get a flavor for the program.

Regardless of the language of instruction in these particular programs—either Spanish or English—the students' home language was accepted at all times. Spanish, English, Khmer, Chinese, and Czech were considered valid for solving problems, asking for clarification, reading, and writing. When there was limited proficiency of the language either on the part of the teacher or the student, various strategies were used to facilitate comprehension, such as translation by bilingual individuals, use of pictures, gestures, hands-on activities, and having students work in cooperative groups in which more proficient bilinguals facilitated communication.

Teachers used methodologies appropriate for students with a variety of language levels, both in their native and second languages. Teachers usually introduced the daily lesson to the whole class. Bilingual teachers alternated between languages, whereas the English-speaking teachers would ask a bilingual student, student teacher, or teacher aide to translate. Following the introduction, students worked in groups on specific tasks. The teacher and any other adult in the class walked around the classroom answering questions, clarifying tasks, and checking comprehension. Group work is an essential form of organization for heterogeneous classrooms (DeVillar & Faltis, 1991). Because of the variety of literacy and math ability levels, cross-age projects (see Appendix) were organized to reinforce language and math skills. Students in the fifth- and seventh-grade clusters taught reading, writing, and math in either English or Spanish to kindergarten, first, or second graders in either bilingual or mainstream classes. Older students acted as expert tutors rather than learners in need of remediation. In being trained as tutors for the younger students, their basic literacy and math skills were reinforced.

Teachers coordinated curriculum in several ways. Thematic units, coordination of content across disciplines, and interdisciplinary class projects were among the strategies used. A bilingual and a mainstream first-grade teacher developed monthly units involving all disciplines around a particular theme. They shared materials and ideas and they implemented these units in their own classrooms and chose opportunities to bring the students together.

Students were assigned to classes based on language ability and needs rather than random choice of students to work with the bilingual or mainstream teacher. Students were discussed during teachers' weekly meetings and adjustments in their schedules were made when necessary. When Carlos, a recent arrival from El Salvador, entered fifth grade, the teachers decided that he would take reading, language arts, and social studies in Spanish, math bilingually, and some units of science bilingually and others in English. He also received 30 minutes of ESL instruction daily. Thus he was receiving most instruction in his stronger language, but was also exposed to English through language teaching as well as content area courses. On the other hand, Jennifer, an English-speaking student, took all her classes except for math with English-speaking teachers. Taking math with the bilingual teacher met Jennifer's needs to take advanced math and to experience Spanish in an academic context.

Integrated programs recognize the special abilities of bilingual teachers. Bilingual staff can assist mainstream teachers in working appropriately with bilingual students by suggesting instructional strategies and giving a more complete evaluation of the students based on what they do in their native language as well as English. Language skills of bilingual teachers can fulfill second language instruction for English-speaking students. The bilingual staff facilitates communication with parents of all the bilingual students in the school, not only those in the bilingual program. Usually parents of bilingual children who have been mainstreamed lose contact with the school because they do not dare communicate with English-speaking teachers.

Mainstream teachers contribute to the bilingual program with their own talents in particular disciplines and in their role as consistent English models.[1] Having to communicate with these teachers provides a functional motivation to learn English. Students make the effort willingly in the context of schools where care and respect for the bilingual students, their language, and their culture prevails. Mainstream teachers may know other languages. Their linguistic talents should be polled and used to the advantage of the students and families. For example, in a high school a mainstream math teacher was fluent in Spanish and knew some Portuguese. He taught math bilingually in Spanish and English to his mixed class of Spanish- and English-speaking students. He could also help a Portuguese student in his or her own language. He also tutored bilingual students who wanted to take calculus (offered only in English). Thus, an integrated program takes full advantage of the staff of the school for the benefit of all students.

The location of the bilingual classes next to the English-only classes allowed for the participation of students in each other's activities. Proximity of classrooms facilitates movement of students between classrooms and encourages casual inter-action among students and teachers. It never took more than 3 minutes for students to go from one classroom to the other and for the class to start in clusters where the rooms were adjacent to or across from each other. This proximity also allowed the mainstream teacher to seek quick help from the bilingual teacher when there was total communication breakdown. Before or after school or during breaks, students would drop by any of the classrooms in the cluster to talk to the teachers, check on special projects, or socialize.

Commitment of principals and mainstream staff to the program and the students makes it possible for bilingual programs to be integrated into the whole school. All staff and not only the bilingual staff should be responsible for the bilingual students' education. In turn, the bilingual staff should participate in general school activities and decision making. When curriculum improvement or special programs are introduced, the bilingual program should also be included. Regardless of how integration is implemented, school mission, curriculum, and environment must reflect the presence of students of different languages and cultures. Otherwise, integrated and two-way programs that succeed in bringing both groups of students together will remain isolated within the school.

KNOWING THE STUDENTS

Bilingual students need to feel that their school is a community that cares for them, treats them as individuals, and wants them to succeed (McPartland & Braddock, 1993). In effective schools, administrators and teachers know their students and

---

[1]Mainstream teachers who do not feel included in the goals of the bilingual program are less helpful and tend to oppose the program (Cleghorn & Genesee, 1984).

students know each other. Knowledge of the students and personalization of the teaching are keys to good teaching (Graves, 1983; Sizer, 1984). Because teachers relate to students both as learners and as children or adolescents, teachers must establish how they will address these two types of relationships, what they need to know about their students, and how they will acquire this knowledge.

The teacher–learner relationship implies involvement between teachers and students around subject matter, whereas adult–child or adult–adolescent relationships are more personal and intimate (McDiarmid, 1991). Focusing on both types of relationships bridges the gap between school and the world outside it, a gap that is especially important for many bilingual students whose world differs greatly from school. Teachers working with young students have succeeded in combining both types of relationships in the context of the classroom. For example, Cazden, Carrasco, Maldonado-Guzman, and Erickson (1980) observed a Mexican American teacher working with first-grade Spanish speakers. Every morning as they sat in a circle, she collected homework and addressed the children with endearing terms, asking questions about them and their families. In successful high schools these relationships have been somewhat separate with the teacher–learner relationship confined more to the classroom and the adult–adolescent relationship carried out outside the classroom. These boundaries are not rigid; in fact much learning takes place through personal relationships. In St. Mary's boarding high school for Eskimos, the teacher–learner relationship took place within the classroom and was ruled mostly by White cultural norms of behavior. However, personal relationships outside the classroom conformed to Eskimo culture. These relationships were close, informal, and involved much teaching and learning (Kleinfeld, 1979). Those who teach in public high schools have little opportunity to interact with students outside the classroom; therefore they must make a special effort. However, special efforts can be rewarding. In Central Park East Secondary School in New York City, students met daily for an hour with the same adult (including teachers, administrators, secretaries, and other staff) to discuss personal issues. The adult was in charge of communicating with the family and worked with the same group of students for 2 years. These "advisories," as they were called, planned extracurricular activities such as field trips together (Meier, 1995).

Knowing the bilingual students as learners includes awareness of their understanding of subject content, language proficiency, and previous educational experiences. Teachers also must explore characteristics that differentiate any learner, such as learning skills, learning styles, aptitude, level of maturation, and other factors (Sizer, 1992).

Teachers working with bilingual students need to know not only how much each student knows about a particular subject but what their cultural perception of the subject is (i.e., cultural knowledge). For example McDiarmid (1991) recalled a discussion with fourth-grade Yupik Eskimo students about what might have caused the school walk-in refrigerator to break down. They discussed the cooling system, compressor, and gases. Finally "I asked, 'So, why did the walk-in break down?'

One of the students who had been most involved in the conversation replied, 'Ghosts.'" (p. 257). Myth rather than science explained unknown events in this student's culture.

Students' background knowledge is acquired through home experiences. Even humble homes are rich in social and intellectual resources. This knowledge engendered by the home should serve as the foundation for learning (Moll, Amantin, Neff, & González, 1992). Knowing their students' families changed teachers' attitudes. From a perception that culture is fixed, teachers realized that culture is dynamic, changing, and goes beyond stereotypes. Culture encompasses all of the students' experiences. These are not found in books about a particular culture but in the lives of the students and their families (Gonzalez et al., 1993).

No assumptions can be made with respect to students' language skills. Each individual is likely to present a different profile. Age, place of residence, previous schooling, approach to learning languages, and home language use determine bilingual students' language proficiency. Students may speak, read, or write only one language or both and probably have different levels of ability for each skill and each language. Rubén, a student with a hearing impairment was considered by teachers an American Sign Language speaker only. The bilingual teacher visited the home and concluded that he was trilingual in English, Spanish, and American Sign Language. As the oldest in the family, he frequently served as his mother's translator outside the home in spite of his limited hearing (Gerner de García, 1993).

Knowledge of students' language skills is important even when students are fluent in English. Often staff members think that if the students function in English, there is no need to delve into their bilingualism and cultural background. The case of Joseph proves the contrary. Joseph was born in the United States to Korean parents. He encountered problems reading in English in first grade. Frustrated by his lack of progress, his reading recovery teacher tried the critical autobiography approach (see Appendix), which requires students to discuss, analyze, and write about their lives in order to understand how situational factors have shaped their histories (Brisk & Zandman, 1995). With some assistance from Joseph's mother, they produced a rather sophisticated book on Korean language, culture, religion, politics, and economics. In the process of writing this book the teacher realized that Joseph could speak, read, and write Korean; that he struggled with a number of cultural conflicts; and that his parents pondered the issue of bilingualism and language use at home. Through this process, Joseph was allowed to show his whole self to his teachers and classmates. Eight weeks after the book writing project started, Joseph graduated from the reading remediation program. What the teacher could not do in 4 months of dealing with Joseph as an English speaker, she was able to do in 2 months of working with him as a bilingual individual.

Students' language and academic development, approaches to learning, and classroom behavior are to a great extent the result of previous educational experience. For example, José, a seventh grader, was having problems in an English language arts class. When asked about his previous educational experiences, he recounted that he had gone to first grade in his native New Jersey in a school system with no bilingual program. As a native speaker of Spanish, his first encounter with learning to read in English was not successful. By second grade, his family moved to Puerto Rico, where his second-grade teacher was unhappy with his inability to read in Spanish. Two years later, the family moved to New England. Having made some progress in reading Spanish, he again had to face school in English. By seventh grade, José spoke English and Spanish fluently but still had problems with reading—a result of his history as a reader rather than an innate lack of talent. In addition, he had a very distinct self-image of being a "bad reader" established in first grade with respect to English and in second grade with respect to Spanish. With this information, the teacher established a plan to give José a chance to have small reading victories, develop his reading ability, and gain confidence as a reader.

Students acquire ways of learning promoted by particular school systems. For example, in systems where text is to be studied instead of analyzed and questioned, students tend to read word by word, look up words they do not know in the dictionary, and make meticulous summaries of what they read. These students often use the exact words from texts in their written work without quoting or crediting the author. This is not considered plagiarizing, but a demonstration of accurate knowledge and hard work (Ballard & Clanchy, 1991).

Personal knowledge of bilingual students includes attitude toward the languages and motivation to learn them, degree of sociocultural integration, and influence of situational variables on them and their families. Teachers need to understand students' feelings with respect to their languages, desire to learn them well, and perspective toward the culture of their community as well as American culture. In order to help students become adjusted bilingual and bicultural individuals, teachers must determine areas of conflict. On the surface, Gabriel was just another student failing high school due to indifference and unwillingness to work. Language was not an apparent issue because he was fluent in English. A bilingual teacher, however, uncovered a very confused individual. He considered himself Puerto Rican but "it's just the language that changes me," he said, referring to the fact that his Spanish ability is limited (mostly colloquial oral). One day he wrote he was 100% Puerto Rican and another day he claimed he was Puerto Rican just because his family told him so. Although he talked about family celebrations with pleasure, he wrote that "I don't really celebrate any holidays because they don't really mean anything to me." He refused to use Spanish and participate in Spanish class, yet he claimed that being bilingual was an advantage to get jobs. Talking about his previous schooling brought painful memories of attending a school in English as a young child when Spanish was his strong language.[2] He did like his American teachers: "I liked learning English with them." He valued education and wanted to go on to college, yet he was flunking ninth grade. Settling Gabriel's language and cultural conflicts was intrinsic to help him change his attitude toward school and improve his academic performance.

---

[2]Gabriel attended English-only programs through eighth grade. A social worker referred him to a multicultural high school in the hopes of improving his performance.

Individual characteristics do not affect bilingual students exclusively. Linguistic, cultural, political, economic, and social factors do as well. Exploring these situational factors deepens the understanding of students and their families. It even helps experienced teachers work with new populations. Students may speak the same language as those already in the United States, but they may have very different reasons for coming, previous school experience, and status in the society.

A number of strategies will help teachers know their students and improve their teaching. Instructional strategies that serve the dual purpose of delivering instruction and providing a window into the characteristics of the students are critical autobiographies, dialogue journals, student-directed sharing time or discussions, the icebreaker (see Appendix), and prereading and writing activities that elicit students' background knowledge. Simply interviewing students produces a wealth of information. When interviewing, it is important to be flexible about language choice. By simply codeswitching initially, the interviewer signals to the student that both languages are accepted.

To learn about the students in the context of the home, teachers can either do home visits or carry out cooperative projects with the parents. Teachers also find out through home visits many important things they did not know about the families, such as the sacrifices that many of these families make for the sake of their children's education, their strength when confronted with adversity, and many other qualities that contradict the typical view of poor families (Gonzalez et al., 1993).

Parent–teacher cooperative projects allow teachers to learn what and how their students learn at home. For example, the Intergenerational Literacy Program in Chelsea, Massachusetts, uses portfolio parent–teacher conferences as a tool for discovering home literacy practices. Parents are asked to develop literacy portfolios reflective of literacy activities conducted at home. The classroom teachers develop their own literacy portfolios. During parent–teacher meetings the portfolios are discussed. As a result, teachers changed their expectations of some students when they realized that at home these students were already doing things that had not yet been taught at school (Paratore et al., 1995).

As teachers learn about their students, students learn about each other. Students must care for each other in all their similarities and differences. For example, the Puerto Rican students in Angela's class, while discussing their critical autobiographies with their Central American peers, learned about the killings of close family members, the parents' agony of long separation from their children, and the Central American students' feelings of abandonment by parents. Their own life problems seemed less harsh when compared with those of their Central American classmates. When students know each other and care for each other, they do not need to act out to make themselves known and popular. McCollum (1993) reported on middle school Mexican American students who were in a school that had developed a culture in which being bad made them popular. Part of being bad for bilingual students was refusing to speak Spanish. If students know each other and there is a sense of community developed in the school, there is no need to resort to behavior that is detrimental to the students' own academic and linguistic success in order to be noticed. In a community of learners, everybody is equally important and known by others.

To facilitate knowledge of students, schools need to be of a human scale; that is, a size that permits all individuals to know each other (Meier, 1995; Sizer, 1995).[3] For example, a new multicultural high school in the Boston area consisted of five teachers and 80 students.[4] The students appreciated not being invisible and considered their experience very different from that of their previous high schools (Brisk, 1996). The teachers knew all students by name and frequently discussed individual cases among themselves. If students were absent, the teachers contacted the families. The size and organization of the program fostered frequent and close contact between teachers and students. A daily school opening activity, the "town meeting," allowed the entire school community to interact. Students, teachers, volunteers, and visitors gathered for general announcements, celebrations, outside speakers, and student presentations. Often students came early to socialize or check on their homework with each other or with teachers. Teachers knew each other well and supported each other. They shared responsibilities, met frequently to discuss students and curriculum, and worked together in solving problems and addressing discipline cases.

A school that treats all students as equals treats all students as individuals. Such schools give all students the same chance to reach the standards of excellence they have set for their students. Because students differ from one another, they will reach those standards following different paths. Knowledge of the students is essential to address individual needs. In the case of bilingual students, this knowledge must go far beyond just concern for English language proficiency.

LEADERSHIP AND SUPPORT
FOR THE BILINGUAL PROGRAM

All studies on effective schools point to the importance of leadership (Edmonds, 1979; Mace-Matluck, 1990). Administrators must support the bilingual program, its teachers, and its students. They must understand the conditions for quality bilingual education, foster collaboration among teachers, and gain community support and participation.

Bilingual program teachers need to secure the support of the school administration as well as the district administrator in charge of bilingual education. The role of the principal is important to promoting the program as well as defining staff roles. Support from the principal is essential to create acceptance for bilingual education within the whole school and community.

Actions that show a principal's supportive actions include:

---

[3]Sizer considered 400 students the maximum acceptable size.
[4]The school was a satellite of a larger high school but was housed in the campus of a community college.

- Hiring bilingual staff members from students' cultures.
- Encouraging parents of [language minority] students to participate in the school activities.
- Encouraging staff to participate in staff development focused on [language minority] students.
- Participating in such staff development himself or herself.
- Including [language minority] program staff on meeting agendas.
- Promoting programs and services for [language minority] students in district and community meetings.
- Working with the district bilingual staff to design school curriculum.
- Allowing district bilingual staff to plan with school staff. (Lucas, 1993b, pp. 105–106)

District and school bilingual directors play a key role as "the driving forces behind successful programs" (Lucas, 1993a, p. 137). District coordinators provide a network for bilingual staff and spread specialized knowledge of the field by disseminating new instructional practices, materials, and assessment strategies. They often serve as mentors for new bilingual teachers (Torres-Guzmán & Goodwin, 1995). Their support is particularly crucial for schools in which there are few bilingual and ESL teachers as well as for schools with principals who are not very knowledgeable about bilingual education.

The trend toward school-based management enhances the principal's role as it decreases the influence of district coordinators. Principals must exercise their authority to improve the bilingual program and make the education of bilingual students a priority where it has been neglected. On taking over a high school in California, a new principal

> discovered that bilingual classes were "remedial," that the school offered bilingual life science rather than biology and bilingual math rather than algebra. He quickly set out to "amend" the situation. Sections of physics, chemistry, and calculus were added along with summer sessions of geometry; the requirements for athletic participation were raised; the number of bilingual staff was increased from eight to thirty three; the bilingual program was expanded to include advanced courses such as economics, biology II, and honors chemistry as well as lower division bilingual courses. (Lucas et al., 1990, pp. 328–329)

To promote what is right for bilingual students, principals must be familiar with research and practices in bilingual education (Carter & Chatfield, 1986; Garcia, 1988). In effective schools, the principals are leaders in promoting instructional practices and supervising instruction. To propose particular instruction and evaluate teaching for bilingual students, principals must know what appropriate curricular and instructional practices are. They can gain this expertise through personal and professional growth and by tapping the bilingual teachers' expertise.

Principals in good schools secure the support of teachers to carry out the school's mission. Support does not imply control. Teachers find a sense of ownership and autonomy crucial to their effectiveness (Carter & Maestas, 1982; Garcia, 1988, 1991; Lucas et al., 1990; Pease-Alvarez et al., 1991). Teachers need to be allowed to implement their own educational philosophy and have support in doing so. "[W]hen they [the teachers] wanted to implement something new in their classroom, they have gone to their principal with carefully thought-out rationale and have eventually enlisted his support" (Pease-Alvarez et al., 1991, p. 358). Promoting teacher collaboration and sharing decision making with faculty were some of the key characteristics in effective schools (Carter & Chatfield, 1986; Lucas, 1993b). This collaboration among all teachers is essential for bilingual teachers who find themselves alone promoting notions of education unknown to the rest of the staff. In a magnet school in California, teacher collaboration occurred through three structures: (a) support groups for curricular innovation; for example, a whole language support group; (b) weekly grade-level meetings to discuss specific features of their instruction; and (c) schoolwide staff meetings (Pease-Alvarez et al., 1991).

The principal is in a unique position to create community support in carrying out the mission of the school. Not only bilingual parents but all parents must understand the place of the bilingual program in the context of the school's goals. They must understand that the use of bilingual students' home language and culture is essential to achieve the school's mission for all students.

HIGH EXPECTATIONS OF STUDENTS

Having high expectations of students and providing opportunities for success are vital for educating bilingual students (Gault & Murphy, 1987; Mace-Matluck, 1990; McPartland & Braddock, 1993). High expectations should not be limited to bilingual personnel. All teachers and staff in the school should have these high expectations. When bilingual students participate in English-taught classes, they need to be fully included in the activities of the classes. As a fifth-grade teacher once told me, for her having bilingual students was a real challenge because she did not want to water down the curriculum. Instead she kept searching for different teaching strategies that would help her communicate the content to her students. Teachers who have high expectations of their students:

- Do not let personal circumstances of the students affect their belief that students can develop to their highest potential.
- Provide challenging curricula.
- Use teaching strategies that allow students to grow and learn such as:
  - Fostering critical thinking.
  - Grouping students heterogeneously.
  - Using the native language.
- Do not use English proficiency to judge intellectual ability or determine a lesson's level of difficulty.

- Engage students regardless of English proficiency.
- Recognize students' accomplishments.

As one bilingual teacher put it: "No 'pobrecito' syndrome here—I want all my students to learn and I know they can learn even though they may come from very poor families and may live under 'tough' conditions" (Garcia, 1991, p. 139). This teacher did not accept excuses for not completing assigned work.

"The idea of 'watering down' the curriculum was flatly rejected as unacceptable" to teachers with high expectations (Moll, 1988, p. 467). For example, in the Carpintería preschool program for 4- and 5-year-old Spanish-speaking students, the teachers emphasized language and concept development. Students were presented with problems and asked to verbalize their experiences. They were asked, for example, to show how they would pick up a pile of trash with a broom and dustpan. During the process, the teacher asked the students to explain what they were doing and their reasons for doing it in the particular way they had chosen (i.e., with assistance from a friend, each tool in a hand, or using hands and feet). Almost exclusive use of Spanish allowed these students to fully verbalize their thoughts and continue to build vocabulary as new concepts were introduced (Campos & Keatinge, 1988).

Instructional strategies should be based on the optimistic assumption that all students can grow and learn. Teachers who use an analytical approach that fosters critical thinking avoid eliciting one-word responses to questions. For example, Katherine, a seventh-grade bilingual teacher, uses response journals (see Appendix) in which students reflect on and analyze what they read. In addition, after reading two books of the same genre, they compare and contrast them. The ability to expand, infer, and make connections evident in their journals was applied by students in other content areas.

Teachers who trust their students' ability allow them to work in heterogeneous groups, challenging them to contribute whatever knowledge they have to the group and allowing them to grow regardless of initial ability. Variety in life experiences allows students with less accomplished skills to participate. In a group project about Desert Storm, a student with low English proficiency contributed the most insightful views. He had been raised in Kuwait and had particular understanding of the problems of that part of the world.

Occasional "needs-based" groups help students practice and overcome specific problems but do not lock them into a particular level permanently (Radencich, McKay, & Paratore, 1995). Pinellas County, Florida adopted a flexible grouping policy. Grade 1 teachers, for example, start reading lessons with the whole class, introducing vocabulary, stimulating background knowledge, and introducing reading using the shared reading approach (see Appendix). Later, students are grouped by needs. Teachers work with one group to address their needs, while the other students work independently or in a learning center with audiotapes. Teachers switch groups to direct different activities with other groups. Students are not in the same groups for all lessons, but it changes depending on particular performance needs. Additional whole class activities, heterogeneous cooperative groups, or pair work follows (Radencich, McKay, Paratore, et al., 1995).

Use of the native language maintains a higher level of intellectual performance in class. For example, written reactions to readings by seventh graders contained more examples of higher level thinking skills when they were done in Spanish than in English, even when the readings were in English.

When staff has high expectations of bilingual students, deficiencies in English do not interfere with their appreciation of their students' capacity.[5] In South Boston High, bilingual teachers ensured that bilingual students, even recent arrivals, took the courses they needed to match their career aspirations. If the bilingual program did not offer needed courses, the bilingual teachers offered individualized courses or enrolled students in courses taught in English. Fluent bilingual students assisted with translations and clarification and bilingual teachers closely supervised progress of students (MacDonald, Aldeman, Kushner, & Walker, 1982).

Instead of lowering the intellectual level of lessons when students are not fluent in English, teachers should change the instructional strategies to help students function. Observing an English reading teacher who focused mostly on decoding and pronunciation because his students spoke English with an accent, Moll and Diaz (1993) suggested a different strategy. With grade-level-appropriate readings, the teacher reads the text aloud, thus avoiding problems of pronunciation. Text-bound as well as text-free questions were asked to assess student comprehension of text. An elementary school in Chelsea, Massachusetts eliminated low-track materials and gave teachers grade-appropriate basal readers as well as trade books. Teachers assisted students in comprehending these materials through flexible grouping including needs-based (before and after reading), cooperative, and peer groups (Radencich, McKay, Paratore, et al., 1995). High school teachers did not talk down to bilingual students with limited English proficiency but "spoke clearly, with normal intonation, explaining difficult words and concepts as needed" (Lucas et al., 1990, p. 328).

Regardless of English fluency or willingness to use the language, teachers must include students who are not fluent or afraid of performing in English. For example, Linda, an elementary ESL teacher, consistently engaged one of her first-grade students in reading activities even if she would not speak English. At the end of the year, the student scored among the highest grades on the English reading test.

Demanding teachers recognize students' accomplishments promptly. At some high schools, the principal congratulates students for particular accomplishments; others hold a "Student of the Month Lunch," and others invite parents to assemblies (Lucas et al., 1990). At the Hurley Elementary School in Boston, the principal established a monthly award to promote writing in either English or the home language.

---

[5]It is often the case in unsuccessful programs that expectations are lowered for bilingual students who are not fully proficient in English, tracking students in less demanding curricula (Minicucci & Olsen, 1992; Wong-Fillmore, 1989).

The dilemma of high expectations is equity and particular needs. Bilingual students need help to achieve what is expected by recognizing their needs. The most admired teachers are those who are caring but demanding at the same time. Chang, a Vietnamese refugee, recalled his bilingual teachers as "very helpful . . . without them, I don't think I would have survived." But, he commented, "they really pushed us" (Brisk, 1994a, p. 9).

The notion of helping students to achieve has been proposed in different ways over time. Vygotsky (1978) suggested that learning takes place at the *zone of proximal development*, where students can function assisted by adults or more experienced peers. This assistance is crucial to the developmental process. Cazden (1988) demonstrated how through *scaffolding* a teacher can model and direct students through the steps of a particular task until they function independently. The notion of *strategic teaching* (Jones, Palincsar, Ogle, & Carr, 1987) has been endorsed by researchers working with bilingual learners because it explicitly teaches learning strategies required in U.S. schools (Bartolomé, 1993; Hernández, 1991; Mehan, Hubbard, Lintz, & Villanueva, 1994). Explicit instruction and modeling of how to go about reading a text to extract information, structuring a particular type of writing, solving a math problem, setting up a science experiment, or taking standardized tests helps students function in the U.S. educational system and achieve commensurate with high expectations. These strategies are unfamiliar to many bilingual learners and parents.

Teachers cannot assume that students will receive help at home. Parents (due to language ability, cultural differences, level of education, or work schedules) may not be able to help. An elementary teacher used older students as tutors when parents were unable to help their children with homework (Garcia, 1991). In the case of high school students, neither the students nor the family may understand the complicated American process for qualifying for college. Counselors who can speak the students' native language are crucial assets to advise them on what courses to take, help them get information and fill in applications, and prepare for exams. They talk to the parents about the opportunities for their children (Brisk, 1994a; Lucas et al., 1990).

School administrators demonstrate high expectations for students when they publicly recognize bilingual students' accomplishments and when they hire personnel of the same ethnic group as the students to serve as role models. The importance of role models cannot be exaggerated. Their presence overcomes students' cynicism regarding their chances of getting ahead because of historical inequity in employment. While watching a video, a group of mostly Dominican and Puerto Rican middle school students realized they could aspire to be something other than professional athletes. The video, *Quality Bilingual Education,* is narrated by a young immigrant Dominican doctor who recalls how as a child he thought he would be a baseball player.

Offering bilingual students advanced programs and courses is another way schools show their belief that these students can reach high standards. Some high schools in California offer Advanced Placement courses in Spanish that give the students the opportunity to earn college credit (Lucas et al., 1990). A high school in New Mexico added advanced math and science courses taught in Spanish and English for its bilingual students. College preparatory courses for bilingual students not only reflect high expectations, but are an important factor in lowering the dropout rates among high school students (Alva, 1991).

For too long, bilingual students have been perceived as students with educational problems. Schools that switch from this attitude to one of hope and success with sensible support for the students are more likely to be rewarded with improved performance. High expectations must be an important agenda for the whole school. Impediments caused by teachers' lack of proficiency in the students' language and students who are still not fully proficient in English are a weak excuse for lowering curricular and instructional standards.

QUALITY OF PERSONNEL

In addition to having the will and motivation to help students succeed, staff working with bilingual students need the academic and linguistic preparation to help them achieve it. In schools with well-integrated bilingual programs, the entire staff knows the bilingual students, feels responsible for them, and is adequately prepared to contribute to their education.

Will to Educate

Educating and caring for bilingual students requires strong commitment and energy. This commitment extends beyond the classroom and lasts over years. Personnel with the will to educate students monitor quality of instruction, embrace innovation, and persist in their commitment to students and to improving education. They do not despair in the presence of difficult situations and find ways to change them.

Staff commitment goes beyond delivering the curriculum. For example, teachers in a Vietnamese elementary bilingual program acted as translators, tutors, intermediaries, advocates, and role models (Brisk, 1994a). A study of high schools in California and the southwest United States revealed that support for bilingual students included counseling students after school and providing outside activities that helped develop leadership and participation, such as clubs, newspapers, and cultural activities. Often the staff took leadership positions within the communities as advocates for students (Lucas, 1993b).

Teachers committed to the well-being of their students are always available to them. For example, Susan, a kindergarten Chinese bilingual teacher, follows up high-risk students long after they leave the elementary school. She is always available to the families that call her when their children are in need (Brisk, 1990). Felicia, a former bilingual student who holds an associates degree, commented that her fifth-grade bilingual teacher still calls her to encourage her to finish her undergraduate education (Brisk, 1994a).

Personnel who want students to succeed constantly look for ways to improve the school, curriculum, and instruction. Often these teachers operate on their own initiative. At a New Mexico high school, an English teacher who had a number of bilingual students in her class asked the ESL teacher to come to her class for several weeks to show her how to teach bilingual students (Lucas, 1993a). Other teachers respond willingly when innovation is suggested. When I introduced to Chelsea, Massachusetts the notion of clustering bilingual and mainstream classes, two clusters of teachers quickly formed and worked hard to ensure its implementation. They organized the clusters, adapted the curriculum, communicated with parents, and constantly revised the implementation. Although it was my idea, there was no question that it quickly became their program (Brisk, 1991c).

Teachers determined to improve education work hard at implementing innovation, and persist for as long as students flourish. For example, John joined a group of teachers in developing and implementing a college preparatory ESL program for bilingual high school students. The initial program was federally funded and was implemented in several schools. A few years later, with federal funds gone, only John was implementing the program—which he continued until he retired. His students developed strong academic skills that opened doors to college opportunities. Many received full scholarships to prestigious universities. These students not only entered college but successfully completed degrees (Abi-Nader, 1990; *Bilingual Education*, 1983).

Exceptional principals with will create good schools for bilingual learners. When a new principal took the reins at the Quincy School in Boston he found the Chinese students thoroughly neglected. There was no effort to provide good education for these students. The previous principal gave Chinese students a number because she considered their names too difficult to pronounce. Neither the school nor the curriculum fully recognized these students, who constituted about half of the school population. The Chinese students and teachers were largely segregated in their own classrooms. The new principal promptly set out to change the system. The curriculum was revised to update its content and to include the students' culture. Computer labs were installed to provide up-to-date technology instruction. The school was organized in clusters by grade level with a Chinese bilingual class in each cluster. The cluster teachers worked together and planned activities for the whole cluster. Some of the Chinese-speaking teachers were transferred to the mainstream program to give mainstream students the opportunity to interact with Chinese authority figures. New bilingual teachers and a Chinese vice principal were hired. Teachers were required to attend workshops to improve their general skills as well as specific skills for teaching bilingual students. Workshops on computer use, literacy for bilingual students, and Chinese culture were offered. The principal was at all the workshops in order to become equally informed. Aspects of Chinese, Irish, and other cultures represented in the school were embedded into the curriculum and school celebrations. Personnel who disagreed with the new school philosophy were encouraged to transfer. This school has since received several awards for excellence and the performance of its students is outstanding.

This will to educate, to improve themselves, and to improve education provides the foundation for successful teachers. Without it, preparation gives techniques but not the strength needed to sustain the work involved in educating children. Committed personnel have created good schools for bilingual students. As one high school principal put it, "You can force compliance, but you can't force commitment" (Lucas et al., 1990, p. 330).

Qualifications

All staff working with bilingual students should be appropriately prepared. Good teachers are not only important for the students but for other teachers. Staff members, adequately prepared to work with bilingual students and their families, understand how bilingualism, cross-cultural experiences, and situational variables affect academic and linguistic development of bilingual learners. In addition, specific qualifications apply to bilingual (National Association for Bilingual Education, 1992), ESL, and mainstream teachers, as well as other staff and administrators.

Ideal bilingual teachers:

- Are bilingual and biliterate.
- Appreciate their students' culture and American culture.
- Have the theoretical background to support classroom practices.
- Master content of what they teach.
- Use appropriate instructional strategies.
- Are totally dedicated.
- Are caring yet demanding.
- Constantly and appropriately comment to their students on their academic progress.
- Demonstrate commitment to the program and the students, actively promoting program and services for bilingual students.
- Devote extra time and energy to the program and students.
- Use classroom strategies that increase student involvement.
- Organize the classroom, communicate with, and discipline students in culturally effective ways.
- Relate effectively with students' families (De La Garza & Medina, 1985; Garcia, 1991; Lucas, 1993b; Saravia-Shore & Arvizu, 1992).

Good preparation for ESL is not unlike preparation for bilingual teachers. In addition to knowing how to teach English, they need background in second language acquisition and the methodology of second language teaching. The most valuable ESL teachers have a certain level of expertise in content area and students' culture. Knowledge of the students' language is desirable when working with beginners. ESL methodology that promotes teaching language through content areas requires familiarity with various disciplines. Awareness of the students' culture facilitates communication and highlights possible sources of difficulty in learning a new language and culture. Knowledge of the language of the students is particularly helpful when teaching beginners because communication flows regardless of students' English ability. By allowing students to use their native language, teachers can provide the vocabulary needed to express themselves in English, either orally or in writing.

Staff members who are not part of the bilingual program but participate in the education of bilingual students need to understand bilinguals and learn strategies to work efficiently with these students. They should understand bilingualism, second language learning, and the effects of culture on learning and behavior. They need to understand that students' concepts are rooted in their cultures. Students will resort to this cultural knowledge when encountering new concepts. Teachers must avoid making assumptions as to the students' background knowledge or lack of it. Instead, they should explore and clarify it (Floden, 1991). These teachers need to acquire different teaching strategies to ensure classroom participation of bilingual students (Faltis, 1993) and must make their English comprehensible to students with different levels of proficiency. Teachers' attitudes toward the bilingual students, their languages, and their cultures can encourage learning if positive but breed apathy if negative (Ramirez, 1985). Attitudes toward languages, for example, will influence the teachers' reward systems when a student uses one or the other language, which in turn will influence language learning. Cortés (1986) suggested that a detrimental effect can result from just the students perceiving prejudice without any real evidence of it.

All personnel working with bilingual students should be competent in the academic subjects they teach; not all need to be fully fluent in the language and culture of their students. Bilingual students need good models of their home language and of English. This can be accomplished by having some teachers fluent in the students' home language and others fluent in English. These teachers can work in teams to provide good models of both languages. For example, at the Gardner School in Boston, the first- and second-grade bilingual teachers cooperated. The first-grade teacher was a native speaker of English with moderate fluency in Spanish, whereas the second-grade teacher was a native of Puerto Rico. They each instructed both grades in their native language. Although both teachers were capable of speaking in both languages, they chose to teach in their native languages. There are many cases in which bilingual teachers are totally fluent in both languages and can serve as good models of both, but there are perhaps many more cases in which teachers are not perfect models of language (Wong Fillmore, 1992). This does not make them bad teachers, but students developing languages need the opportunity to interact with native speakers.

Integrated schools naturally provide bilingual students with native speakers of both languages. For example, in a fully integrated elementary school in Southern California, classes were team taught by a Spanish-speaking and an English-speaking teacher (Carter & Chatfield, 1986). At an elementary school in Chelsea, Massachusetts in which the bilingual, mainstream, and Chapter 1 teachers worked together, the bilingual teacher stopped worrying about having to promote and model both languages. She could focus more on the students' home language because her colleagues were in charge of developing English and bilingual students interacted daily with English-speaking students (Brisk, 1991a).

A combination of teachers of different languages and cultures provides added advantages. First, both cultures are represented and students receive the benefits of both sources of knowledge. Second, native English-speaking teachers (bilingual, ESL, Chapter I, specialists, or mainstream) are often better able to confront the system and to orient students and families through American bureaucracies such as summer programs, extracurricular activities, and college applications. Teachers who come from their students' ethnic group usually understand the students well and know culturally congruent strategies to demand of the students and discipline them. They also provide an important bridge to the parents and community.

Administrators working in schools with bilingual programs should have an understanding of curriculum needs and instructional practices that will help bilingual students succeed in school. Such understanding is essential to develop school goals sensitive to bilingual students' needs and to provide appropriate support to the bilingual program.

All administrators do not need to be bilingual, but the administrative staff should include a combination of language abilities. Complementary language skills allow the administration to serve all students and reach out to all parents. When Carol was appointed principal of an elementary school with a large bilingual Spanish population, she promptly hired a bilingual secretary with ties to the community and promoted a bilingual teacher to be assistant principal. Working with them allowed her to make informed decisions and to communicate with Spanish-speaking parents, but she did not have to relinquish her responsibility for the whole school, including the bilingual program.

Administrators need to develop strategies to work effectively with personnel of different cultural backgrounds. School management is facilitated by understanding ways of communicating, teaching, and disciplining by staff from different cultures.

Personnel working in schools with bilingual students need to combine commitment, leadership, and preparation to create the appropriate school environment, to develop quality curriculum, and to implement instructional strategies conducive to learning. Their willingness to provide a good education sets the tone of the school and invigorates students often discouraged by experiences in the larger society.

RELATIONSHIPS WITH THE PARENTS AND COMMUNITIES OF THE STUDENTS

Families provide for the basic emotional and physical needs of their children. They should be encouraged to contribute to the formation of bilingual, bicultural individuals by developing the home language and culture and motivating their children to learn English and learn to function in the American cultural context.

Parental participation in the education of their children is critical for successful education. The types of home–school partnerships vary and so do the results. Communication between school personnel and families improves students' reading achievement (Snow, Barnes, Chandler, Goodman, & Hemphill, 1989), helps students feel enthusiastic about their education, and helps teachers better understand the culture of the home (Ruiz, 1993). Parental participation in family literacy programs results in increased parental involvement in community and educational activities affecting them and their children (Ada, 1988; Delgado-Gaitán, 1991). Participation in the governance of the school increases parental support for school goals (Carter & Chatfield, 1986). The more diverse the connections, the broader the benefits (Goldenberg, 1993).

There are six major types of activities commonly found in home–school participation in education: home–school communication, volunteering, home activities, governing, collaboration with community organizations (Goldenberg, 1993), and "across the border" activities. When dealing with families of bilingual students, these activities need to recognize issues of language and culture.

Home–School Communication

Home and school need to communicate to learn what each is doing for the children's education. Schools with personnel who can speak various languages are obviously more successful at home–school communication. Schools must let parents know the goals of the school, programs, and innovations, as well as their children's academic progress. Schools must also listen to parents. They need to find out parents' own educational goals, their efforts to help children with their education, the home language (or languages), and home cultural characteristics.

Schools must find ways to communicate their goals and purposes to families. They should explain to parents the curriculum, nature of the offerings, teaching approach, and uses of home language and English for instruction. Parents involved in defining and revising the mission and goals of the school gain a clear understanding of the school's philosophy and practices (Carter & Chatfield, 1986).

Teachers establish strong and consistent student–home communication in different ways: periodic informal communications, telephone contact, monthly parent meetings, or biweekly newsletters. Because levels of literacy among parents vary and personal contact is often more culturally congruent, face-to-face or phone contacts are essential.

Traditionally, home–school communication was stressed with elementary students but ignored for older students. However, high schools also need to communicate and welcome parents. Meetings in the school or the neighborhoods assist communication. Effective high schools tried monthly meetings either for breakfast before parents went to work or in the evening. These meetings were organized around a theme, and students presented plays or they were honored for their work. Students were involved in the activities and the native languages of the parents were used. One administrator organized the meetings in the parents' neighborhoods (Lucas et al., 1990). In an alternative high school in Boston, one teacher from a team was in charge of calling the homes of the absent students every morning. This allowed the families and faculty to stay abreast of the students' schoolwork. Many high schools keep in touch through newsletters in the languages of the homes (Lucas et al., 1990).

Schools must learn about educational activities at home, as well as cultural values and language use.[6] Ethnographies of home life, parents sharing portfolios of home activities with teachers, and critical autobiographies inform the school of families' interests and activities. Teachers and researchers in Arizona have studied bilingual students' home and community life as a way to relate classroom instruction to the homes' "funds of knowledge." Teachers visited their students' homes to collect information on family activities, networks, job skills, and interests. Assisted by researchers, they analyzed the information and found ways to incorporate it into their curriculum. Rather than ignoring what children learn at home, this knowledge is transformed to be the basis for instruction (Gonzalez et al., 1993). In Chelsea, Massachusetts, parents create literacy portfolios for their children. They observe and record literacy activities at home and include them in their portfolios. These portfolios are discussed during parent–teacher conferences. Parents and teachers participate in these conferences as equal providers of education to these children (Paratore et al., 1995). Doing critical autobiographies often requires input from parents. Issues discussed in connection with the lives of the students need to be clarified by parents who are more knowledgeable than the teacher about the linguistic, cultural, social, political, or economic factors affecting their ethnic group. Sharing knowledge with teachers gives parents power, a feeling of being respected by teachers, and also a chance to clarify their own concerns and understand those of their children (Brisk & Zandman, 1995).

Schools and homes may not always agree on how or what students should be taught. When disagreeing with the home, schools need to do so respectfully (Meier, 1995). Respect for parents and caring for the students engenders trust in the school. With bilingual students' families, conflict is often rooted in cultural differences. School staff members need to talk with parents to understand their values as well as to help them understand American cultural values that are beneficial for their children. Patricia's mother would not let her participate in a summer Upward Bound program because she opposed her daughter's overnighting outside the home. A bilingual teacher went to Patricia's home, explained the benefits of this program in preparing Patricia for college, and succeeded in obtaining the mother's permission (Brisk, 1994a).

Volunteering

Volunteer activities that bring parents to the schools enhance their understanding of the school and vice versa. Traditional parent volunteering such as assisting in school functions or in the classroom open an avenue for parents to become closer

---

[6]For specific suggestions see Pease-Alvarez and Vasquez (1994).

to the school and provide an extra hand to often overworked teachers. Anne, a first-grade bilingual teacher, taught parents to bind books. Toward the end of the year, they were in charge of binding the books their children had produced. Parents enjoyed the time together and took great pride in their children's products.

Parents particularly enjoy volunteering for activities that involve sharing their knowledge or enhancing their own knowledge. By getting to know the parents, teachers in an Arizona school arranged their curriculum to allow parents to present in their classes their own knowledge or to assist teachers in preparing units: "[P]arents and others in the community [were invited] to contribute *intellectually* to the development of lessons" (Moll, 1992, p. 23). For example, a teacher prepared a unit on the curative power of plants assisted by the families' extensive ethnobotanical knowledge (Moll & González, 1994). Parents particularly enjoy helping in school when it improves their own education. At the Hurley Elementary School in Boston, Spanish-speaking and English-speaking parents volunteered in a two-way bilingual science program. By attending workshops on the curriculum and working as teacher aides, they learned about science and about first and second language development.

Often parents appear uninvolved in their children's education because they do not participate in school activities. Home research has demonstrated that they are indeed very involved with their children's education, but only at home because it is difficult or threatening for parents to participate in the schools (Nieto, 1992). Circumstances such as work also impede attendance to school activities. Schools should accommodate parents' schedules or intervene to facilitate this participation. One teacher sometimes called employers to arrange release from work in order for parents to participate in school activities (Delgado-Gaitán, 1991). Treating parents with respect, making them participate in interesting activities, and allowing use of their native language all attract parents to schools.

Home Activities

Schools should encourage parents to participate in the education of their children at home. In a successful preschool program, parents "were convinced by the teacher that they were their child's most important teacher and that their viewpoints were valuable in their child's classroom" (Delgado-Gaitán, 1991, p. 31). A crucial aspect of this collaboration is the development of the home language. For example, a home training program for Portuguese parents encouraged them to carry out a number of activities at home to reinforce knowledge of Portuguese. Parents engaged their children in conversations in Portuguese, pasted Portuguese words on cereal boxes and milk cartons, talked about shared experiences, read together, and played language games. Their children's performance in reading tests significantly improved within 3 months. Use of the home language enriched the linguistic and intellectual environment surrounding these children (Medeiros, 1983). Schools should not counter the home's role in first language development by sending home activities that are exclusively in English. Rather, they should strengthen the families' role in native language development as well as assist families in motivating their children to learn English and become bilingual.

Teachers can take two approaches to working with parents. One is to prepare materials to be used at home and train the parents how to use them. Materials sent from school are particularly helpful in homes where parents cannot afford to buy books. In the Carpintería preschool program for Spanish-speaking children of migrant workers, the parents were instructed to be the "other" teacher. Through monthly workshops, participation in the program, and weekly phone conversations, these parents were prepared to work with their children on academic activities. They were provided with materials that would help them work with their children at home (Campos & Keatinge, 1988).

Another approach is for the teachers to observe how parents naturally teach their children given their own philosophy of learning, encouraging the parents to continue to do so as the teacher provides what the children are not receiving at home. A group of Latino parents in Los Angeles were given books to use at home. Rather than reading for meaning and discussing the stories with their children, they focused on teaching their children decoding skills. Teaching reading in the classroom centered around reading for meaning and talking about the stories (Goldenberg, Reese, & Gallimore, 1995). Parents and teachers together provided the full range of literacy activities needed to learn to read. Thus rather than go against the grain of what parents believe they should do, teachers should build on their contribution.

Many parents—especially those of high school students—because of language, lack of familiarity with the U.S. educational system, and their own limited educational experience, often cannot help their children with homework. Many parents find it easier to help when homework is in the home language (Stergis, 1995). These parents help their children in other ways: They monitor that homework is completed, limit activities outside their studies, and insist that they complete their schooling (Brisk, 1994a; Lucas et al., 1990; Stergis, 1995).

Governing

Parental participation in school governance occurs through districtwide or school organizations as well as independent parent organizations formed specifically to consider educational issues. These organizations are of two types: those just for parents and those for parents and staff. Many school systems have parent advisory councils (PAC) that include bilingual parents or are just for bilingual parents. The level of involvement or power of these organizations also varies from deep involvement in the governance of the school to planning occasional activities. In Lauderbach, an elementary school in southern California, parents participate in the formulation and promotion of the school's goals. The staff and parents work together constantly, revising and improving their vision of education (Carter & Chatfield, 1986). An active bilingual PAC was crucial in monitoring the quality of the bilingual education program in Milwaukee (Arvizu, Hernández-Chavez, Guskin, & Valadez, 1992). In an effective high school in California, PAC parents meet monthly to organize activities and are instrumental in reaching out to other parents to get involved in these activities (Lucas et al., 1990).

In Carpintería, California, Spanish-speaking parents formed an organization to have active parents help less involved parents. The group helped parents understand their rights and develop strategies to talk to school personnel. They not only improved their ability to support their children but also to support each other. This organization helped parents bring up issues of concern to the school authorities and follow up when they felt no appropriate action was taken (Delgado-Gaitán, 1991).

Collaboration With Community Organizations

Collaboration with health services, libraries, after-school programs, and other social service organizations contributes to the general support for the family. One school in California housed a legal services office on its premises. While visiting the office, parents were also encouraged to visit their children's classroom. Attending to urgent personal concerns brought parents to school.

Community workers can facilitate the communication between parents and school personnel who do not speak the language of the families. An English-speaking teacher engaged community workers who spoke Spanish, Chinese, Korean, and Vietnamese to explain to her students' parents the purpose of Back-to-School Night, the activities that were going to take place, and how the parents could contribute. She also asked them to give parents each other's phone numbers to discuss among themselves the purpose of Back-to-School Night. The attendance at the event was high (Faltis, 1993).

Activities Across the Border

The participation of school personnel in the community and of parents in school-initiated programs for adults increases the opportunities for communication and for learning more about each other. Teachers' attendance at soccer games, birthday parties, and other community and family gatherings allows for casual conversations with the parents and signals that they are interested and care for their children (Garcia, 1991).

Adult education programs allow parents to enhance their own education and thus be more effective educators for their children. In addition, these services attract parents to schools and open natural communication. Often teachers in these programs are also school teachers. Parents get to know the school and the teachers in contexts other than direct involvement with the children. The bilingual education program at Pajaro Valley Elementary school in rural California organized monthly literacy activities with the parents. They gathered to discuss children's literature and to read stories and poems written by the parents and by the children. This program brought parents and children together at home around literacy activities, improving children's and parents' motivation to read and write; it fostered pride in Spanish, their native language; it brought the parents closer together enhancing community support; and it made parents more interested in school activities (Ada, 1988).

Parent involvement requires commitment from both parents and schools. Schools that include parents in curriculum development, program evaluation, and mission design enjoy high levels of participation. Teachers and active parents are instrumental in assisting reluctant parents. To enhance participation, parents must be informed, establish a personal connection, and feel that they have a role in the education of their children (Alvarez, Hofstetter, Donovan, & Huie, 1994).

The contribution of the home should be approached by the school as complementary. The home is an important partner. Their teachings should be respected and used as the foundations to provide what the home cannot. Schools need to know what the students receive at home to complement their education. When school and home are at odds, it behooves the school to work with the parents to resolve any conflict to avoid tearing the student apart.

CONCLUSION

[T]he Basic School is an institution held together by something far more than connecting corridors and a common schedule. It is a community for learning with a *shared purpose, good communication,* and a climate with *justice, discipline, caring,* and occasions for *celebration.* (Boyer, 1995, p. 29)

Schools with bilingual students can achieve such goals only if they consider the bilingual students and their education an inherent part of their agenda. These students and their families must be respected. Their languages and cultures must be woven into the fabric of the school.

The school, in coordination with the home, has the duty to develop educated individuals with good language skills and strong bicultural identity, helping them to function in their communities and the larger society. To achieve these goals, schools must focus on academics, use the students' languages and cultures to their educational advantage, and sharpen their ability to function in English and the American culture.

"Teachers are, without question, the heartbeat of a successful school" (Boyer, 1995, p. 31). Bilingual teachers have a special role in translating their school's mission to their students' reality. To do their jobs successfully, they must engage other teachers in the mission. When considering improvements in curriculum content and delivery as well as instructional practices, the bilingual staff must be part of the planning and development process and considerations pertinent to needs of bilingual learners must become part of the general agenda.

School reform that incorporates the essential conditions for a good bilingual program strengthens the quality of the school as a whole. The differences in language abilities and cultural backgrounds of bilingual students force educators to look at students as individuals and to find creative and diverse ways to convey knowledge. Learning to collaborate with colleagues of different languages and cultures prepares English-speaking students for the realities of a society characterized by diversity in the workplace. Collegiality with teachers of different languages and cultures enriches the work experience of English-speaking teachers and better prepares them to deal with the increasingly diverse student population.

Improvement of bilingual education cannot be sustained in isolation but must be carried out within the agenda of improving education for the whole school. A good bilingual program is more likely to exist within a good school. A school has a better chance to develop global qualities when it incorporates in its mission the needs of bilingual populations.

4

Creating Quality Curricula

Quality curricula accessible to all student reflects high expectations of the education system. On graduation bilingual students must be able to be thoughtful, solve problems, and make good use of their language abilities and breadth of cultural experiences whether they opt for academic or vocational programs. Teaching bilinguals means more than just teaching their language and culture. A good bilingual program includes all the academic offerings appropriate for each grade level, uses both students' home language and English for instruction and assessment, takes advantage of the students' culture to facilitate and enrich instruction, and introduces students to the intricacies of American culture and the American way of life. Curricula should also include the development of thinking and study skills to help students become good learners.

In devising effective curricula for bilingual students, schools confront difficult choices beginning with how to use and how to teach language. Schools must make choices with respect to courses taught in each language, introduction of English, number of years of instruction in the home language, bilinguality of the courses, and approaches to teaching students who are not literate in either language. Factors such as students' age, educational background, and native language literacy as well as availability of personnel and materials have determined language use in the curriculum. Most important is designing a consistent language policy embraced by all personnel, students, and their families. Students' progress should be carefully monitored to evaluate the effects of a particular policy on students' academic, linguistic, and sociocultural development.

Schools must consider the following policies when planning and implementing curricula appropriate for bilingual learners:

- The curriculum should be bilingual, meaning that:
  - The native language should be used for an extended number of years to develop literacy and for teaching academic content.
  - English, the second language (L2), should be fully developed.
  - Languages are used to maximize instruction.
  - Language choice and student assignments should be consistent.

- The curriculum should be cross-cultural, meaning that:
  - Native culture is included.
  - Personal experiences are tapped.
  - American culture is explicitly taught.
  - Cultural conflicts are analyzed.
- All bilingual students should participate in a comprehensive and quality curriculum, meaning that:
  - All content areas are covered.
  - Content, language, and culture are integrated.
  - Thinking and study skills are explicitly taught.
- Materials should be varied, of high quality, interesting, and in the native languages as well as English.
- Content and language assessment should be ongoing, authentic, and fair.

BILINGUAL CURRICULUM

A bilingual curriculum takes advantage of both languages to teach language, literacy, and content areas. There is variation with respect to when each language is introduced and for how long, and the choice of language in which to initiate literacy and to teach subject matter content. Within variation, effective programs underscore the importance of strong home language development and ensure that when English is used students are actually learning. Language policies adopted by a school must be followed by all teachers in order to provide consistent language development. In planning bilingual curricula, language, literacy, and subject content need to be addressed. Ideally, teaching of language, literacy, and content are closely integrated.

Bilinguals learn best when they have at least one strong language, when both languages are used in the curriculum, and when elimination of the native language is not considered as a precondition to learning English. A strong native language provides grounding for language and literacy development. Instruction in the native language and ability to use the native language allow students to work at their own cognitive level. Introduction of English should not come at the expense of the native languages. Effective programs continue native language development long after English has been introduced (Medina, 1993; Ramírez, 1992; Thomas & Collier, 1996). This can be done through content area courses taught in the home language. Rock Point students who had started their development of native language literacy in the first grade continued through sixth grade with one class in Navajo literacy. When they went on to junior and senior high school, their language was maintained through one social studies or science course a year (Holm & Holm, 1990).

Language and Literacy Development

Bilingual students need to develop academic ability in both their home language and English. Offering a content-based language curriculum in both the native language and English is an effective and meaningful way to teach language and literacy. This approach is particularly valuable in preparing students to handle content courses. A content-based language curriculum covers language development goals through themes drawn from the social studies, science, and math curricula. Lessons include language and content objectives (Christian, Spanos, Crandall, Simich-Dudgeon, & Willetts, 1990).

Students also need English as a social language to use in personal interactions with English speakers. Schools should structure settings for developing communicative English through natural interaction with English-speaking peers and teachers. School-based social interaction with English speakers becomes crucial for students who have limited contact with English speakers outside school. Girls especially are often restricted from participating in activities outside their home or their family (Brisk, 1994a). Integrated programs in which bilingual and English-speaking students and teachers come together in academic and social settings provide the ideal context for natural and functional development of English among bilingual students (Brisk, 1991c; Smith & Heckman, 1995).

Research has demonstrated the value of strong native language literacy on the development of literacy in the second language, even when languages have dissimilar writing systems (Cummins, 1991). Positive results have been found when literacy in the native language is introduced first as well as when literacy in both languages is introduced simultaneously. Immigrant students who received at least 2 or 3 years of home language instruction before immigrating performed better than immigrant students who were completely educated in English (Collier & Thomas, 1989). With Spanish-speaking and Navajo students completely schooled in the United States, research indicates that strong intensive development of their native language for 2 or 3 years, followed by continuous use of their native language after English is introduced improved academic achievement in English and English language literacy (Campos & Keatinge, 1988; Holm & Holm, 1990; McConnell, 1983; Ramirez, 1992; Thomas & Collier, 1996). Intensive introduction of both languages from the very beginning have also shown positive results (McConnell, 1983). The issue is not when English is introduced but what happens to the native language once English is introduced. Snow, Cancino, Gonzalez, and Shriberg (1989) found that elementary students who came from homes where English was not the native language performed better in certain language tasks in English when the homes had maintained the native language than when they had switched to using English. When the native language is neglected (at home, school, or both) it ceases to support second language development, which in turn can result in language and literacy problems. Elementary students who after a year of native language instruction received their education only in the second language showed difficulties in reading typical of students with reading problems (Bossers, 1991). Moreover, Beebe and Giles (1984) found that if learning a language is perceived as requiring the neglect of one's own language and cultural group, it becomes difficult to acquire the second language to a high level of proficiency. Therefore, when the native language is strong and encouraged, it facilitates academic achievement and English language and literacy development. Even students equally weak in both languages benefit from intensive instruction in their home language (Medina & Escamilla, 1992a). Bilingual students benefit the most when they receive long-term instruction in both languages (Collier, 1992; Cummins, 1981; Ramírez, 1992). Research among junior high school students showed that the more years they had attended bilingual education programs, the better students performed in school and the lower the dropout rate (Curiel, Rosenthal, & Richeck, 1986).

Programs for young students introduce L2 literacy after first language literacy has been acquired or start students in both languages simultaneously. For example, in Rock Point, students were taught to read first in Navajo, relying on locally developed materials and methods. In the second grade, students were introduced to reading in English: "We did not replace reading in Navajo; we added reading in English. Thereafter, students were expected to read and write in both languages" (Holm & Holm, 1990, p. 177).

Two-way schools that emphasize development of both languages for a number of years introduce literacy in both languages at an early age. In the Amigos Program in Cambridge, Massachusetts, native speakers of Spanish and English spend half of their time in Spanish instruction and half of their time in English instruction. Literacy is introduced in both languages in kindergarten (Cazabon et al., 1993). Yu-Lan, a Chinese bilingual first-grade teacher, introduced literacy in both languages simultaneously because she felt students did not confuse the English alphabet and Chinese characters.

Students with low levels of language proficiency in both languages benefit from a bilingual approach, contrary to the common belief that they are best served by English-only programs. These students seem to benefit from using their whole linguistic repertoire rather than being restricted to just one weak language. In an elementary bilingual program in Arizona that emphasized Spanish initially, slowly increasing English instruction, low-proficiency bilingual students "acquired significant knowledge of English while being exposed to large amounts of English and Spanish (Medina & Escamilla, 1992a, p. 264).

Introduction of literacy in English to older students depends on their level of literacy in the home language. Students fully literate in their home language can be promptly introduced to literacy in English, but students with limited or no literacy in their native language face a dilemma. They benefit from instruction in the native language, but they feel a great urgency to develop English literacy. Such students can benefit from a bilingual approach where all their linguistic resources are used to develop literacy. Moran, Tinajero, Stobbe, and Tinajero (1993) recommended a number of strategies for educating the older student with limited schooling. Based on their long-term experience, rather than empirical research, they recommended a number of strategies. They underscored the importance of using the native language and students' personal experience as the foundation to introduce students to the new experience of schooling in a different language and culture.

The language curricula for the native language and English should be integrated. Speaking, listening, reading, and writing are taught in relation to one another and not as separate skills. The different components of language such as pronunciation, spelling, grammar, discourse, and text structures are taught in context rather than as isolated components. Students discuss, read, and write about a subject. Aspects of the language that cause problems or that are needed by students to express themselves are taught. There is no separate time for reading, writing, or speaking; they are all practiced together to reinforce each other.

Language Use in Content Area Instruction

To learn in content area classes, students must, of course, understand the language used for instruction.

> The modifications to the instructional program required to [teach] . . . content in a manner appropriate for students [does] *not* entail a dilution in the conceptual or academic content of the instruction, but rather require the adoption of instructional strategies that take account of students' academic background and ensure comprehension of the material being presented. (Cummins, 1994, pp. 42–43)

Schools teach courses in the native language of the students, in English, or bilingually. Content area offerings in the native language and in English are organized depending on the age and second language proficiency of the students and the availability of personnel and materials in the native language of students. Most research on successful bilingual education programs, however, underscores the value of offering content courses in the native language in order to give "students the opportunity to progress through the content areas while developing their English skills" (Lucas et al., 1990, p. 323). Therefore, schools should make every effort to find teachers who can teach in the language of the students.

Programs need to make choices about when to introduce each language, which subject to teach in each language, and how to alternate the languages. Some programs start with content area instruction mostly in the native language, gradually introducing instruction in English. Others teach in both languages from the very beginning. Degree of difficulty varies with different subjects, especially for students starting in upper elementary and secondary levels where the demands to function in English are greater. Mathematics is the subject that students can handle with greatest ease, followed by science (Spanos, 1993). Social studies and literature are the most demanding for linguistic and cultural reasons (Short, 1994).

Programs with bilingualism as a goal tend to teach all subject areas in both languages. Other programs, to accommodate busy schedules, or because of the nature of the native language, teach some subjects in the native language and others in English. In a fourth-grade two-way program, Spanish reading and language arts are integrated with science and taught in Spanish; English reading and language arts are integrated with social studies and taught in English; and math is taught in English. Teacher preference and 3 years of trying the arrangement in different ways led to this particular language distribution. The students have been in the program since kindergarten; therefore their second language is developed and they have experienced the different subjects in both languages. At the fourth-grade level at which there is so much to learn, teachers felt that they needed long chunks for integrated time dedicated to each language and content area. Programs with languages for which there are less written materials may also choose to teach just some subjects or some aspects of a subject in the language. In the Rock Point Navajo bilingual program, at the high school level the social studies course in Navajo relates to Navajo government (Holm & Holm, 1990).

How the languages are distributed ranges from alternating languages by classes to alternating languages within a class to allowing students language choice. In programs that separate the language of instruction, the languages are alternated on a daily, weekly, or monthly basis (Christian, 1994; De La Garza & Medina, 1985). During each period, all subjects are taught in one language and in the following cycle they are taught in the other. Thematically organized curricula alternate the languages within the thematic unit. Activities are done in one or the other language, depending on students' language level and availability of materials. The new concurrent approach allows teachers to alternate language, but under strict criteria. Language switches can only occur between concepts, rather than haphazardly in the middle of sentences or just for a word (Jacobson, 1990). Yet another approach is the "preview–review," in which language alternation occurs within each lesson. Material is previewed in one language and presented in the other, along with a subsequent review in the preview language. Thus a lesson introduced in the home language is then taught in English and then reviewed in the home language, or vice versa.

Yet another approach to language use in content classes is to teach bilingually and allow students freedom of language choice. In the elementary science curriculum known as *Descubrimiento,* students work on science and math projects in either language. Materials are provided in both languages so that students choose the language in which they write (Cummins, 1984).

School choices are limited when there are no teachers in a particular language or content area specialization. Schools must find ways to facilitate learning and communication. Some schools offer courses in English with the assistance of bilingual aides and cross-age tutors. In a Choctaw bilingual program, paraprofessionals taught mathematics, assisted by classroom teachers who reinforced concepts in English. Both teachers and paraprofessionals participated in workshops on Choctaw mathematics terminology (Doebler & Mardis, 1980).

Effective high schools offer courses in the native language or in English. Content courses taught in English use sheltered methods (i.e., teaching the content area with an ESL approach). Both basic and advanced courses are offered in the native language to ensure that bilingual students are not trapped in low-level courses (Lucas et al., 1990).

In secondary schools, where the variety of languages and the dearth of personnel specialized in content areas are prevalent, flexible strategies may be necessary. These include allowing students to use their native language, providing resources in the native language, adapting instruction in English, working in coordination with ESL teachers, and stocking the library with books in the home language (Lucas & Katz, 1994). At the Multicultural Middle College High School there were no content classes formally taught in any native language. Native languages, however, were constantly used by students and teachers in many circumstances. Students, for example, used their native language to assist one another, to tutor other students informally, to ask and answer questions, and to interact socially. Students had access to English–Spanish and English–Arabic bilingual dictionaries. Teachers used Spanish to check comprehension, to explain activities, to provide instruction, and to interact socially. Because the only native language known by the teachers was Spanish, it was the only one used by teachers to facilitate learning content (Brisk, 1996).

Language Boundaries in a Bilingual Curriculum

In a bilingual curriculum, the languages of instruction may be strictly separated so that neither teachers nor students are allowed to use the other language. A more flexible approach restricts teachers but not students, allowing the students to use the other language when they cannot express themselves in the language of the class. In the bilingual French immersion program in Holliston, Massachusetts, adults must use French. Visitors, parents, or administrators must address the teachers and students in French inside the classrooms; if they cannot, they may politely ask the teacher to step out into the hallway, where English is allowed. Students are strongly encouraged to use French but when they cannot express themselves in French, they speak English and the teacher repeats it in French to model how to say it in French. Students are expected over time to rely less on English.

Other bilingual programs allow language alternation or codeswitching within class for clarification, to introduce the vocabulary in the other language, or to facilitate expression. Materials may be in both languages. Some programs use alternation within content areas because "bilingual children engaged in cognitively demanding academic learning must be allowed to access their entire scope of linguistic resources in order to achieve full potential . . . particularly when the primary focus of an activity is cognitively oriented" (Milk, 1993, p. 102).

Jacobson (1994) studied the effects of language separation and language alternation in student achievement in English and found no difference except for slightly improved performance in mathematics when the language alternation approach was used. Ferro (1983) confirmed these results among Cape Verdean middle school students.

Language separation is recommended for young learners developing both languages (McLaughlin, 1984) and for language instruction, especially oral language. For literacy development, on the other hand, bilingual students' use of both languages is to their advantage. Homza (1995) found that the writing process among first-grade Spanish-speaking students acquiring literacy was highly bilingual, especially when they were writing in English. They often planned and rehearsed in Spanish stories that were eventually "published" in English. Their class emphasized freedom of language choice, allowing students to make the most use of their bilinguality.

There is no empirical evidence to favor either strict separation of language or language alternation except in the case of mathematics. Problems emerge when language alternation results in constant translation or neglect of the home language or when language separation is carried to such an extreme that students do not experience bilingualism.

Consistency of Language Use and Student Assignment

Schools must establish the language policy for their curriculum and keep it consistent for all teachers in all grades. Thus, if the school chooses to teach 80% of the time in the home language for the first 3 years of the students education teachers must abide by this policy. Inconsistent policies may result in a different language emphasized at each grade level, jeopardizing the development of both languages.

Student participation in a bilingual curriculum must also be consistent. Students should follow the bilingual curriculum as planned by the school. Premature main-streaming or switching a student back and forth between the bilingual and mainstream programs can be detrimental. Escamilla (1994b) compared three students: one who progressed through the bilingual curriculum from greater emphasis on the native language to more emphasis on English; a second who switched twice in 4 years from the bilingual to the mainstream program; and a third student who was transferred after kindergarten to the mainstream program. Although such a study of only three students may seem to lack significance, the results were quite startling and suggestive. The first student made steady progress in English language literacy, the second showed no improvement between first grade and third grade (the two grades when he was in the mainstream), and the third was referred to special education when she entered third grade. Consistent participation in a good bilingual program benefits students linguisti-cally and academically. Parents or school systems who are concerned mostly with English language development often switch students to English-only instruction. When the student begins to fail, they send him or her back to bilingual education, having lost precious time. More frequently students end up in the irreversible path of special education. These students seldom progress to high academic levels in English and have lost the opportunity to be bilinguals.

Abundant research varies, as do classrooms with specific circumstances, but certain principles are present in effective programs:

- Long-term use of the native language, especially at the elementary level.
- Rich oral and written input in both languages.
- Opportunities for consistent and intensive use of each language separately.
- Focus on academic language skills when teaching English.
- Content taught using comprehensive English.

- Bilingual students make use of both languages to learn.
- Consistency of language policy and program participation.

The key seems to be balancing these principles. Thus opportunity for consistent use of each language can coexist with use of both languages to learn. If certain areas of the curriculum are offered in one language, free language use may be allowed in others. Rich exposure to both languages is considered over the span of several years. Thus intensive exposure to the home language may occur initially, whereas intensive exposure to English comes later. In true bilingual programs neither language is neglected completely at any time.

CROSS-CULTURAL CURRICULUM

A cross-cultural curriculum blends or contrasts the students' culture and life experiences with aspects of American culture. The incorporation of students' native culture and personal experience is the best way to introduce the new culture because "[a]ll that we know about learning insists that previous knowledge and skills are intimately involved in the acquisition of new knowledge and skills" (Corder, 1983, p. 95). Students' culture must be embedded in the curriculum. Thus, literature includes works from the culture of the students, social studies explores the nations of origin of the students, sciences considers beliefs of their families, and mathematics accepts different ways of solving problems.

Students may or may not be familiar with American culture. Teachers need to teach not only American values, but also ways of thinking and behaving to help students function in a new environment even as they are encouraged to maintain their own identity. A cross-cultural curriculum blends and compares aspects of the home culture and American culture and openly discusses cultural conflicts (Nieto, 1992). Bilingual students greatly benefit from cross-cultural curriculum because it makes learning meaningful, it helps them cope with cultural conflict, and it makes them capable of functioning in both their ethnic community and the larger community (Kleinfeld, 1979).

Incorporating Native Culture

Every aspect of the curriculum can have elements of the native culture of the students. Incorporation of the native cultures needs to be ongoing and substantial. An annual Puerto Rican week or multicultural festival tends to trivialize culture (Nieto, 1992).

The literature of every culture differs, reflecting particular beliefs and concerns. For literature selections "teachers use literature that reflects the culture of their Latino students. They also encourage students to share favorite stories, poems, and sayings that they have learned at home" (Garcia, 1991, pp. 138–139).

Writing styles vary by culture as well. Japanese written text lacks clarification and full explanations. In Japanese culture, it is the responsibility of the reader to interpret rather than that of the writer to be clear (Hinds, 1987). Korean writing is characterized by indirectness. An essay contains topics unrelated to the central theme and often the purpose of a paper is not stated until the very end (Eggington, 1987). Arabic prose is close to the oral language with long elaborate sentences (Ostler, 1987). The language arts curriculum needs to include contrasts in the writing system to help students become proficient bilingual writers.

History, geography, and social and political organization abound in contrasts. Central to the social studies curriculum in a Navajo bilingual program was teaching Navajo clanship, history, government, social problems, and economic development. Students from this program "left high school with some formal preparation for participation in the Navajo political process" (Holm & Holm, 1990, p. 178). The incorporation of the students' culture allowed them to understand and participate fully in their community.

Different scales such as the metric system, Celsius for measuring temperature, clothing sizes, and shoe sizes give students a different sense of numbers. Even mathematical operations differ culturally. When Alex, a recent arrival from Czechoslovakia, went up to the board to do a long division problem, he set up the dividend and divisor differently from the expected American way. The other students claimed it was wrong but the teacher just asked Alex to explain to the class how it was done in his country.

Science instruction should explore traditions of the students' culture. Using herbs for medicinal purposes, as in Mexican culture, can be an important addition to the science curriculum of a school with Mexican students.

Incorporating Personal Experiences

"Any learning a child encounters in school always has a previous history" (Vygotsky, 1978, p. 84). Culture includes students' personal experiences. These are a pure reflection of neither their ethnic culture nor American culture, but rather of the daily lives of the students influenced by cultures in contact, complex family situations marked by problems of immigration, cultural adjustment of parents, language proficiency of adults, safety of neighborhoods, and many other issues that barely resemble these families' experience in the country of origin.

Relating the students' experiences to the content of the classroom can facilitate understanding of subject matter. In a language arts lesson in an alternative high school in New York, students were asked to read about the Civil Rights movement. Prior to reading, the teacher put on the board a number of words taken from the selection: *racism, discrimination, segregation, integration,* and so forth. The students, mostly Latinos, had looked up the definitions of these words for homework. The teacher asked the students for examples from their own lives that would illustrate the concepts expressed by these words. Their responses included a discussion of racism, discrimination, and ghetto life. The class examined one particular example of segregation: a neighborhood Hasidim school that segregated boys and girls. Only after this association of important concepts in the reading with students' personal lives was completed did the teacher proceed to having students read the selection. This strategy not only follows recommended steps in the reading process, but acknowledges students' personal experiences as knowledge (Torres-Guzman, 1992).

Teaching American Culture

Bilingual students may or may not be familiar with American culture, depending on how much contact with the culture they have had. Thus teachers cannot assume knowledge or understanding: American culture needs to be taught. There is, however, very little evidence about how bilingual programs successfully teach American culture.

Krasnick (1983), Nieto (1992), Zanger (1993), and Met (1994) advocated systematic teaching of culture especially through cultural contrasts. Zanger (1993) developed a curriculum for students to act as cultural anthropologists, researching and contrasting their cultures with American culture. They learn American culture by interviewing their American peers and analyzing the results. Nieto (1992) considered multicultural education a major aspect of school reform that covers a broad range of aspects of the curriculum and structure of schools.

Observation of five middle school and high school ESL classrooms within bilingual programs in a large urban area underscored the need to promote systematic teaching of American culture. The classes were observed with respect to teaching of general knowledge and of behaviors and to planned, spontaneous, or missed opportunities to teach culture. Except for one teacher who planned to teach American culture, most of the instances of explicit teaching were spontaneous and related to behavioral norms:

Teacher (asking a student who seemed distracted):   Isn't that right, Qaiss?

Qaiss: Excuse me?

Teacher: I like the way you said that, Qaiss! That's exactly how you should speak to your teachers.

The few instances of planned teaching related to general knowledge such as art, music, literature, politics, and history. In a discussion of Romeo and Juliet, a teacher compared the fight between the Montagues and the Capulets to urban gang wars. However, teachers often missed opportunities to teach culture, perhaps because they took for granted many of the unique qualities of American society. Cultural characteristics such as the informal style of American classrooms, promotion of critical analysis rather than rote memorization, and free participation in class rather than passivity are instances in which American classroom behavior invites comparison with students' own experiences of classroom norms in their country of origin.

One teacher acknowledged that she never planned teaching of culture for two reasons: First, she was not sure what American culture was, and second, she was afraid of creating stereotypes of American culture. Defining American culture is not easy. Nieto (1992) defined it as:

> Neither simply an alien culture imposed on dominated groups nor an immigrant culture transposed to new soil. Neither is it an amalgam of old and new. What is "American" is the complex of interactions of old, new, and created cultures. These interactions are not benign or smooth. (pp. 232–233)

Thus American cultural knowledge with respect to art, history, politics, and philosophy needs to be presented in all its complexity. Behavioral norms, especially those that govern behavior in educational institutions and the world of work, are vital if we want students to interact successfully in our institutions. Although the possibility of stereotyping culture is ever present, the solution is not to avoid explicit teaching of culture, but rather to present it as dynamic rather than static and inflexible.

Blending Cultures

Kleinfeld (1979) believed the curriculum should be bicultural. Instead of focusing on one culture or the other, classroom content should present aspects of both cultures in content and style of delivery.

An elementary school teacher with a multicultural classroom developed a unit on superheroes. The starting point was the cartoon characters the children constantly talked about (personal experience). These heroes were analyzed and classified according to several characteristics such as name, age, gender, and so forth. Their speech was analyzed. Later, heroes of the students' home countries (ethnic culture) and famous American men (American culture) were analyzed in comparable ways. Finally, heroes of Greek mythology (typical American curriculum) as well as the mythology of the students' own countries were studied (ethnic cultures; Enright & McCloskey, 1988). This teacher successfully engaged students in a traditional American curricular topic through first tapping into their personal experiences and ethnic cultures.

Most classes in a high school for Eskimo students in Alaska "were a mixture of factual information, personal experiences of the teacher, references to Eskimo village life, delightful in-jokes, and broad humor" (Kleinfeld, 1979, p. 34). In these classes, teachers taught the traditional American curriculum, relating it to the students' cultural knowledge and delivering it using a combination of typical American classroom strategies with the more personalized and casual interactions typical of an Eskimo village.

Managing Cultural Conflict

Cultural diversity creates conflict when values collide. Awareness of cultural differences plays a role in the ease of communication. The first step to resolving cultural conflicts is realizing that the problems come from cultural differences rather than judging behavior or values as incorrect or unworthy. It is important to recognize that culture is arbitrary. Beliefs and behaviors are the result of knowledge handed down in interactions with people's life experiences. Because the history and lives of different groups differ, so do their cultures. American and bilingual students and staff need to understand their own culture, learn about each others' culture, and accept that there will be some conflict when there are differences between the two (Wurzel, 1981).

Recognizing conflict and exploring different points of view are essential to developing a successful school climate that bridges cultural diversity (Nieto, 1992). For example, a number of students from East Africa arrived at a high school in Boston. American and Spanish-speaking teachers and students were disturbed because the African students were not in the habit of bathing daily. The conflict was discussed openly. Americans and Spanish speakers realized that the African students were not "dirty," but were behaving according to norms learned in their own country. In turn, the African students learned the American norms.

Cultural conflicts can create serious dilemmas for bilingual students who find themselves caught between conflicting values of the school and their families. These conflicts must be discussed among teachers and families for the sake of bilingual students. For example, the drama and music teachers in a school in Arizona complained about Leticia as irresponsible. Leticia, a very good student, had missed chorus rehearsal and drama club meetings. The bilingual teacher pointed out that Leticia had acted responsibly by staying home and caring for her younger siblings while their mother was hospitalized (Gonzalez et al., 1993). Students, teachers, and families must work through cultural conflict and reach certain compromises. In Leticia's case, teachers needed to show understanding of her family needs and allow for some absences. Families need to understand how their values affect their children in the new cultural context. Leticia's mother could have asked a neighbor or relative to help out so that Leticia did not have to miss as many activities.

Schools need to work systematically to make the curricular content cross-cultural. Over time the whole curriculum can be completely cross-cultural. Schools also need to be open and use strategies that encourage students' and families' input to facilitate quick incorporation of new cultural groups.

COMPREHENSIVE CURRICULUM

In effective schools the curriculum is demanding, clear, and comprehensive. A comprehensive curriculum is not necessarily a smorgasbord of courses but "a limited number of centrally important skills and areas of knowledge" (Sizer, 1984, p. 225). Bilingual students must have access to offerings in all content areas and should participate in extracurricular activities. One way that programs have addressed breadth of curricular offerings for the bilingual program is to make it identical to the mainstream program. Lauderbach, an elementary school in San Diego, utilizes a well-developed and quite specific curriculum continuum in both Spanish and English. Goals and objectives are detailed and grade-level expectations are clear. This curriculum is used by the entire school. Teachers work together to incorporate innovation and variety (Carter & Chatfield, 1986).

Bilingual teachers need to adopt educational innovations that allow students to be better prepared to function in further studies and the world of work. Present curricular reform emphasizes developing thinkers, problem solvers, and learners with good habits. Instead of teaching disciplines as discrete units, they are combined in coherent units around themes, essential concepts, important literature, or relevant research projects. Such integrated instruction facilitates learning (Sizer, 1992).

Bilingual programs integrate teaching languages and culture to content areas. Curricular integration is a solution much sought after by programs in order to offer a complete program that covers content, languages, and culture. In order to coordinate content with instruction in both languages it is better to keep students within their grade level (Met, 1994).

Because integration of instruction requires planning, organizing, and coordinating with other teachers, administrators must allow teachers time to meet. While students are at gym, music, art, or computer lab, teachers can meet to plan and prepare their integrated instruction, sometimes with outside specialists. Teachers can concentrate on developing one or two integrated units each year with the goal of eventually having their whole curriculum integrated.

Integration of instructional content takes place within a self-contained classroom or across several classes. At early childhood and elementary levels, integration is logistically easier because one teacher is usually responsible for all instruction or two teachers are responsible for all disciplines, with each teacher handling one of the languages. In upper grades, teachers tend to teach specific disciplines. Therefore, integration requires coordination among teachers or clustering of disciplines, so that one teacher teaches more than one subject in an integrated fashion. Demanding curricula require good coaching. Teaching students how to learn should be embedded in content area and language instruction. The curriculum needs to be periodically updated for content and methodology of teaching.

Content Area Subjects

Content area subjects are integrated through different strategies:

- Thematic units.
- Literature-based curriculum.
- Key concepts.

- Combining disciplines.
- Interdisciplinary projects.

In *thematic units,* a main topic gives coherence to everything that is taught during a period of time. Mathematics, social studies, sciences, literature, and the languages are studied around a unifying topic. Anne, a first-grade bilingual teacher, organizes her curriculum around themes in order to integrate disciplines as well as native and English language instruction. She develops objectives and plans activities for each one of the disciplines in relation to this theme. English and Spanish are practiced throughout the disciplines. Most of the instruction is done in the native language. The second language is introduced relative to students' ability and also as a reaction to students' own initiatives. Students learned about each one of the senses (science), developed empathy and respect toward deaf and blind people (social studies), read fiction and nonfiction work involving the senses (language arts), created puppets representing the characters of one of the books they read (fine arts), counted, created graphs, identified geometric forms using the senses as the topic (mathematics), and carried out miniprojects at home with their parents (homework). Both languages were used in different ways when covering the various disciplines. For example, students conducted a number of science experiments and read books on the different senses in Spanish, and read very simple English books on the topic. Students wrote and illustrated their own individual books in Spanish on senses using the process writing approach (see Appendix). The whole class produced a "Big Book" in English on the senses by dictating ideas to the teacher.

A *literature-based curriculum* uses specific books to bring coherence to the curriculum. The themes studied emerge from the contents of the book. One bilingual and one mainstream first-grade teacher coordinated their curriculum around favorite books. The organizing book for their first unit was *The Very Hungry Caterpillar* by Eric Carle (1987), which has been published in English and in Spanish. They collected related literature in English and Spanish. The bilingual teacher purchased a cocoon for the children to observe and study metamorphosis. The metamorphosis of frogs was also studied. For a whole month, these two classes individually or together covered reading, language arts, social studies, math, and science around the themes emerging from the central book. The bilingual students were developing these concepts in their native language and English depending on the materials and context.

Some schools organize disciplines around *key concepts.* Mathematics, sciences, and social studies are explored within each concept. Immigration is a topic of great interest to bilingual students. A cluster of seventh-grade bilingual and mainstream teachers in Chelsea, Massachusetts incorporated it in the various disciplines they were teaching. The language arts and reading teacher had found an appropriate novel about an immigrant child to share with her students. The social studies teacher introduced the topic of immigration in the context of the students' own town as well as the United States. The science teacher chose to complete the immigration theme by studying animal migration. A mural, writing projects, and a field trip to the science museum brought closure to the unit (Brisk, 1991c). In Liberty High School, a ninth-grade newcomer school in New York City, themes such as school life, survival skills, New York City, and the immigrant experience tied the curricula of the various subjects together (Marsh, 1995).

Instead of dividing middle school and high school curricula into a multitude of subjects, Sizer (1984, 1992) proposed that teachers teach more than one *discipline in combination.* For example, he recommended a curriculum simply divided into humanities and sciences. Combining content areas allows for having longer periods in which disciplines are integrated (Lucas, 1993b).

Interdisciplinary projects present excellent opportunities for students to develop knowledge across disciplines. In an alternative high school in New York, the environmental science curriculum integrated science, social studies, and language development. The focus of the investigation was a neighborhood storage facility for radioactive and toxic waste. The plant had deposited several hundred barrels of toxic waste on an empty lot. The students photographed the lot, counted barrels, read their labels, and took samples of spilled liquid for analysis. In class they learned about cell structures, toxicity, chemicals, and other scientific concepts. They discussed the effects of hazardous materials on humans and the environment, the role of government in regulating activities, and the power of citizens to pressure government. They studied key decision makers and wrote to them. They also prepared a presentation (including charts, videotapes, and maps) for a conference of the Citizen's Committee of New York (Torres-Guzman, 1992). This project-driven curriculum integrated a number of disciplines and skills in a meaningful way. Students in the end felt satisfied not only because they had learned academic concepts but because they had influenced policy that directly affected their communities. Perhaps as a result of their work, the plant processed all the barrels with toxic waste and cleaned up the lot.

Integration of Language and Culture
With Content Areas

Language and content instruction can be integrated through any of the approaches described by providing language-sensitive content classes and content-based language classes.

In a *language-sensitive content class,* the subject matter teacher presents content at the cognitive level of the students, but matches communication strategies to the students' language level. Thus, in addition to teaching subject matter, teachers must teach the vocabulary of the discipline, reading and research skills, writing, and oral expression. Students learn to present and defend an argument, persuade others, express the process and results of an experiment, ask for clarification, and answer questions. Content classes that use English must be language sensitive for bilingual students in the process of acquiring the language.

Social studies courses taught in English are particularly difficult for bilingual students because they rely on books and on many abstract terms difficult to explain and understand. Several language teaching strategies help middle school students cope with American history classes. These include identifying essential terms, such as *liberty, taxes, rebel, disguise,* or *protest* that are rarely defined by the texts prepared with native English speakers in mind; teaching vocabulary and transition marks that help infer cause and effect; and teaching temporal words that indicate sequencing (Short, 1994).

Of course the mere fact that students are native speakers of a language does not guarantee that they are proficient in the academic variety of the language. Students arrive in school with diverse educational backgrounds, including no schooling at all. Thus content classes in the home language must also be language sensitive. Angela, a fifth-grade teacher, read science and social studies texts aloud to her class to overcome her students' difficulty with comprehension. Angela read aloud with expression, checked for comprehension, clarified difficult and new concepts, and prompted students to associate the topic of the readings with their own experience. Her students learned to understand the language and the content, were able to consult the books in conducting projects, and learned to express themselves orally and in writing.

In *content-based language classes,* language teachers integrate instruction with content. Language becomes the medium of learning rather than the only focus of learning (Mohan, 1986). In these classes there is direct instruction in the specialized language of subjects and a focus on the disciplines as well (Crandall, 1987). A language class using science as its content will teach basic processes in scientific inquiry (observing, classifying, comparing, communicating, predicting, inferring); logical connectors such as *because, however,* and *consequently*; and appropriate scientific terminology (Kessler & Quinn, 1987).

One content-based ESL approach widely used in preparing upper elementary, middle school, and high school students is the Cognitive Academic Language Learning Approach (CALLA; Chamot & O'Malley, 1986). Initial lessons use simple language to introduce a new concept and then increase language complexity to review each concept. Students work in cooperative groups to solve problems with the assistance of directions spelled out on a worksheet. The teacher focuses on the aspects of content, language, and learning strategies that cause difficulty in order to teach them.

A high-intensity language training math course was developed for a high school with a large number of Spanish and Vietnamese students and speakers of other languages who had limited math skills and were only beginning to learn English (Spanos, 1993). Based on CALLA, this course was designed to teach basic math concepts, relations, and operations and to develop skills in solving mathematical problems. Language skills included mathematical vocabulary, reading, and writing. The teacher distributed problems to groups who attempted to solve them using a worksheet called "Word Problem Procedure" (Spanos, 1993, p. 392). This worksheet listed a series of instructions including writing the name of the members of the group, copying the problem they had chosen to tackle, reading the problem aloud, clarifying vocabulary, writing what the problem asks them to find and the operation(s) they need to perform, solving the problem, explaining the problem to the other students, writing down an explanation, and writing a similar problem. The steps on the worksheet included learning strategies for beginning ESL students. Teachers could determine what students did correctly as well as areas of difficulty with respect to language, content, and learning strategies. The teacher prepared minilessons and additional exercises to overcome students' difficulties. What the teacher inferred from these worksheets and conferences with the students about the results of the worksheets helps to determine students' progress in all three areas: learning strategies, English, and mathematics.

Culture should be present in the objectives of lessons and integrated into language and content instruction. Curricula should systematically include relevant aspects of students' culture, highlighting opportunities to teach American culture explicitly, and all content should be connected to the students' personal experience. Moll et al. (1992) and Freire (1970, 1973) advocated the systematic study of the communities or homes of the learners in order to incorporate the students' personal experience to curricula.

Preparing a unit on the American Revolution, the teachers focused on the concept of protest. Protest was discussed in relation to the Los Angeles riots, which were part of the students' personal experiences. Flags were analyzed as symbols of protest. The students drew and explained the flags from their own countries of origin. With the backdrop of their personal experience and cultural background, the class explored in depth the history, significance, and influence of the American Revolution here and abroad (Short, 1993).

Development of Thinking and Study Skills

Bilingual students aspire to enter the workforce but need skills to succeed. In this information age, they need to learn more than facts: They need to learn how to solve problems and think independently. Critical thinking is an essential skill for jobs that require creativity and independence. Especially in teaching in English, it is important to develop learning strategies, thinking skills, and problem-solving abilities (Thomas & Collier, 1996). Because many bilingual students come from school systems or societies that do not emphasize these skills, they need sensitive teaching to adjust to the American way of dealing with problems. Development of thinking skills should be part of the instruction regardless of the actual or perceived intellectual qualities of the student.

Finding Out/Descubrimiento is a bilingual (Spanish–English) science and math curriculum designed to teach thinking skills rather than the facts of science or routine arithmetic operations. Math and science activities are organized around different themes, such as measurement, optics, water, pendulums, and photography. Students work individually and cooperatively in a laboratory setting. It takes about 14 weeks to implement the whole curriculum (DeAvila & Duncan, 1982).

Bilingual students must be taught how to learn. Strategic teaching and teaching learning strategies and study skills are among the ways that successful programs have provided assistance. Strategic teaching incorporates a series of steps to help students become good independent learners (Jones et al., 1987). After assessing students, teachers explain new content and learning strategies. The strategies are modeled by the teacher and practiced in assisted groups. Slowly the teacher gives students more responsibility for carrying tasks on their own until they can do them independently. Hernández (1991) successfully used strategic teaching to improve reading comprehension skills of Spanish-speaking sixth-grade students. He added two important components to the strategic teaching model developed by Jones et al. (1987). First, the strategies were taught using the native language. Students learned how to ask questions, summarize, and predict by reading Spanish text and performing these tasks in Spanish. Second, when assessing content knowledge, he considered students' cultural knowledge because "the interpretation provided by their prior experiences may not make new knowledge comprehensible" (Hernández, 1991, p. 94). He found that strategic teaching in the native language not only improved reading comprehension in Spanish, but helped students carry out the strategies when attempting to read English, a language they barely knew, thus underscoring the value of bilingual education when implementing new successful practices with bilingual learners.

A distinguishing feature of the CALLA approach mentioned earlier is that in addition to language and content, students are taught learning strategies, including advance preparation, organizational planning, selective attention, resourcing, deduction, elaboration, inferencing, questioning for clarification, and cooperation (Spanos, 1993). While focusing on these strategies, students learn English, mathematics, social studies, or science.

A program that integrated social studies and language teaching for middle school bilingual students also incorporated learning strategies. Social studies texts used a number of visual aids to accompany text. Teaching middle school bilingual students to interpret timelines, charts, and maps facilitated comprehension of text. Another helpful strategy involved synthesizing information through graphic organizers that highlight important concepts and show hierarchies and relationships (Short, 1994).

The "Achievement Via Individual Determination" (AVID) program, designed for low-achieving high school students, had a special course offered as an elective. This course taught specific academic strategies needed to succeed in college preparatory courses. No skill was taken for granted. Teachers and tutors taught note-taking techniques, study skills, the inquiry method, how to work collaboratively, and how to apply all these skills to the academic classes. Students learned to use writing as a tool for learning, to become independent thinkers, and to use their knowledge and experience as well as their study skills to solve problems (Mehan et al., 1994).

MATERIALS

Good materials support implementation of a quality curriculum and facilitate instruction. Inappropriate materials frustrate students and make the work of teachers more difficult. To overcome inadequacy of materials due to language and culture, bilingual programs use not only commercially produced materials, but teacher-made and student-made materials as well.

Quality bilingual programs use a variety of materials including literature, subject area textbooks, visuals (pictures, films, student projects), and technology.

These materials need to be of varying degrees of difficulty because bilingual students have different cognitive and linguistic abilities. Teacher- and student-made materials can fill the gaps left by the lack of appropriate commercially produced materials. A Cambodian kindergarten teacher in Lowell, Massachusetts produced all the materials she needed to introduce her students to literacy in Khmer. Her colorful big books, alphabet charts, and word games attracted not only the Cambodian children, but also the English and Spanish speakers who shared her classroom. Frustrated by the lack of science materials in Spanish, one teacher encouraged her fifth-grade students to produce science lessons. For the unit on insects, each student chose to study one insect, wrote about it (using the computer), and illustrated the work with accurate and elaborate drawings. The final products were bound in a volume for the whole class to use. Classroom-produced materials not only fit the needs of a particular group of students but, of course, involve them intellectually with more intensity than if they merely studied texts. The process of making them is very educational.

Quality materials can facilitate comprehension, particularly when they are in the students' second language. Some characteristics of good books include text coherence, appropriate headings and illustrations, and aids to facilitate reading such as vocabulary overviews, graphic organizers, and prediction guides. English materials produced for native speakers are often difficult for bilingual students because they assume background knowledge bilingual students may not have. A fifth-grade mathematics text contained a word problem based on doing the laundry at a laundromat using quarters. Several recent immigrant students from Central American could not solve the problem because they were unfamiliar with the concept of the laundromat or the value of a quarter.

Teacher-produced adapted materials help fill the gap found in social studies textbooks used at the middle school level (Short, 1994). Adapted materials include background knowledge necessary for understanding the lesson, vocabulary development, and aids such as graphic organizers, hands-on activities, and other devices to facilitate comprehension of the basic content of the lessons.

It is best to use a combination of adapted materials to facilitate comprehension and textbooks produced for English speakers to familiarize bilingual students with books used in mainstream classes.

Materials should be accessible in both the native language of the students and in English, regardless of the language of instruction. Bilingual materials are especially useful for initial stages of language development. Libraries should contain materials in both languages. When there are no materials in the native language, programs can develop their own materials. For example, the Cherokee Bilingual Education Program in Oklahoma developed materials in Cherokee for all elementary grades (Bacon, Kidd, & Seaberg, 1982). Unless locally produced materials are attractive, however, students may reject them. An alternative is to use second language materials with instruction in the native language. Teachers or students can write summaries of the chapters in the native language for their own and future use.

Materials should reflect the bicultural nature of the programs. Literature and storybooks should reflect American culture as well as the culture of the students. Books in English with cultural content familiar to the students are particularly good for the early stages of language development. They can be easier to comprehend because the students are familiar with the content. A number of stories traditional to other cultures have been produced in English. Students and parents enjoy reading or looking at these books and can easily grasp the content in spite of language difficulty.

Bilingual students should become familiar with stories and literature being used by their English-speaking peers because they are an important aspect of the assumed background knowledge of students as they go through the grades. ESL classes should introduce bilingual students to popular American stories, poems, and songs.

Short (1994) argued that English materials prepared for native speakers need to be culturally inclusive. This in turn facilitates use by bilingual learners. For example, she illustrated the dearth of information with respect to the role of African Americans and Native Americans in the revolutionary wars (Short, 1993, 1994). The United States has always been a cultural mosaic, yet books rarely reflect the cultural variety of the country.

Books with universal themes are useful in multilingual classes. A high school teacher used *It Can Always be Worse,* a story of a Jewish family in turn-of-the-century Russia. Her ESL students enjoyed discussing how life can seem worse than it is. Village life was familiar to many of her students (Marsh, 1995). This type of material presents new and yet familiar cultural information. Students find it easy and enjoyable to draw contrasts and similarities with their own cultures.

In addition to textbooks, bilingual classes make use of videos, kits, magazines, and visuals. Videos containing plays, films based on books, or content area subjects are extremely helpful with comprehension of books and textbooks. It is often advisable to show videos before students do the readings to establish background knowledge. Videos with subtitles can be very helpful in teaching reading, especially when the videos are in the home language and the subtitles are in English (Lambert, 1986). Kits with a variety of materials about a topic offer the opportunity to read, touch, conduct experiments, listen to tapes, and watch videos reinforcing the concept through multiple media. Monthly magazines add variety, currency, and expectations to a class.

Technology increasingly offers a variety of materials for all disciplines and some in the home language. Access to the Internet provides an invaluable resource to bilingual classes, not only for tapping into databases in different languages, but for connecting with classrooms throughout the world. Electronic mail makes bilingualism useful, motivating students to develop and maintain their home languages (Cummins & Sayers, 1995).

Classroom learning is enriched by field trips and use of community resources, such as museums, businesses, and community centers. The Oyster School in Washington, DC, an exemplary bilingual elementary school, takes full advantage of local organizations. Students participated in Project Satellite sponsored by a television station and a hands-on science program sponsored by the Department of Education. Their geography curriculum was developed in cooperation with the National Geographic Society (Fern, 1995).

Schools with clear goals and a well-established curriculum can profit from a variety of resources. By making the resources fit the needs, the students, and the curricular guidelines, students can enjoy a rich experience.

ASSESSMENT

Assessment requires measuring what students know. Purposes and methods of assessing are at the center of a great controversy between those who support standardized tests for the purpose of accountability and the more recent trend toward authentic (also called performance or alternative) assessment to evaluate "how and what students know and can do in real-life performance situations" (Darling-Hammond, 1994, p. 6). The main purpose of performance assessment is to determine students' growth and to inform instruction. Standardized tests are defended as objective measures that can be easily administered to large numbers of students for the purpose of accountability. On the other hand, defenders of performance assessment believe that students are individuals whose potential needs to be carefully examined in real-life situations.

Systematic assessment is an important component of effective schools (Mace-Matluck, 1990). Bilingual students are frequently assessed by schools that take learning seriously. Regrettably, bilingual students are either excused from testing because of their limited proficiency in English or they are tested only in English. Neither policy is fair to these students. Exempting students from assessment in a language they do not yet master may be motivated by fairness, but "it literally creates a kind of systemic 'ignorance' about the educational progress" of these students (LaCelle-Peterson & Rivera, 1994, p. 70). Schools must establish appropriate assessment policies in both English and the home languages.

Assessing bilingual students is associated mainly with determining eligibility for bilingual programs or moving students to the mainstream. Such tests emphasize, sometimes to the exclusion of other relevant factors, assessment of English language ability. Based on scores on English language proficiency, students are assigned to bilingual or mainstream programs. Only students who demonstrate low levels of English proficiency are enrolled in bilingual education, a mostly political and fiscal policy. Research has demonstrated how whimsical this policy can be because eligibility often depends on which test is used. Although 44% of a group of first graders tested with the Language Assessment Scale were classified as non-English speakers, only 8% of the same group of students tested with the Bilingual Syntax Measure qualified as non-English speakers (Durán, 1989).

Assessment of bilingual students must expand its purpose, scope, and strategies. Good bilingual programs focus on students as individuals, providing the education they need to achieve language proficiency, academic achievement, and sociocultural integration. Such programs erase boundaries between bilingual and mainstream programs, utilizing the resources of both to serve all students. Assessment evaluates students' growth and directs instruction. The use of English tests for assignment to bilingual or mainstream programs becomes secondary.

Valid assessment of bilingual students includes background information, performance in both languages, academic achievement, and ability to function in both cultural contexts.

To interpret students' performance, schools must first obtain background information on language proficiency, level of schooling, and level of native language literacy (LaCelle-Peterson & Rivera, 1994). Such information helps in understanding performance. It is very different to have difficulties in English because the second language is in the process of development, than to be unable to perform because of lack of schooling. Students arriving in Arlington, Virginia public schools are assessed in English and their native language to obtain information on language proficiency and previous schooling. Parents are interviewed in their native language. When nobody on the staff speaks the language of a new arrival, assistance is sought from the community or consulates (Chamot, 1995).

Language testing covers not only grammatical competence (grammar, vocabulary, and pronunciation) but also sociolinguistic competence (ability to use language appropriately given the circumstances), discourse competence (ability to use extended language), and strategic competence (ability to be resourceful when language ability fails; Swain, 1984). Because nonlinguistic context can facilitate language use, the specific context defines the level of difficulty for language assessment. Most students understand the language used around a science experiment more readily if it is presented in the laboratory rather than in a book. In the laboratory, language explanations are clarified by watching the experiment being carried out (context embedded), whereas in the book only the language carries the meaning (context reduced; Cummins, 1984).

Students' literacy needs to be assessed with respect to their general ability to read and write as well as their ability to read and write in a specific language. To ensure development, it is important to determine that students have strong literacy skills in at least one language. Literacy testing to determine general ability does not have to be done in just one language. Students write better in the language they know best or in the language in which they have learned a particular topic. Students recalled more facts about a reading they did in English when they were allowed to express themselves in their native language (Lee, 1986).

Assessment of academic achievement includes the ability to think (cognitive skills) as well as perform tasks in mathematics, science, and other content areas. The focus should be to measure students' ability to solve problems by using their knowledge of the content areas. Sizer (1992, 1995) believed that measuring long-term intellectual habits is essential in determining students' preparation to perform later in life.

Most programs focus on language and academic assessment. Bilingual programs should also help students adjust to functioning in two cultures. If sociocultural integration is a goal of the bilingual program, however, assessment of students' attitudes toward their home language and culture and English as well as their ability to feel comfortable in both cultural environments should be a component of assessment. Sociometric choices that evaluate students' preference for interaction in a variety of social settings, their self-esteem, and their attitude toward bilingualism can define the level of adjustment to the two cultural groups (Cazabon et al., 1993).

Schools need to consider fair strategies for assessing bilingual students that take into account language and culture because both English language proficiency and cultural constraints often lead to misperceptions of students' abilities. A Spanish-speaking student looking at an item on an intelligence test that showed a picture of an apple with a bite out of it answered affirmatively to the question, "Is the apple whole?" He interpreted the question as "Does the apple have a hole?" lowering his intelligence score as a result. A kindergarten teacher considered a student from India behind in his development because he could not tie his shoelaces at the end of kindergarten. In India, children do not wear shoes with shoelaces so it has never been considered a developmental benchmark (Schmidt, 1995).

Fair assessment strategies include:

* Assessing in the home language.
* Assessing in both languages.
* Allowing students to choose the language in which they will perform.
* Using limited- or nonverbal measures when testing in English.
* Incorporating elements of students' culture using multiple assessment strategies.
* Coordinating assessment by various teachers.
* Involving the community.

To obtain credible results in tests of academic and cognitive ability, students should be tested in their stronger language. Bilinguals process information more quickly and accurately in their stronger language because they concentrate on understanding the item rather than decoding the language. Content area tests in both English and the home language produce higher scores than tests in English. Bilinguals often learn some things in one language and some in the other. The opportunity to follow assessment instructions in both languages and to respond in either language affords bilinguals a greater chance to succeed. Bilingual Spanish speakers who took the National Assessment for Educational Progress tests bilingually performed better than they did when the test was in one language. When skills in a particular language are not being assessed, bilingual students should always be given the choice of the language in which they want to give evidence of their ability. Writing projects, responding to tests of reading comprehension, and demonstrating content knowledge can be done in any language. When students are forced to do it in one language it becomes a language proficiency test rather than evidence of literacy ability or content knowledge.

When testing in the students' weaker language, it is important to use oral or written language, hands-on demonstrations, or other means to ensure that language does not act as a barrier to expression of their ideas. Ideally, when interpreting academic tests in English, results should be given separately for the academic area and language proficiency. In the case of intelligence tests, nonverbal measures are better predictors than verbal measures (Durán, 1989).

Use of a variety of instruments (observations, conferences, students' products, checklists, teachers' narratives, tests, student demonstrations, and long-term projects) gives students the opportunity to demonstrate their skills in a variety of styles, increasing the chances that the type of measure is not a factor in the outcomes.

Incorporating elements of the students' cultures and personal experiences in the assessment strategies can facilitate the students' performance. Familiarity with the concepts and expected behaviors allows the students to concentrate on solving the problem at hand and fully demonstrating their skills. It is a well-known fact, for example, that students' knowledge of the topic can raise performance scores in tests of reading comprehension.

Assessment of bilingual students should be a coordinated effort. All teachers (bilingual, ESL, and mainstream) need to communicate with each other and be aware of the students' skills as measured by all teachers in order to make fair decisions about the students' language, literacy, and academic achievement performance and needs. The results should be kept in individual students' portfolios that include clear learning objectives. Ideally each student should have one portfolio where the assessments carried out by the various teachers in English and in the native language are collected. Thus, teachers become aware of all the skills bilingual students have rather than just the ones each teacher tests in the language they can test.

The Urban District Assessment Consortium administered performance tests in a number of Boston schools. Participation of community members facilitated the administration of assessment measures bilingually (Gonzalez & Cress, 1994).

Assessment of bilingual students is a complicated matter, yet it can be done fairly if there are no restrictions on the linguistic and cultural characteristics of the assessment measure. In order to make the process feasible, schools need to involve teachers, community, and any resources that will permit the implementation of bilingual assessment.

> Assessment and accountability are worthy goals. The task is to create a system that usefully and fairly assesses what we care about and that does not distort the process of learning. Such a system cannot be done on the cheap. There is no shortcut to a fair and full understanding of a human being. (Sizer, 1995, p. 58)

CONCLUSION

Developing a quality curriculum is a complex enterprise because of the need to combine content, languages, and cultures. Much reform is needed because most existing curricula lack linguistic and cultural breadth. Innovations carried out for the benefit of bilingual students would also benefit all students. The inclusion of beliefs, knowledge, and contributions of other cultures would expand the knowledge of all students, simultaneously making the curriculum more relevant for bilingual learners. Learning additional languages through contact with speakers of these languages would enhance foreign language education for English speakers.

Educational changes require time and support from educators and families. Long-range planning engaging educators, families, and students can help accomplish the goals of curricular innovation and bring schools and communities together to collaborate and learn from each other. Curriculum content, of course, often foments ideological and political disputes. For the benefit of students, such disputes should be sublimated so that the focus is on developing individuals—bilingual and monolingual—capable of facing the challenges of a world in which people of different languages and cultures increasingly find themselves working together.

5

Creating Quality Instruction

Quality instruction is in the hands of teachers. They choose instructional practices, administer assessment, and set standards for their students. Teachers also organize the classroom, utilize resources, create links with parents and communities and, through their own behavior, create models (positive and negative) that may remain with student for the rest of their lives. In classrooms with bilingual students, teachers decide, consciously and unconsciously, how to use the native language and English and how to incorporate disparate cultures.

Teacher background and preparation, societal factors, school policies, and curricula choices, of course, set parameters for teachers. Despite such external pressures, teachers choose practices and implement them in their classes. For that reason, this chapter does not dictate unvarying formulas to be applied regardless of circumstances or characteristics of the students. The intent of this chapter is to highlight good instructional and assessment practices. Teachers need to be flexible, to accommodate their students' needs, and to incorporate new ideas that emerge from new research or from their own experience of observing students. Most important, teachers should be guided by the goals and expected outcomes of language development, academic achievement, and sociocultural integration.

Teachers must develop a philosophy of teaching that includes the following principles:

- Instruction should respect students, their language, and their culture.
- Instruction should be engaging, challenging, and supportive.
- Special strategies are needed for teaching English and teaching in English and for educating students with limited literacy and schooling.
- Class objectives should include language, culture, and academic content.
- Students should play an active role in learning.
- Classrooms should be organized to maximize learning, collaboration, and participation.
- Assessment should be integrated with instruction.
- Resources should be varied and serve the basic goals.

- Family and communities should be partners in the classroom.
- Teachers should maximize their skills and backgrounds.

One complication to implementing the recommendations in this chapter is that many bilingual students and teachers have been previously exposed to teaching methodologies that fundamentally differ from those used in U.S. classrooms. For example, when students are accustomed to language lessons centered around grammar topics, they have great difficulty with thematic units or content-based language lessons. Transitional strategies can be used to help students adjust. It took 8 weeks for Alice, a Haitian teacher, to transform her social studies class from lectures with practically no student participation to student-directed discussions (see Appendix). For several weeks, Alice stayed in the circle, helping direct the discussion and encouraging student participation. Gradually Alice participated less and slipped outside the circle to become an observer. Initially only the assigned student leader spoke from a prepared speech. Week after week, more students participated spontaneously and finally the very quiet ones were induced by the leader to participate. The transition was needed by both teacher and students. They adjusted well, enjoyed the new style, and understood its benefits.

The recommendations included in this chapter are useful for language and content-area teachers whether they instruct in the native language or in English. These recommendations emerge from what teachers have used successfully at the early childhood, elementary, and secondary levels. Specific examples from real classrooms illustrate the recommendations. Because each classroom is a unique universe, teachers must be flexible, adjusting lesson content, teaching methods, resources, and language use not only to age and grade level but to cultural backgrounds and the particular language proficiency of their students. Individual teachers ultimately decide what is best for their specific group of students but such decisions should follow understanding of principles outlined in this chapter, knowledge about their students, and particular circumstances of their classroom setting.

RESPECT FOR STUDENTS, THEIR LANGUAGE, AND THEIR CULTURE

Language and content area teachers need to create bilingual and cross-cultural environments in their classrooms regardless of what language they use for instruction. Classrooms become communities of learners where individual students are valued, all languages are considered valid media for communication, and cultures are accepted as the legitimate bases for knowledge and behavior. Teachers also must extend the students' language abilities and cultural knowledge beyond their experience. Student development should be additive; that is, students develop their language and learn English. The knowledge they bring to class is a valid basis for presenting new knowledge. Often the use of students' language and culture in education is seen as wasteful because it is perceived as not taking the students beyond the stage they are at. It is important to use the resources of the students, but equally important to expand those resources. One does not preclude the other.

A healthy classroom exudes respect from the teacher toward all students and among students themselves. Individual students' characteristics are accepted, ideas are welcomed and challenged in a scholarly manner, and personal interests (of the students as well as of the teacher) motivate learning. Ruben, a bookworm type of student, expressed interest in reading a book about Michael Jordan. Another student interjected:

> "Ruben has no business doing that—he doesn't know anything about sports." Truman [the teacher] overhears this remark and intervenes. He says, "That's not true. Ruben and his brother watch soccer and basketball games all the time. He knows a lot about basketball." (Gersten, 1996, p. 238)

Truman not only welcomed an idea from a student but also taught other students to be more accepting. Later, this teacher not only accepted a suggestion from a student but turned it into a lesson for the whole class. When a student sought permission to reread a book because she felt her English was better and she would now understand more, Truman not only agreed, but also told the whole class that it is a good idea to reread something because as better readers they would understand more (Gersten, 1996). This teacher responded well to his students and taught them to behave in a civil manner toward each other.

Respect for languages requires that no language or dialect is rejected. Many teachers restrict language use in the classroom because they believe the use of the two languages should be clearly separated and, thus, classes should be either in one language or the other. Others think that it is acceptable to use more than one language. Both points of view are acceptable, depending on the circumstances. Separation of languages is more important for oral language development, whereas literacy and content area teaching benefit from the use of both languages. As language models, teachers need to be more careful with language choice and students, as functioning bilinguals, should be free to choose the language. Therefore, teachers should:

- Use the language of instruction defined by curriculum planning with flexibility for literacy and content area instruction.
- Consistently model language (L1 or L2) in language development classes.
- Never forbid students to use either language.
- Encourage students to use the language of the class to develop fluency.
- Objectively explain language varieties (academic, social, and regional).

The language of the classroom should be the one defined by the curriculum for the particular subject being taught. All teachers need to adhere to the curriculum plan and employ language consistently. These broad parameters allow considerable flexibility in content area classes. When working with a group that had been in the

United States for a year or less, June, an English-speaking social studies teacher, started each week presenting the basic vocabulary in Spanish and English and gave readings in Spanish. A bilingual paraprofessional and graduate student assisted in the class. Every effort was made to ensure that the students understood the material while maintaining English, the language of instruction assigned by the overall plan for the cluster. These same students attended Alma's science class taught in Spanish.

Bilingual instruction helps literacy development. Ms. Andrade's assignment was to teach literacy in English to an elementary class of 27 English-speaking and Spanish-speaking students. She focused on literacy development and chose to use both languages to reach this goal. Checking comprehension in Spanish, allowing discussions of English readings in Spanish, and direct instruction in Spanish helped the bilingual students. In the early part of the year students wrote mostly in their native language. Later in the year many Spanish speakers started to write in English, and several English speakers solicited help from their classmates to translate their English stories into Spanish. There was no pressure for students to use their second language, yet most of them did (Reyes, Laliberty, & Orbanosky, 1993).

When one of the goals of their class is the development of a particular language, teachers should consistently model that language. Jody and Margaret teach in a fourth-grade two-way program that integrates Spanish and English speakers. For the sake of efficiency, science is also the Spanish language development class, whereas social studies is the English language development class.[1] Jody uses only Spanish in the science class and Margaret use only English in the social studies class. Students are free to use either language. The teachers gently encourage them to practice Spanish in science classes and practice English in social studies lessons.

When developing oral language, teachers should encourage use of the language of the class. Encouraging the use of one language can be done without forbidding students to use the other. For example, a French immersion teacher reinforced the notion that the thing to do was to speak French. The children themselves encouraged each other to use the language. When we went to film the class for a television show, the children talked even to the cameraman in French. When children could not express themselves in French, they spoke in English and the teacher repeated it in French. Thus students learned how to say what they wanted to say even if, at first, they did not know how to say it in French.

On the other hand, when developing literacy and content area, students should take advantage of both languages to engage fully in the classroom activities. The social context encourages students to move into English as they become fluent in it. In order to encourage the advantage of strong native language development, teachers should dedicate a time, discipline, or topic specifically for consistent development of the native language. Cynthia's first-grade bilingual class spent part of each day in a writing workshop in which they enjoyed complete freedom of language use. Most children wrote, read, and discussed in Spanish for the first half

---

[1]Students in these classes are native speakers of Spanish and of English who have attended this two-way program since kindergarten.

of the year. Later in the year some attempted writing in English, often planning what they wrote in Spanish. Others continued to write in Spanish even if they admitted they could do it in English. When a monolingual English-speaking teacher visited the class during author's circle, the children accommodated their visitor by translating what was read and communicating with the visitor in English (Homza, 1995). These students started each day reading and discussing books in Spanish.

Freedom of language use paves the road for literacy development and positive attitudes toward both languages, and the presence of monolingual English speakers promotes the natural development of English. Literacy activities in the native language continue the development of a strong language basis.

In an ESL high school class for students with minimal literacy, the students told their stories in Spanish and with the help of their teacher they wrote them in English (Marsh, 1995). Although the purpose of the class was to teach English literacy, the teacher took advantage of the students' ability to express themselves orally in their native language as a foundation to develop English literacy.

Students' choice of language depends not only on their level of proficiency, but also on their personality, the topic, and their notion of whether it is appropriate or desirable to use one language or the other. Different students will make different choices. Students find it helpful to use the native language during the early stages of English language learning. Some students are fearful of using the second language because they do not want to make mistakes, whereas others find it challenging. Topics often sway the choice of language. Amal's students found it easier to talk about Ramadan in Arabic and smoking in English because of the cultural associations of those topics (Bou-Zeineddine, 1994). Students who have been taught not to use one language when learning the other will refuse to make use of both languages even if it is helpful. Students who choose the native language in ESL lessons gradually use more and more English (Brisk & Bou-Zeineddine, 1993). This flexibility of language use by students extends to classes in which the teacher speaks only English. Students should be able to use their native language to help each other. It is very natural to ask bilingual students to help students who are not fluent in English in a class in which there is language flexibility. A fifth grader felt proud of being able to help her English-speaking teacher: "When kids don't understand in English I explain in Spanish. . . . My mother and father will be proud of me because I will learn a lot. This is awesome!" (Brisk, 1991a, p. 23). When bilingualism is not seen as desirable, students resent requests for translation and students who need it resent being singled out.

Respect for students' languages extends to the dialects they actually speak. Teachers must accept students' dialects and teach them about the existence of these language varieties, the reasons for their development, and when it is appropriate to use which variety and why. Contrasting dialects or sociolinguistic studies of language use in neighborhoods, media, and literature help diffuse unwarranted attitudes toward different language varieties and ways people speak. For example, an advanced Spanish language class for native speakers developed a dictionary of contrasting dialects. When a student used orally or in writing an expression or grammatical structure different from standard Spanish, the teacher wrote it down on an index card. She then solicited from the other students the version in their own local dialect and added it to the card. At the end, the teacher gave them the standard version. An elementary bilingual teacher in Chicago had a class glossary with four columns: Puerto Rican, Cuban, Mexican American, and standard Spanish. Students learned that the language of the books is different but not necessarily better than their own language variety.

No language variety is better than another in absolute terms, but one may be more appropriate than the other relative to the circumstance. Teachers must point out that in school, the world of work, and other formal situations the standard variety is considered more suitable, whereas in their homes and neighborhoods, dialect is accepted and appropriate. Authors also use community dialects when they want to identify a character as belonging to a particular community.

Respect for students' culture encompasses accepting their ideas, knowledge, values, and behaviors. In addition, educators must extend this knowledge by incorporating elements of not only American culture in their lessons, but elements of the students' ancestral cultures as well. Often bilingual students born in the United States have little knowledge or are ambivalent about their families' culture. Essential to achieving sociocultural integration is a solid grounding on personal experience and ethnic culture. Respect and knowledge of American culture is more successfully attained when students are secure members of their community and are respectful toward their own ethnic culture (Kleinfeld, 1979).

To achieve respect and extension of culture, teachers need to:

- Acknowledge personal experience as knowledge.
- Elicit students' background knowledge before presenting new material.
- Accept students' styles of learning and culturally based classroom behavior.
- Adjust management style for effective classroom climate.
- Expand students' cultural experience through education.
- Familiarize students with classroom behaviors expected in an American classroom.
- Act as cross-cultural interpreters for academic and social purposes.

Topics need to be related to students' personal experience to facilitate comprehension and recall. The introduction of a topic starts with the assumption that the students know something about it, but teachers cannot assume specifically what students know because it will be based on their cultural background. Eliciting this background knowledge is the first step in any lesson or unit. Semantic mapping (see Appendix) where the key word is written on the board and students brainstorm ideas associated with the concept is a useful strategy. As students call out words, the teacher writes them on the board around the central theme. They discuss the terms, clarifying, relating, and categorizing. Through this strategy the teacher learns students' notions of a concept. Another strategy appropriate for students who can write requires students to jot down everything they know about a topic. With the paper in hand they discuss their ideas in small groups. These private notes give the students the opportunity and time to think and then express themselves about the topic.

Another strategy is student-directed sharing time or discussions (see Appendix). Alice organized her sixth-grade social studies curriculum in broad topics such as religion, education, politics, and so forth. Discussion took place at the beginning of each topic. Before the day of the discussion, she directed her Haitian students to find out everything they knew about the subject. She encouraged them to interview family members, read newspapers from their country, and make notes of their own ideas. While the students were discussing, she sat outside the circle and took notes. What Alice learned from the student-directed discussion served as the basis for preparation of the rest of her lessons on that particular topic. She admitted that until she started trying this strategy she never realized how much her students knew. Incidentally, Alice was also Haitian, yet she still had a lot to learn about her students.

Students differ in the way they receive and process information. In other words, each student has a particular learning style. Ethnicity, cultural background, and social class as well as individual preferences are among factors influencing these differences (Heath, 1983; Nieto, 1992; Sizer, 1992). To accommodate differences in learning styles, teachers need to present lessons in a variety of ways to match the various ways that students best absorb the material. Teachers should constantly guard against stereotyping students and lowering standards in the name of adapting their teaching to students' learning styles.[2]

Students' notions of appropriate classroom behavior derive from what they have learned at home about adult–child interactions. Students schooled abroad have acquired the rules of behaviors established in other school systems. Teachers working with students of the same ethnic group have successfully incorporated into their classroom the rules of behavior from their students' cultures (Au & Jordan, 1981; Cazden et al. 1980; Philips, 1972). When the teacher arrives at school in a Hawaiian village, several students are waiting to help him or her bring materials to the classroom. The teacher puts out the work and the children arrange the classroom, distribute the work, and finally ensure that everybody is in class when the lesson begins. Not much is said, but everything is organized and all students are settled as the lesson seamlessly begins. Different students help throughout the year without having specific assignments. This Hawaiian teacher, like a Hawaiian parent, minimizes verbal directions and close supervision, and allows students to organize, select, and "assign" specific tasks (Jordan, Tharp, & Baird-Vogt, 1992). Using culturally congruent means, the teacher achieves an orderly classroom atmosphere in which students thrive.

When teachers are of a different culture from their students, they maintain some of their own style, but must make adjustments. A teacher working at the Odawa Indian Reservation used the typical American style of whole-class presentation with questions directed to individual children. Through coaching and imitation, he gradually incorporated a style more congruent with these children's culture. He

---

[2]See Nieto (1992) for dangers of stereotyping and adapting to students' learning style.

organized students in groups and would call on a whole table. When addressing individual students, he would do it in a more private setting (Cazden et al., 1980). At St. Mary's boarding high school in Alaska, the American teachers conducted American-type classrooms, but outside-of-classroom teaching continued in the personalized and casual style characteristic of Eskimo village life (Kleinfeld, 1979).

Classroom management also presents challenges. Students accustomed to discipline strategies practiced in their homes and previous schooling experiences may misinterpret discipline strategies used by American teachers. Hispanic teachers use very different strategies from White American teachers to indicate disapproval of their students' behavior in class (Hernández & Santiago, 1983). Their appeals are indirect, peppered with polite forms such as "excuse me" and "please," and call for respect toward the teacher and others. The White American teachers use direct and short commands. For example, whereas a Hispanic teacher said "Juan, please do not get up," a White American teacher said "Sit up, Ana" (Hernández & Santiago, 1983, pp. 106–107). Students happily obeyed the Hispanic teacher, but they perceived the short and direct order of the White American teacher as disrespectful and rude. Consequently, teachers of the same culture as the students are usually efficient classroom managers because students understand their expectations. Incongruent management practices become ineffectual. Ballenger (1992), a White American teacher working with Haitian students, discovered that incorporating Haitian discipline strategies helped her gain control of her class. She developed an eclectic style that included her own strategies as well as those of her Haitian colleagues. She concluded that:

> The process of gaining multicultural understanding in education must, in my opinion, be a dual one. On the one hand, cultural behavior that at first seems strange and inexplicable should become familiar; on the other hand, one's own familiar values and practices should become at least temporarily strange, subject to examination. (p. 57)

Cultural adaptations to accommodate classroom interactions and management are more difficult when students come from a variety of cultural backgrounds. Good teachers, however, intuitively make modifications to improve communication and classroom climate: "[A]lthough all schools cannot become *culturally compatible,* they can nevertheless become *multiculturally sensitive* (Nieto, 1992, p. 120).

Students' cultural experience is expanded through education. Students' background knowledge must be expanded to comprehend and assimilate topics. Lessons expose students to new literature and ideas unfamiliar to them and their home culture. The students' original culture is used as a bridge. In a program for Asian high school students, storytelling was used as a bridge for reading literature traditionally used in U.S. schools. Students were asked to tell traditional stories of their country of origin. Next teachers focused on storytelling techniques and analysis of elements of stories such as conflict, resolution, main character, and others. Students then read Aesop's Fables, Greek myths, and classic stories such as

The Old Man and the Sea and *Clash of the Titans.* Reading was supplemented with videos of these stories. More advanced students explored works of other times and cultures such as *The Iliad, Arthurian Legends,* and *Rhyme of the Ancient Mariner* (Werner-Smith & Smolkin, 1995). These teachers introduced the students to the genre of fiction through the analysis of stories of their own culture. With these tools at hand, they were able to take on the tasks of reading and understanding stories very foreign to their cultural experience.

Many bilingual students come from homes with little written material available to them (Goldenberg et al., 1992). Teachers need to expose these students not only to traditional textbooks but all sorts of written resources found in the real world (Heath, 1986). These can become the basis for literacy development and they are often free. An ESL middle school teacher had her students write to various consulates and embassies requesting information. Students studied a map of the world to choose their country, practiced letter writing techniques, and finally mailed their letters. The room was alive with excitement every morning when the responses started to arrive. Students read, shared information, and produced brochures about their chosen country. A high school bilingual teacher used the study guide for taking the driver's license test as her ESL text. Although the language level was higher that what her students could handle, the strong motivation to get a driver's license and the numerous explicit diagrams and pictures made it a viable text.

Another strategy for expanding students' experience is field trips. Bringing parents as chaperones can also expand the parents' knowledge of the community. Trips to museums, libraries, and colleges in connection with class projects gives students broader perspective but also teaches them what is in the community. An ESL high school teacher blended photography with language learning when working with new arrivals. Students took pictures of famous places around Boston, using public transportation to get around. Lessons were built around those pictures. The students became familiar with the city and its public transportation and, in the process, also learned a good deal of English. Mei, a high school student from Hong Kong felt these activities were crucial because "you don't know the place when you are a recent immigrant, and you don't know any places around. Besides you don't have a car, you don't know how to take the T [subway] to go, even if the Museum of Science is easy to go to (Brisk, 1994a, p. 25).

Teachers also need to familiarize students with cultural norms of social behavior in the American context. Marsh (1995) worked with Spanish-speaking high school students who were recent arrivals and had limited schooling experience in their own countries. She taught them norms of behavior and interaction by modeling and direct instruction. She taught them how to behave with other students, with classroom visitors, and with teachers. She taught them common courtesy norms and how to listen and greet other students. She taught them how to maintain an orderly classroom, how to ask permission to leave the room, what to do when they were late, how to ask for help, and how to show respect for the teacher. Learning English is not enough to know how to behave in a particular society. Students need to know appropriate ways to relate and act in specific contexts.

Other classroom routines that can be confusing for bilingual students are selecting lunch, answering the teacher while sitting down, and addressing the teacher by name. These students may be used to going home for lunch, standing up to answer the teacher, and addressing the teacher by saying "teacher" (Clayton, 1993). Teachers of bilingual students play demanding roles. On the one hand, they cannot make any assumptions about behavior. On the other hand, they need to teach and present a model to their students of what is expected of them. The goal is to demonstrate the differences in behaviors without proposing that American norms are better so that students learn what works in this society.

Teachers serve as cross-cultural interpreters, helping students analyze, compare, and contrast knowledge from their culture and American culture. Teachers who come from a different community from the students must elicit cultural information from the students, their families, and community in order to succeed in explaining and analyzing cultural contrasts. This undeniable challenge, to learn from students, is one of the factors that can make teaching in multicultural classrooms so rewarding. Many of my finest students have, as experienced teachers, actually spent time in the communities from which some of their students immigrated and have returned to their classrooms with fresh insights into their roles.

ENGAGING, CHALLENGING, AND SUPPORTIVE INSTRUCTION

Classroom activities and the content of lessons should be interesting and challenging (García, 1963; Sizer, 1992). In the case of bilingual learners, lessons must be pitched to students' cognitive level, taking their language and literacy needs into consideration. Students in a bilingual classroom may be in the process of developing English but they are capable of handling material at a higher intellectual level in their native language. In other cases they may have had limited schooling for political or economic reasons but they are mature with rich life experiences. Teachers should implement strategies that allow for differences in abilities to present challenging content either in English or the native language to students with diverse language and literacy levels. High dropout rates for too many bilingual students may be attributed to low expectations in designing curriculum. Too often, teachers wait for students to achieve English proficiency before demanding serious work in their native language.

Lisa had students of Spanish, African, and American backgrounds in her high school humanities class. She worked very hard to make the curriculum challenging and comprehensible for students with very diverse backgrounds and language abilities.

The students had been studying about the Holocaust. They had read about the topic, had seen the movie "Schindler's List," and had listened to a presentation by a survivor of the Holocaust. The teacher started the class with a review of the issues raised by their visitor from the previous session. The discussion moved on to Israel. The teacher showed a map which she said was from 586 B.C. Immediately she asked how long ago that was. An argument ensued between a student who said it was 2,570 years ago and another who said it was 2,580. Lisa showed the class how the process both students used was correct, except the first one had made an addition error. Then, the students were divided into groups to explore one of the following topics: culture, politics, history, and problems in Israel. . . . After the groups had shared, Lisa asked further questions to clarify some points:

Lisa: . . . Do you remember Mr. Kline last year?
Debbie: Mr. Kline is from Cuba. Can he be Jewish?
Lisa: Can anyone from any nationality be Jewish?
Whole class: Yes.
Lisa: Why is this?
Judy: They move around. (Brisk, 1996, p. 13).

Lisa accepted the students' opinions but also challenged them. By working in both the whole class and in small groups, all students had a chance to participate regardless of language background. When working in small groups, students used their native languages and/or English.

Current teaching strategies that encourage more student creativity and involvement require adjustment for teachers who are accustomed to traditional methods. Rather than use watered down, uninteresting, and unchallenging material to allow students to cope on their own, it is better to employ vital material that may need instruction not only from the teacher but also from peers (Reyes, 1993). Students learn the material as well as language and study skills, which in turn allows them to work independently and creatively. Direct instruction with full engagement of the students in the learning process is very different from the much criticized transmission model.[3] In the transmission model, students are passive learners. In new approaches[4] involving direct instruction, students are fully engaged while they are helped in gaining skills to function independently. Participation with help is considered an important step in the development process. After a group of sixth-grade Spanish speakers who were beginners in English finished reading *The Fat Cat,* their teacher asked them:

If you were the teacher and I was the student what would you ask me about the story?
S[tudents]: Why did the cat go to the lady's house?
Why did the lady give the cat some soup?
Why did the cat get so fat when he ate the soup? (Hernández, 1991, p. 101)

---

[3]See Cummins (1984) for a critique of the transmission model.
[4]Some of these approaches have been called *scaffolding* (Cazden, 1988), *strategic teaching* (Jones et al., 1987), and *reciprocal teaching* (Hernandez, 1991). They are largely based on Vygotsky's (1978) theory of learning.

This interaction occurred in Spanish. The teacher instructed the students on how to go about thinking about a story, but allowed them to create their own questions. Students had to understand the story in order to ask such pertinent questions.

Teachers need to balance allowing for creativity in the context of interesting and challenging instruction in the students' native language or in English. Providing structure and skills to carry out creative activities steers students down the path of success without thwarting their motivation and avoiding unnecessary frustration. Sensitive teachers who know their students can adjust the amount of support as needed or desired by individual students.

SPECIAL STRATEGIES
TO PROVIDE FOR NEEDS

Successful instructional practices consider students with different needs. Acquiring English and learning to function in an academic setting in English require strategies different from those used with native English speakers. Students who have not been socialized to a school environment and have limited literacy also need to be approached in a different way. In adjusting to needs, the goal is still success and expectations are not lowered.

Teaching English and in English

Good first language development strategies also apply to second language teaching. The English language teachers, however, must take an especially active role, because often they are the main source for this language. Good practices for teaching literacy and content area subjects can be applied for instruction in the second language. Literature and social studies are the most difficult subjects to take in English. Literacy skills are needed and the main source of information is books. However, most books assume a considerable amount of cultural background. On the other hand, mathematics uses manipulatives and science uses hands-on experiments to facilitate comprehension and learning. The following strategies facilitate learning of and learning in English:

- Establish that students understand the goals of each lesson, general expectations, and homework assignments.
- Thoroughly explore background knowledge.
- Use direct instruction.
- Use interesting content when teaching language.
- Provide opportunities for meaningful language use.
- Use "gentle" correction strategies.
- Encourage participation by all students.
- Balance difficult with less demanding tasks.

- Choose what is most crucial.
- Modify language by speaking clearly.
- Paraphrase.
- Support verbal explanations with visual organizers and nonverbal cues.
- Check comprehension frequently.
- Read texts and tests aloud.
- Allow students to use L1 to help each other.
- Make materials in L1 available.

Teachers not only need to clearly explain goals and expectations for the lessons, but they need to make sure that all students understand them. Lessons can start with a simple agenda written on the blackboard. The teacher takes time to discuss it, asking students to talk among themselves to clarify and make sure that all understand what is expected of them. Teachers or students can use their native languages to ensure comprehension. Setting consistent routines also helps students know what to expect in the class. If students know what is expected of them they will be able to function better with less confusion and fewer discipline problems. Homework also needs to be clearly explained. Students not only should know what the assignment is, but how to carry it out.

Before starting the lesson the teacher should check background knowledge without making assumptions. Because bilingual students have a different cultural experience, they may not know relevant information assumed in books written for U.S. students. A reading about the Navigation Act imposed by Britain on the colonies confused Benny, a high school student from the Dominican Republic who was unfamiliar with the history of colonial America. The teacher engaged in an explanation about the colonies and their relation to Britain. Only then could Benny begin to understand the reasons for trade restrictions required by this Act.

Direct instruction is essential in a class in which all students are learning the language because the teacher is the only person who knows the language well (Wong-Fillmore, 1989). The teacher models the language, encourages students to repeat, verbalizes actions and processes, uses the language used by students and expands on it, and provides oral and written scripts for students to use. In activities in which students participate in group projects, research, or discussions the teacher actively monitors the students' work. Aurora closely observed student-directed discussions, providing vocabulary when necessary to continue the flow of the discussion. Holdaway (1979) proposed use of the structure of a story read by students as the basis for creating a story (see Appendix for shared reading). Especially for the early stages of language development, students have a richer experience with language if they are assisted in working with the language than if they are given a simple nonverbal activity to do on their own. In a student-centered class, the teacher provides direction as needed and allows for self-directed activities as feasible.

Instruction needs to be supplemented with exposure to other models of language such as film, tapes, and other English speakers. Students need to be exposed to peers who are native speakers of English because children learn different aspects of the language from children than from adults (Hatch, 1978). The use of the Internet has enhanced written communication among native and second language learners (Sayers, 1989).

Teacher- or self-directed activities must be done with interesting content and meaningful use of the language. Teachers must present both social and academic contexts for language use. Students need to interact with friends, carry out school routines, and get along in the outside world as well as understand lectures, answer teachers' questions, take notes, read texts, write papers, and take tests. Strategies such as projects, role playing, taking advantage of circumstances, and even becoming language detectives or ethnographers can be used for productive and interesting language learning. A third-grade teacher developed The Valentine Factory as a 1-month lesson rather than the traditional cutting and pasting to make cards. The class decided to produce Valentine cards and sell them in the school. To carry out this project, they read about factories and discussed such issues as setting prices and making profit. They visited classes to market their product and take orders. Finally, they produced the cards. The activity was not only engaging; it also provided functional use of written and oral English. They read to learn about producing an item, they used oral language to discuss and market their product, and they had to write the cards. The teacher taught them specific aspects of language that they needed to carry out this project. For example the structure "X units of Y" (3 yards of ribbon, 6 sheets of paper) was needed to calculate the materials they needed. The question "How many Valentines do you want?" was essential to take orders. They had to be able to answer the question "How much will it cost?" (Wong Fillmore, 1989). This activity provided the opportunity for learning and practicing both oral and written English and for interaction with the teacher, peers in their class, and native speakers of English in other classes.

Role playing brings outside context to a classroom. To simulate, for example, in the context of a visit to the doctor, students develop listening skills that allow them to answer questions posed by the doctor or nurse. They practice speaking skills to explain health problems, set up appointments, and order medicine. They also learn to read signs that direct patients to different departments in a clinic or hospital and read and respond in writing to health questionnaires. There are literally hundreds of situations encountered by the students that offer opportunities to teach the functional use of English.

Taking advantage of circumstances is another way to practice real language. For example, an elementary ESL teacher, before sending a tardy student to the office, took advantage of the opportunity to practice the language they needed to notify the office and to understand what they might be told (Leone, 1995).

In all these examples, teaching of all four language skills was accomplished by demonstrating the use of each skill in the appropriate context (Heath, 1986).

Speaking, listening, reading, and writing were done for the same reasons that they are done in the real world.

Teachers can structure activities to encourage participation by all students regardless of their English level or willingness to participate. A teacher can structure responses for the students to respond to with an action ("Show me X") or a word ("What do you need?"), a whole sentence or question (Tell me about this Valentine?"), or extended speech (What can we say about this Valentine to sell it?) depending on their level of English ability (Wong Fillmore, 1989). Cooperative learning activities, such as The Jigsaw (see Appendix) are appropriate for students helping each other with language (Slavin, 1970).

"The teacher was careful to call on the extremely reticent students only when she was fairly certain they would be successful" (Gersten, 1996, p. 235). Fourth-grade students had read a story about a bad man transforming himself into a good man. There were about 30 examples in the story to illustrate this transformation. The teacher asked the students to give examples. Taking advantage of the momentum generated by students calling out examples, she succeeded in obtaining responses from even the most reticent students. Another strategy is to work individually or in small groups with students with limited language or willingness to speak out. Once they gain confidence and practice in expressing their ideas in English in small groups, they participate around more vocal students.

One dilemma that teachers often voice in relation to second language teaching is what to do about correction or feedback. On the one hand, language and literacy acquisition is developmental. Abundant meaningful exposure and opportunity for practice makes learning possible. Learners improve their speaking and writing skills with time and use. Constant correction blocks the natural process. Yet second language acquisition theory proposes that incorrect forms can "fossilize" and become part of the permanent linguistic repertoire of the learner. Teachers should not be afraid to give students the correct form of the language. Timing and manner of correction as well as nature of the error are what matters. When encountering errors in writing, the teacher should try to first understand the message and then help students with the language that will clearly convey their message. There is no point in correcting language until the message is clear and organized. Often, clarifying the message improves the quality of the language. Rather than interrupt students while they are talking to correct them, the teacher can note important errors. With this information, the teacher can plan minilessons, point the problems out to students individually at a later time, or model the correct form when responding to a student. However, for some students minilessons or modeling is not sufficient. They need a specific explanation of what is wrong in their work and how it can be corrected (Reyes, 1992, 1993).

When working on grammatical and mechanical errors, it is important to highlight how these errors affect meaning. Charles, a high school teacher, connected all corrections to meaning. Looking at Duk's work on the computer he read aloud, exaggerating the error:

Charles: . . . paintful . . . What's the problem?
Duck: the "t."
Charles: Yes. . . . She is full of pain.

Whether commenting on content, vocabulary, grammar, or spelling, Charles always explained how the error affected meaning.

Sometimes teachers are hesitant to correct for fear of embarrassing students, "[y]et the acceptance of responses that are improper is likely to convey to students that teachers do not hold high standards and expectations for them" (Gersten, 1996, p. 237). Teachers must convey to students that they want them to improve their language without humiliating them.

In order to keep the material at the cognitive level of the student teachers should mix difficult with less demanding tasks and choose essential concepts rather than water down content. Ms. Leonard, a fourth-grade English literacy teacher, discussed stories with her students by mixing higher order thinking questions with description of the characters and other key elements of the story. She chose a few words crucial to the understanding of the story for students to study, find the definition of in the dictionary, and use frequently (Gersten, 1996).

Explanations in English are difficult to understand when students are still in the process of acquiring the language. Supporting explanations with visual organizers and nonverbal clues facilitates listening comprehension. Ms. Tapia uses a blackboard and prepares charts to reinforce oral activities. When asking the students to predict before reading a story, she writes down each student's predictions on the board. After the story is read, the students review their prediction. She also has a chart to analyze characters in a story. Actions, speech (or dialogue), and how characters look are listed on the chart as sources of support to make inferences about a character (Gersten, 1996). These visual resources enhance student participation. Objects, maps, graphs, and other nonverbal cues help students understand oral and written English.

Teachers cannot assume that bilingual students understand everything they say. They should check comprehension frequently; once a student loses track it becomes harder and harder to comprehend the rest. This is not an easy thing to do because constant interruptions also interfere with comprehension of the key points. Angela was reading a passage from a science book on invertebrates. At the first encounter with the word *invertebrates,* she asked students to define the word, provide examples, and relate their firsthand experiences with these creatures. She read the rest of the passage without interruption. The explanation of the key concept helped the students tackle the rest of the paragraph.

Reading text aloud makes it a lot easier for bilingual students to understand. In reading aloud, the teacher pronounces difficult words correctly, adding meaningful expression. June always read the directions of her tests aloud and she watched the students carefully. Whenever she sensed that somebody was not comprehending she would repeat and double check.

As discussed earlier, use of the home language facilitates both literacy and content area instruction in English. Corky, who taught math in English, asked her students to choose the English or the Spanish version of the math textbook for completing homework assignments and for other exercises required in the class.

Teaching Students With Limited Schooling

Students from abroad who enter American schools with no or little prior schooling are at special risk. Insightful teachers realize that such students have to develop language and behavior appropriate for their new schools. Programs that work successfully with these students use their native language and English, relate lessons to the students' experience, integrate language skills, integrate teaching academic language with content area instruction, and use instructional strategies typical of elementary schools regardless of the students' age.

The native language is the best medium for introducing all new concepts and creating a base for learning in English. Before introducing a story in English, a high school teacher reads it in Spanish, stressing reading strategies such as previewing, predicting, making inferences, and finding the main idea. Once those functions are introduced, the teacher then reads the story in English, asking students to talk about the plot and characters, and relate the story to the students' culture and experiences (Marsh, 1995).

Relating concepts to the students' culture facilitates comprehension and allows for the use and development of higher order thinking skills. Gerner de García (1995) developed a unit around the book *Growing Vegetable Soup* by Lois Ehlert (1987). Her students came from rural Central America where they learned how to grow and care for plants at an early age. Concentrating on what they already knew, the students could effectively practice reading, writing, and developing science projects while gradually expanding their English vocabulary.

Public oral language is another source of difficulty for these students. Often they are reluctant to speak, even in their native language. Formal oral language needs to be taught and should be integrated with the practice of written skills. Marsh (1995) used a number of strategies to get her students to speak (in any language) in her ESL class. Dramatizations, impromptu speaking, and performances from scripts were used. Students prepared dramas based on topics from their culture that they rehearsed in their native language to ensure comprehension. The plays were then presented either in the native language or in English. For impromptu presentations, the students were given a topic on which they had to speak spontaneously for 2 minutes. Scripts selected from a variety of sources or produced by the students were used to practice oral language and performances were videotaped.

Curriculum, materials, and strategies used at the elementary level assist these students. They need not make them feel childish if they are relevant to the knowledge and skills that they bring to school. A program for middle school students in Texas organized curriculum around literature-based units and theme-oriented activities. Students read aloud, wrote in journals, engaged in cooperative learning, and developed key vocabulary in content areas. For science they used the program *Finding Out/Descubrimiento* (DeAvila, Duncan, & Navarrete, 1987) developed for elementary schools (Hewlett-Gómez & Solís, 1995). Attractive children's books are useful and enjoyable (Gerner de García, 1995) because many such students have rarely seen such books that are common in the United States.

Teaching reading, writing, and the inquiry method as a tool for thinking and learning helps low-achieving students acquire academic skills. At the AVID program, high school students were taught how to identify main ideas, take notes in academic courses, and write questions on those notes. Questions were then used for discussions. They were taught to write their own thoughts, either as they came up or as reflection after a class and after reading a text. These students also learned how to solve problems and clarify thoughts through their own questions and collaborative research (Mehan et al., 1994).

LESSON OBJECTIVES

The challenge of teaching bilinguals is the need to integrate content, language, and culture in every lesson. These three objectives need to be explicit so that students know what they are going to do in each lesson. A science lesson on plants for the elementary level, for example, might have the following objectives:

1. Content: to identify various characteristics of plants.
2. Language: vocabulary related to plant parts, describe plants orally and in writing, recognize names of plants when reading.
3. Culture: compare local plants with plants from students' places of origin.

Teachers should be flexible in implementing their objectives by being open to pursuing a topic or a problem elicited from a student. During a high school ESL lesson, a student mentioned that he was tired because he had not slept all night due to a shooting in his neighborhood. The teacher asked the student to narrate what had happened: "[S]everal writing, reading, and listening activities emerged such as role-playing the shoot-out, reporting an emergency via 911, drawings of sequences of events and writing an action packed story" (Marsh, 1995, p. 419).

Teachers should have broad objectives, but they also need to record what actually was taught. Attached to the lesson plan teachers can keep a form on which they record material covered each day or week (see Fig. 5.1). Students could keep their own list.

Content	Language	Culture
Week 1		
Week 2		

FIG. 5.1 Lesson content record form.

STUDENTS' ROLE

Effective teachers engage students in learning by creating active learning opportunities, at the same time displaying active teaching behavior (Garcia, 1991; Lucas, 1993a; Mace-Matluck, 1990; Pease-Alvarez et al., 1991; Tikunoff, 1983; Tikunoff & Vasquez-Faría, 1982). Teachers encourage students to participate in classroom activities, to interact with each other, and to collaborate among themselves. Student collaboration and interaction should be structured and monitored by teachers to ensure both full participation and learning. In a classroom where interaction and collaboration are encouraged, students talk and move freely but purposefully. To make collaboration productive, teachers need to model how to ask questions, how to give constructive criticism, and how to listen. In Cynthia's first-grade class students start the afternoon writing session with a writers' meeting at which they discuss with the teacher their plans. Students usually share their ideas with a partner, write drafts in consultation with other students and with the teacher, periodically choose one piece for publication, and share with the class their final product. Cynthia provides a structure and coaches and encourages students. Students, however, are allowed creativity in their writing and are supported when assisting other students. Students in this class collaborate during the planning, writing, revising, and sharing of their stories (Homza, 1995).

Good teachers give their students freedom and responsibility for their work. Thus, students:

- Self-direct work and keep constantly engaged.
- Keep work organized and orderly.
- Learn from each other as well as from the teacher.
- Learn to provide constructive criticism.
- Actively participate in learning.

These habits need to be established through practice and direction from the teacher early in the school year.

Once accustomed to the writing sessions, Cynthia's students carried out their activities without constant prompting from the teacher. They kept their work neatly organized in folders. Every day at the beginning of writing workshop they reviewed their folders to determine plans for the day. Sharing their stories involved helping each other edit. Noriliz read to Dianis her bilingual story:

N: (reading) Mi mamá me llamó para comer. . . . My mommy told to come fom [sic] eat.

D: *To* eat not *for* eat. (Homza, 1995, p. 152)

To keep studer s constantly engaged in learning, teachers must train their students to look for additional work when their task is finished. Students need access to interesting books, games, and activities for "fill-in" time. Dedicating space to a listening, reading, and writing corner encourages such additional work.

Engaging students in classroom activities should occur regardless of language and literacy proficiency. Lessons that have clear objectives but allow students flexibility in what each produces permit students with limited language or literacy skills to participate at their own level. First-grade Spanish speaking students were assigned to write stories in Spanish. Madeline's initial stories were all just one sentence long. The teacher encouraged her to illustrate them, find titles, and put covers on them including the author's name. Her books looked like the others even if the other students' stories were longer and more elaborate. When being taught in English, students should also feel included even if they cannot produce much in that language. For example a kindergarten teacher used the word card strategy (see Appendix) for students ranging from native speakers of English to Gina, a Chinese girl who had been in the United States for 2 weeks. Gina could fully participate in this activity because all she had to do was bring one English word to class each day.

Students may have difficulty participating in class not because of language but because of culture. They may come from systems that frown on active participation based on a transmission model in which teachers lecture and students listen. Teachers should encourage such students to listen and learn while they help them to become more active in the classroom.

All students need to be given a chance to be experts in the class. It gives them the confidence and motivation to learn. The jigsaw, a cooperative learning strategy (see Appendix), relies on expert groups to put the puzzle together. Each expert group becomes knowledgeable in one aspect of the material to be learned and each group is responsible to teach the other students. Cross-age projects (see Appendix) allow older students to experience their expertise when they teach younger students. To use this strategy, teachers must prepare the older students well before they confront their charges.

CLASSROOM ORGANIZATION

Physical organization of the classroom supports principles of learning. As the roles of teachers and students have evolved from lecturers to coaches, facilitators, and managers, the traditional classrooms (rows of seats facing the blackboard) have yielded to a variety of room arrangements designed to suit particular activities. Modern classrooms are very active, even chaotic.

To ensure that learning takes place in this seemingly unstructured atmosphere, teachers vary students' grouping to adjust for activities, styles, and language needs and also to coordinate participation of outside help. Classrooms are organized to provide opportunities for flexible groupings and constant engagement of all students. Work takes place in the whole class, in small groups, in pairs, or even independently. Such variations allow students to interact with their teachers and with each other. In a literacy project in Chelsea, Massachusetts, classes start in whole-class groups to introduce new vocabulary, make predictions, and define purposes for reading. Sometimes students work in pairs to make predictions and set purposes. Then students are divided in two needs-based groups. The composition of these groups changes for each reading selection. Students who have the background knowledge and interest in the topic as well as reading proficiency work independently. Others work with the teacher who reads the selection aloud and further reviews vocabulary. After reading silently and aloud in cooperative pairs, the class discusses the reading as a whole class or in heterogeneously cooperative groups. They work together on a writing activity. Needs-based and student-led groups are formed to carry out writing or follow-up activities. A number of different groupings and activities complete the cycle (Radencich, McKay, & Paratore, 1995). Students are not placed in permanent groups. The composition of the groups constantly changes depending on the purpose and students' specific needs. Having students of different abilities in a group allows more advanced students to practice their skills by teaching others as the less advanced students benefit from this. Homogeneous grouping should be directed to the specific needs of a group of students.

Often paraprofessionals, volunteers, and college students work with a teacher. It is essential that their work be coordinated by the teacher so they are all working for the same goals. When teachers do not speak the native language of the students, they should yield to the paraprofessional to provide background knowledge and literacy in the child's first language.

CLASSROOM ASSESSMENT

To make assessment productive, meaningful, and fair it needs to be coordinated with instruction. Relating assessment with instruction avoids the pervasive sense that time dedicated to assessment is stolen from instruction. Assessment prepared by teachers in conjunction with instruction has a dual role: to improve teaching and increase learning. Teachers need to collect information, interpret it, and make decisions about instruction and students (Genesee & Hamayan, 1994; O'Malley & Valdez Pierce, 1996[5]).

It is difficult but necessary to distinguish content and language assessment. Language ability should not interfere with students' ability to demonstrate knowledge of a subject. In a bilingual classroom, teachers:

- Plan assessment and instruction simultaneously.
- Assess students while teaching.
- Become familiar with background characteristics of the students.
- Evaluate process and products.
- Assess academic achievement bilingually.
- Use authentic activities in addition to tests for assessing language and academic achievement.
- Give positive but realistic feedback.
- Target students' evaluation appropriately depending on whether it is presented to administrators, parents, other teachers, or students.

Teachers need to plan assessment and instruction simultaneously. In planning their goals for lessons, they should develop strategies to monitor the students' progress. Teaching techniques can serve assessment purposes. In turn, the information acquired through assessment can direct instruction to areas that need improvement. For example, student-directed discussion is a highly recommended strategy for language and thinking skill development. Teachers can observe students, assessing their language proficiency, ability to think, and knowledge of content. They can give students feedback and incorporate language and content activities in lessons that cover problems evidenced during the students' discussions. Amy, an ESL teacher, audiotapes her students' discussions and transcribes portions of them. She then discusses with the whole class the language problems in the transcripts and prepares all her grammar lessons based on collected data from these discus-

---

[5]Both of these sources have excellent and clear descriptions of assessment strategies for language and content area learning. Although addressing English, these suggestions can and should be applied to native language assessment.

sions. Amy uses her students' knowledge to evaluate their performance and inform her instruction.

To assess students' performance accurately and meaningfully requires three sets of data: (a) familiarity with their background characteristics, (b) an evaluation of process required to perform, and (c) evaluation of outcomes. Obtaining each set of data requires its own strategies. Basic background information includes the amount of previous schooling, literacy level in the home language, understanding of the school culture, interests, and level of English proficiency. In addition to noting classroom behavior and reviewing records, teachers use a number of strategies to get to know their students: talking to the students, their families, and community members' reviewing journals and critical autobiographies, and eliciting observations from researchers or student teachers.

To understand "process," teachers need to know how a particular student arrived at a particular solution. When Carmelita wrote "el conejo brown" (the brown rabbit) it appeared that she did not know the Spanish word for *brown.* By observing while she was writing and asking her about what she was doing, however, I found out that she chose the English word because the Spanish *café* (brown) has an accent mark that the word-processing program she was using could not produce. I also was able to suggest that she could write in Spanish and then add the accent marks by hand. Thus, observing the process avoided an incorrect assessment of the student's language ability and provided an immediate teaching opportunity. To evaluate process, teachers observe and interact with students as they are reading, writing, solving a math problem, or completing a science experiment. The time to discuss process with students is critical. It is done while students are still engaged in the tasks, when the teacher may learn why students do the task their way. However, reserving comments until students have completed the tasks is less intrusive.

The process can be bilingual and bicultural although the product, consistent with reality, is usually in one language or the other. Noriliz' first story in English was completely rehearsed in Spanish in her personal journal. Each of the daily expansions were also found in her Spanish journal (Homza, 1995). In order for the teacher to understand how Noriliz could write and revise in English, she had to investigate the process. Noriliz put priority on thinking about the story "Lo primero que hacer es pensar un cuento . . ." (The first thing to do is to think of a story; Homza, 1995, p. 160). However, for her that thinking needed to be done in Spanish.

Oral proficiency needs to be assessed in the language in question. However, literacy and knowledge of content can be assessed in either or both languages. A student can read in English but explain the content in the native language, especially at the early stages of English language learning. Alex, a student from the former Czechoslovakia, joined the English class of an integrated fifth-grade Spanish–English team. Soon after he arrived, the teacher gave a test on bones. Students were to write the names of the different bones on a picture of a skeleton. Alex did it in Czech. Through pointing at the body and using a dictionary, the teacher confirmed his knowledge of the subject and graded him accordingly. As a test to his classmates, she instructed them to teach Alex the English equivalents.

To evaluate language, teachers observe students as they carry out regular classroom activities or activities especially planned to demonstrate knowledge of a language skill. Teachers use protocols reflecting performance goals (see Fig. 5.2 as an example) to facilitate collecting the information. While observing the class, the teacher focuses on a few students at a time to fill in each individual protocol, noting the student can perform the task independently (++), with some help (+) or not at all (x).

For example, observing students during role playing activities, a teacher may note whether they use the appropriate language and respond logically. Reading can be evaluated by observing students directing a shared reading activity, discussing a book, or noting how well they use information from books for research projects. Writing can be assessed as students write and publish their work. Protocols with specific grammar skills and vocabulary can also be developed. Pronunciation and spelling are important in second language development. Special activities such as reciting a poem can be used to check pronunciation. For spelling, the teacher may establish a target for the number of words to be spelled correctly over a period of time. Weekly tests evaluate progress in reaching the goal. Any word misspelled can be part of the test the following week.

In addition to observations, conferences, dialogue journals, learning logs, and tests provide data to measure students' language development (Genesee & Hamayan, 1994). Conferences are usually individual discussions about readings or written work done in class or as homework. They provide the teacher with a deeper knowledge of an individual student's abilities. One teacher discussed a reading (about an Italian American boy whose aunt visits from Italy) with a fifth-grade student who was reportedly able to read English. The student had successfully answered some general questions about the story, but apparently had trouble understanding details. When asked who came to visit, she said "grandparents," drawing from her own experience rather than from comprehension of the text. Following this session, the teacher realized that this student had used her oral knowledge of English and her own intelligence to appear to have a greater reading ability in English. It took a one-to-one conference to accurately access this student's reading ability.

In another instance, when a teacher asked a highly biliterate student about a book she was reading, the student claimed not to understand a word of it. All she could say was that it was about a priest and Indians. The teacher was surprised because this book was well within the student's reading level. She asked the student to read aloud from the beginning. In the third line the book mentions British Columbia.

T: Where is British Columbia?

S: (hesitant) In England?

T: No, it is in Canada.

S: That is what confused me. I could not understand why there were Indians
    in England. Now I understand the whole book.

She went on to give a clear account of the whole book. This student was so
perturbed by what she considered an anomaly—Indians in Europe—that she
doubted that she understood the book. The 5-minute conference not only confirmed
to the teacher this student's advanced reading ability but helped the student
overcome her initial self-doubts.

Examination of students' journals and learning logs provides additional data on
students' language development. Journals can be analyzed for writing fluency,
sentence structure, vocabulary, grammar, spelling, and ability to express complete
thoughts. Learning logs reveal students' level of comprehension of language used
in content area lectures and texts. Teachers keep grids with performance objectives,
on which they enter achievements of individual students obtained from the various
assessment strategies.

Evaluation of content area subjects is best done through projects that require the
application of knowledge to real situations. Sizer (1992) recommended long-term
projects that require thinking, combining disciplines, and consulting with individu-

Name:

Speaking	Time 1	Time 2	Comments
The language is appropriate for the person being addressed			
Pronunciation does not cloud meaning			
No major consistent syntactic problems that cloud meaning			
Can take at least three turns in a dialogue			
Listening			
Responds appropriately to what other students say			
Performs correctly at least five instructions			
Reading			
Reads fluently and with expression			
Makes predictions			
Understands the main idea			
Writing			
No major gaps in meaning or content			
No major consistent syntactic problems			
Comprehensible spelling and handwriting			

FIG. 5.2 Language assessment protocol.

als, books, and other sources. The teacher coaches the students so that they can perform well. Students have the opportunity to demonstrate in front of others the skills they have gained through what Sizer called exhibitions. One such project required students to write an essay in English about a human emotion (fear, envy, courage, etc.). They were also asked to define this emotion through three other media of their choice such as another language, a drawing, photographs, videos, plays, or other art forms. They had to find examples in literature, journalism, the arts, and history. Students were given 4 months to have the exhibition ready. They were also told the criteria that would be used to judge them. Another more pragmatic project involved preparing the federal income tax form for five families. The teacher provided the financial records of these imaginary families to groups of students and gave them a month to provide results. Members of one group then audited the results of members of another group. Both these projects required students to use their knowledge to handle real-life experiences and to combine knowledge they acquire in different disciplines (Sizer, 1992).

Tests can be included as an additional measure rather than the only assessment measure for both language and content area. They provide information to the teacher and other parties and give students practice in test taking as well as demonstration of performance under pressure.

Evaluation of students should also be an opportunity to teach. Teachers should point out first what students have done correctly so that students know what they can do again. Problems and errors should be indicated with the goal of improving students' skills rather than degrading their performance. Teachers need to be explicit to students when commenting on language performance. They need to show them that language development does not always mean that they are able to do academic work in that language. Often students feel frustrated because they are told that they have learned a great deal of English, yet they cannot function at their age- or grade-appropriate academic level.

Teachers need to organize the information collected in different ways depending on who will use the data. Parents and administrators want information that reflects an overall picture of the students' performance. Teachers and students need more detailed and frequent information that will help with measuring achievement. From all the information collected weekly in a class, teachers and students select specific examples that show the content and language that students are learning, instructional strategies used, and the progress students make over time. This information should also support decisions for student promotion.

Teachers should also be concerned about the sociocultural integration of their students. In addition to general observations, they may also consider using students' journals, sociograms, and interviews to measure how their students feel about their language and culture, how they relate to their community, their attitudes toward English, and friendships with American peers. Observing students in situations where they must use the home language and interact with people from that culture, as well as with English-speaking Americans, can reveal ability to function in both cultures. In a fifth-grade integrated math class, the teacher formed groups with recent arrivals, bilingual students, and English-speaking students. She then observed how students interacted. Observations can be corroborated by interviewing the students. Yuka was observed mostly with her Japanese classmates. When interviewed, however, she revealed, "I feel that I am ready to be more with American students. The only reason I am not doing it is that they have their own group[6]" (Interview, March 7, 1996). Yuka had the potential but the American students were not facilitating the process. In schools that promote sociocultural integration, even students with limited English find ways to interact with English speakers because all students are encouraged to interact with people of different cultures.

June used dialogue journals to measure her bilingual and mainstream students' attitudes toward dealing with each other in a seventh-grade integrated cluster. Initially students expressed their wariness about dealing with students of a different ethnic group. Bilingual students who had been mainstreamed revealed embarrassment at having to interact with students in the bilingual program. These emotions had not been openly or orally expressed to the teacher. Over time, and through the express goals of the program, the journals revealed that the students developed more positive feelings.

Sociograms or questionnaires that ask students about their relationships with students of other groups give further insight. In an evaluation of the Amigos program, student were asked such questions as: "Have you made any very good friends who are Spanish-speaking? English-speaking? Would you rather have English-speaking or Spanish-speaking friends?" (Lambert & Cazabón, 1994). Sociocultural integration must be closely monitored and supported, otherwise prejudices can deepen when groups of students are brought together.

Interviews with families also reveal the source of sociocultural adjustment or lack of it. An interview with Rebecca, the mother of a 9-year old Russian student, revealed her own dilemma between promoting Russian cultural values and wanting her to daughter to assimilate. It was thus not surprising that her daughter was also struggling with the pull of the two cultures.

Knowledge of students, accurate interpretation of their performance, authentic techniques, and clear communication of results make assessment essential for the educational process. Schools need well-prepared, sensitive, and organized teachers to carry out this pivotal task.

RESOURCES FOR TEACHING

Resources should serve the teacher's curricular goals instead of driving the curriculum. Teachers need to consider what resources they need, how to use them, and how to organize them in the classroom. Students should be instructed on how to use resource materials, either in the classroom or the library, because they may have never had access to such resources. Using a dictionary, encyclopedia, or going to a public library may be a totally new experience.

---

[6]Yuka (not her real name) was interviewed in Japanese by M. T. Shew, a graduate student at Boston University and a native speaker of Japanese.

Traditionally, classrooms have relied on textbooks for each subject. The modern classroom also employs a variety of other books, magazines, videos, filmstrips, science kits, math manipulatives, maps, posters, student-produced materials, and computers.

A fundamental planning decision involves how to use textbooks. Traditionally teachers supplement textbooks with other materials. Increasingly, however, teachers focus on a variety of materials, using textbooks as a supplement. Availability, teacher experience, and the quality of textbooks influence choice and use of materials. Textbooks can be particularly helpful to new teachers because they provide an organized sequence. In some cases, textbooks are the only materials available in the school. Often teachers themselves purchase additional materials or encourage students to bring books from home to share. Many publishers, responding to the demands for a greater variety of resources, have modified textbooks to include literature, hands-on activities, and science experiments. For the most part, however, textbooks are not as interesting to students, may seem too long and difficult, and give rise to unfair competition when individual students or groups are working at different levels.

Textbooks should be only one of the many resources supplemented by reference books for the content areas and authentic literature in English and students' home language. In one school in Mexico City, in addition to a well-stocked and well-used library, all classrooms (Grades 1–12) had their own reference materials. In each classroom a few shelves running along two or three walls were sectioned and labeled for each of the subjects covered by the class. Students used the materials as references for their various projects. The students themselves are responsible for searching and reshelving the books they need.

An elementary bilingual Spanish class enjoyed the monthly arrival of the magazine *Mi Globo*. Students read and discussed the feature article and developed a number of writing projects around the themes featured by the magazine. Some of their work was published by the magazine, increasing their enthusiasm for these written projects (Leone, 1995).

Bilingual students especially benefit from use of visual media to supplement and clarify printed information. Videos of books to be read fill gaps in background knowledge and also model language for students reading in English. In an ESL program teachers used videos of first-grade English speakers as a source for teaching English to upper elementary Vietnamese students. These students viewed and analyzed the language of the native speakers in the videos. Discussions and written projects in which the fifth graders acted as linguists provided the source for language development (Heath, 1985).

Science kits or programs are especially useful. A fifth-grade integrated bilingual and monolingual class rented science kits from a local museum to teach the various science units. These kits contained a variety of materials. Many came in multiple quantities and could be used by the students, to later be restocked by the museum. Some of the kits were in Spanish. *The Finding Out/Descubrimiento* method developed by DeAvila provides bilingual science materials for a variety of learning centers where students work in groups as well as individually (DeAvila & Duncan, 1982).

Student-produced materials are interesting to students and more accessible because the language level is closer to their own. Anne, a first-grade bilingual teacher, kept student-produced books in the classroom library. Students were furnished with library cards to borrow the books and bring them home.

Most schools now have access to computers. Teachers should blend the use of this technology into their teaching goals and coordinate work with the computer lab. Teachers can train students to use computers in the classroom. A second-grade teacher had parent volunteers working with the children on the one computer she shared with her neighbor. A sign-up sheet helps logistics and avoids conflict. Many schools have computer labs for classes to share. The classroom teacher and computer teacher need to work together to ensure that the work in the computer room is coordinated with instruction. While working on a science project that involved the study of a nearby pond, students conducted research using databases available through the Internet with the assistance of the computer teacher.

Bilingual classes greatly benefit from technology because it gives them access to the world that uses the native language of the students in their daily lives. The program *De Orilla a Orilla/From Shore to Shore* makes use of electronic mail technology to connect bilingual classrooms in the United States with classrooms throughout the world. Teachers in the two paired classes plan their projects together communicating via e-mail. These projects are carried out in individual classes and shared with each other through e-mail as well (Cummins & Sayers, 1995).

Classes should use nonscholastic resources. A newly developed multilingual high school program lacked bilingual teachers with a strong science background. The teachers reached out to the community for assistance. In a course called Science Projects, students developed science-fair type projects. They worked under the direction of one of the teachers with the assistance of graduate students from a well-known university. They often traveled to the university laboratories to work on their projects. For the biology course they secured an instructor from the local Audubon Society and a graduate student from another prestigious university. Together with one of the teachers, the high school students studied biology through preparing themselves to teach science at a nearby elementary bilingual school. The Audubon Society provided basic instruction and materials, the neighborhood became the laboratory, and the graduate student brought the concepts to a high school level (Brisk, 1996).

PARTNERSHIP WITH FAMILIES AND COMMUNITIES

Teachers make connections with the students' homes and neighborhoods by bringing members of the family to share their expertise and by using the neighborhoods as resources for learning. A high school teacher invited parents and members of the community to visit her class. Students asked these visitors about work opportunities in New York City. The students learned to ask questions and acquired knowledge of job opportunities from members of their own community (Marsh, 1995).

The local pond became the science laboratory for students in a multilingual high school class. They studied its

> biology, chemistry, and ecology. They planned and carried out field studies of microscopic aquatic life, developed a hydrogeologic profile of the pond, and analyzed its various chemical and physical properties. . . . The product of the investigation was a field guide of the local aquatic system that they prepared for elementary school students. (Rivera & Zehler, 1991, p. 65)

The assumption of this program is that having students investigate the world around them can motivate them to learn by making science relevant to their immediate surroundings.

Teachers should not only work with community members of the same ethnic group as the students but with other ethnic groups and English speakers. A high school ESL teacher wanted her students to become aware of the presence of other ethnic groups in New York City. She invited a Cherokee into the class who told stories, discussed cultural contrasts with the students, and taught them traditional dances (Marsh, 1995). Fluent speakers of English in the community can also serve the program. There might be members of the staff, or relatives or friends of the children who could volunteer to read once a week or once a month.

Homework can be a good means of involving the family in classroom activities. An elementary bilingual teacher regularly assigned a question related to the class theme that she knew parents would be able to discuss with their children. She also sent books home to read or recommended books that could be found in the local library (Leone, 1995).

Teachers and parents need to work together to offer a complete bilingual and bicultural education to students. Each should contribute what they can. Parents may know the home language better than the teacher and they may be more familiar with the traditions. A literacy program for bilingual parents encouraged them to write for their children the stories that they themselves heard as children. Parents with limited education can still provide motivation and discipline to ensure that their children work hard and succeed in school. Patricia, a high school student, commented in reference to her mother: "I think we learned a lot by seeing my mother working so hard. We had to do well, period. To see her working so hard you had to live up to that standard" (Brisk, 1994a, p. 12). Regardless of their education level, parents are essential partners in education. Their role should be seen as informers, reinforcers, and supporters of the work in the classroom.

To develop students' language and sociocultural skills, members of the ethnic group of the students as well as English speakers and members of other ethnic groups need to support the work of the bilingual program. The best models of sociocultural integration are adults who respect each other and support students' efforts in maintaining their culture while also learning to function in the American culture.

MAXIMIZING THE TEACHER'S SKILLS

Ethnic background and language ability of the teacher also plays a role in instructional choices. Rather than trying to be everything, teachers who are native speakers of English and those who come from the students' cultures should complement each other in their work. Both can contribute to the language acquisition process. Home language teachers' stronger knowledge of the language and culture of the students facilitates learning because they understand students' responses in their native language, introduce topics in the home language, provide explanation with respect to cultural contrasts, and provide a bridge with parents. English-speaking teachers are models of English and interpreters of cultural knowledge implied in materials. They are better equipped to monitor students' creative use of the language. In a fifth-grade integrated cluster, Corky, the mainstream teacher, was a science aficionado, whereas Peggy, the bilingual teacher, loved math. Corky developed their science curriculum and Peggy offered an advanced section of math for bilingual and English-speaking students taught bilingually. Cooperation between teachers creates an ideal context for optimal learning. Teachers need to plan together and develop their own strategies to work in coordination for the benefit of students.

CONCLUSION

Good instructional practices need to be modified by language and cultural considerations in order to make classroom activities suitable for bilingual learners. New instructional strategies and principles of teaching and learning constantly enrich the field. Therefore, teachers need to be prepared to modify their strategies. In addition, teachers need to be researchers to observe and modify accordingly new educational strategies that have not been tested with bilingual students.

Keys to creating the right classroom context are flexibility and organization. Teachers need to be flexible by adjusting to diverse language proficiency and cultures, and modifying practices as needed by their students. Teachers need to be organized to cover rigorous curricula, developing the students' languages and literacy and constantly stimulating students to engage deeply in learning.

6

Beyond the Debate

Much of the debate on bilingual education is wasteful, ironic, hypocritical, and regressive. It is wasteful because instead of directing attention to sound educational practices, it has led to advocating specific "models" based solely on what language should be used for what purpose. It is ironic because most attacks on bilingual education arise from an unfounded fear that English will be neglected in the United States, whereas, in fact, the rest of the world fears the opposite; the attraction of English and interest in American culture are seen by non-English-speaking nations as a threat to their own languages and cultures. It is hypocritical because most opponents of using languages other than English for instruction also want to promote foreign language requirements for high school graduation. Finally, it is regressive and xenophobic because the rest of the world considers ability in at least two languages to be the mark of good education.

The political struggle to defend the existence of bilingual education in schools has wasted much energy in the search fo a "perfect" model. The recent history of bilingual education is replete with various models, all posing as panaceas. Overreliance on particular models often detracts from analysis of what actually happens in schools. When proponents of bilingual education let themselves be drawn into the battle over language choice, they too often lose sight of what should be their central goal: providing quality education to such students in ways that integrate them into both their own and the majority culture. If educators could ignore their particular biases about language use they would discover sufficient evidence to orient them toward providing effective education in any language. They would recognize that the mission of schools is to educate students so that they have choices when they graduate. Educating bilingual students has to go beyond merely teaching them English or merely maintaining their native language. The world of work demands that graduates achieve not only high-level literacy skills in English, and even knowledge of other languages, but also analytic ability and the ability to learn new things. Bilingual students have not only the potential but also the right to be prepared to meet the challenges of modern society.

Criticisms of bilingual education are not all unfounded. Some bilingual programs are unsuitable for delivering quality education even if they have graduated some successful students. Much of the credit goes to the heroic efforts of individual teachers (Brisk, 1990, 1994a). Advocates must admit that many bilingual programs are substandard. Rather than offering a blanket approval for programs on the basis of whether they use the children's native language, advocates of bilingual education need to be selective by supporting only those programs and schools that adhere to the principles of good education for bilingual students. Bilingual education too often falls victim to political, economic, and social forces that feed on unfavorable attitudes toward bilingual programs, teachers, students, their families, languages, and cultures. Such attitudes translate into school characteristics that limit quality education for language minority students. This book attempts to portray specific characteristics of bilingual programs that have succeeded. Research on effective schools demonstrates that schools can stimulate academic achievement for students regardless of how situational factors influence them. Considerations of language and culture facilitate English language development without sacrificing the native language and the ability to function in a cross-cultural world.

Implementation and evaluation of bilingual education programs need to move beyond supporting what have too often become compensatory programs. All students, but especially bilinguals, deserve quality programs that overcome negative stereotypes. Abundant results from empirical research and experience can help show the way (see Table 6.1).

Many bilingual programs exist because school districts must comply with legislation and court decisions. They survive in isolation within unsupportive schools where the attitudes toward the program are negative and the expectations of students are low. Students reject their identity in schools that do not accept their culture, but cannot adopt a new one (Commins, 1989). Such students often become angry and disruptive (Brisk, 1991b; McCollum, 1993). "One wonders what the achievements of such students would be if their energies were liberated by an environment in which they no longer needed to trade ethnicity for school learning" (Secada & Lightfoot, 1993, p. 53). Overworked and unappreciated teachers burn out, leading to turnover and instability in programs.

Schools without clear goals depend on the individual teacher for the quality of the program and are more vulnerable to ideological pressures. Without explicit goals for bilingual education, confusion and dissatisfaction among staff and community are likely results. A contrastive study of a community in California and another in the Midwest illustrate the importance of clear goals (Arvizu et al., 1992). Lack of leadership and inclusion of the program leads to differences in opionion with respect to the purpose of bilingual education. When English-speaking and bilingual faculty do not share goals, a deep gap in communication develops among the faculty members, affecting teachers, students, and language use (Cleghorn & Genesee, 1984).

Although many teachers are well qualified, increasing demands on personnel have resulted in the hiring of poorly qualified teachers or the recycling of mainstream teachers with no preparation to teach bilingual students. Districts experience personnel satisfaction and stability when they develop bilingual programs gradually and maintain strict control of the quality of personnel. Districts that develop quickly

TABLE 6.1

School Characteristics

Promote Quality Bilingual Education	Limit Quality of Bilingual Education Programs
1. Administration in cooperation with faculty and community develop clear goals.	1. There are no clear goals, leaving interpretation open to ideological tendencies.
2. School creates a bilingual and bicultural society.	2. Personnel and students outside the bilingual program have poor attitudes toward program's languages and cultures. There is no explicit instruction on American culture.
3. Bilingual program is integrated with the whole school.	3. Bilingual program is segregated from the rest of the school.
4. Bilingual students are well known by all staff.	4. Only bilingual staff know bilingual students.
5. Administration provides leadership and supports the program.	5. Administration is unsupportive, ambivalent, or indifferent.
6. School staff sets high expectations and supports bilingual students.	6. Staff believes ability to function is related to English language proficiency or ethnic background.
7. School hires quality personnel willing to work with bilingual students.	7. Students are taught by personnel with limited understanding or skills.
8. School enjoys a productive relationship with parents and communities.	8. Parents are perceived as indifferent or uninterested. No effort is made to accommodate parents' language and culture.
9. School curricula make use of the languages and cultures of the students to promote learning.	9. Use of students' languages and cultures is limited and only within the bilingual program.
10. Bilingual students participate in a comprehensive curriculum that benefits from current educational innovations.	10. Bilingual program curriculum does not cover all the same areas as the general school curriculum. Bilingual students do not benefit from special programs brought in for the whole school.
11. Materials are of high quality, varied, and in the language of the students a well as English.	11. Materials in the language of the students are limited and of poor quality.
12. Assessment is fair and authentic and has as a purpose improved teaching and learning.	12. Assessment is mostly standardized tests in English. Its main purpose is to enter and exit students into and from the bilingual program.
13. Instructional practices are consistent with goals of promoting language development, adjustment to both cultures, and academic achievement.	13. Instructional practices are inconsistent, depending on teachers' beliefs and knowledge.

and haphazardly without careful teacher recruitment experience excessive staff turnover, often losing their best teachers who burn out when they find themselves supporting the less prepared teachers (Arvizu et al., 1992). Because the program is often seen as remedial, curriculum is narrow, materials are deficient, and assessment is limited to English language development.

Such bilingual education programs should not be supported. The bilingual education characterized in this book should be supported not merely because it is good for bilingual students, but also because its implementation can benefit schools as a whole.

BILINGUAL, CROSS-CULTURAL
TRANSFORMATION OF SCHOOLS

The rising sense of frustration with public education has called into question our ability to educate our students. The search for better ways to educate children has led to a proliferation of commissions, studies, and government initiatives (Goals 2000: Educate America Act of 1993; National Council on Education Standards and Testing, 1992; National Education Goals Panel, 1991, 1992; National Governors Association, Task Force on Education, 1990) with recommendations to reform education in general.

> [I]n our quest for higher standards and superior academic performance we seem to have forgotten that schools cannot be excellent as long as there are groups of children who are not well served by them. In short, we cannot have educational excellence until we have educational equality. (Oakes, 1985, p. xiv)

One such population that has not been properly served is bilingual students. "Language minority children tend to lag behind language majority children academically and the dropout rate for some linguistic minority groups is as high as 70%" (Ambert, 1991, p. xvi).

Most national educational reform efforts avoid including bilingual education. Bilingual students and educators have been kept in the margins of education reform. There are several reasons for this oversight. First, various commissions' panels do not include experts in bilingual education: those that do give them only a limited voice. Second, bilingual education is perceived as a politically controversial topic to be left up to legislation and court rulings to enforce implementation. Finally, it is seen as a compensatory program separate from mainstream education rather than a sound educational approach that can be integrated to the goal of foreign language development present in most proposals for educational improvement: "If the schools of the twenty-first century are truly going to be characterized by educational excellence for all students, they must be designed with all learners in mind—including those who bring linguistic *riches* with them to school" (LaCelle-Peterson & Rivera, 1994, p. 73, italics added).

Education of bilingual students should be part of general school improvement efforts and should not depend on federal and state legislation. Better education for all students requires educational reform that includes bilingual students. Schools should be arenas where bilingualism is praised, cultural differences are sources of learning, and the main focus is on quality of education. Schools where various languages and cultures are the norm with curriculum and classroom experiences enriched by this linguistic and cultural variety prepare students for the world of the 21st century. All students, not only bilinguals, need to find balance in their quest to become global, preserving their own individual identity as well. A cross-cultural school environment helps form such individuals.

The presence of bilingual personnel enriches staff resources. Bilingual teachers bring added knowledge and teaching and managing strategies that help increasingly multicultural schools. Such teachers contribute to the staff's understanding of bilingual students and to establishing ties with the communities of all students. They also provide added language models for schools promoting foreign-language education.

Bilingual and cross-cultural curricula support the goals of developing bilingual skills in all students. Second language development among English-speaking students is enhanced by a school context that values languages and promotes interaction between English speakers and speakers of other languages. Familiarity with culture not only supports second language learning but enriches factual knowledge and cognitive development. Claims that U.S. students do poorly in geography tests are symptomatic of their general lack of knowledge about the rest of the world. Incorporating in the school curricula aspects of the bilingual students' cultures will by extension improve American students' knowledge of the world in a very tangible manner. People of other cultures approach problem solving, personal interactions, and learning differently. Experiencing and discussing such differences expands American students' perspectives. At a time when technology facilitates contact with people of diverse linguistic and cultural backgrounds throughout the world, it should be obvious that schools need to prepare all students to communicate and relate in an increasingly interactive world.

Most successful bilingual programs have been created not by legislative mandates but by concerned educators and communities working together. Good education for bilingual students should not be the outcome of compliance with legislation. Schools must be willing to create good programs suitable for all students, including bilinguals. To overcome resistance to implementing bilingual education, many communities resort to politics or lawsuits to force school districts to provide bilingual education. However, political solutions create their own problems, paradoxically compromise and rigidity. For example, laws and regulations that impose a 3-year maximum for students attending bilingual education programs arose as a compromise between the forces for and against bilingual education. Research shows time and again that students profit from long-term bilingual instruction, even though some students who stay shorter periods eventually succeed in mainstream education. Kleinfeld (1979), in her study of an effective Catholic high school for Eskimo students, concluded that there was much that needed to be done to offer an appropriate education to bilingual students, but only private schools had the freedom to provide it. Education is not about regulations, but about students.

Educational reform must consider education of bilingual students in order to include it in this country's educational improvement agenda. Advocates cannot accept any longer that the educational well-being of bilingual students is the pawn of linguistic and ideological power battles in Congress, legislatures, and courtrooms.

STRATEGIES FOR IMPLEMENTATION AND
EVALUATION OF BILINGUAL EDUCATION

This book describes a number of fundamental conditions needed to achieve excellence in bilingual education. Successful programs seek to achieve these conditions simultaneously because of their interdependence. Programs, however, can start implementing them slowly within the context of an overall plan that addresses language, culture, and characteristics of effective schools: "By radically simplifying the program to those few things we felt to be most important, we learned to do those few things well. In time we were able to increase the number of things we tried to do" (Holm & Holm, 1990, p. 179).

Outcomes of academic achievement, language development, and sociocultural integration for bilingual students depend on well-developed programs and especially the quality of the instruction. Bilingual programs enjoy well-prepared and committed teachers, but for schools to have consistent and well-coordinated instruction, there is a need for more than the occasional outstanding teacher. Comprehensive curricula with a clear plan for the use of home languages and English and incorporation of cultures guide teaching and learning for all students and do not leave matters to chance. Development of such curricula and language policies require a school in which languages and cultures are respected, bilingual students are known as individuals, the bilingual program is part of the whole school agenda, and all personnel expect bilingual students to reach the desired outcomes. To create such a community, schools need to attract well-prepared personnel willing to implement these programs. Schools with active and supportive leadership and a clear mission developed in consultation with parents and the community provide the foundation to create a quality bilingual education pyramid (see Fig. 6.1).

Achieving specific conditions depends on how situational, individual, and family factors affect specific students or groups of students. For example, how well a school creates a bilingual and bicultural society depends on the status of the languages in question. Where the language of bilingual students has high status—for example French in California—the school does not need to make a special effort to improve attitudes. However, when a language has a lower status than English—for example, French in New England—the school needs to redouble efforts to raise the status of the minority language.

No special effort is needed to promote high expectations for Chinese or Vietnamese students in Boston. Spanish-speaking students, however, have a very different experience. Schools need to make a special effort to instill high expectations among staff working with Spanish speakers. On the other hand, they must ensure that high expectations for Asian students do not result in a lack of appropriate support for such students.

To implement the suggestions given in this book, schools need to plan for the long range; implement innovations gradually; develop a mission, goals, and plans for the school working with staff, parents, and community in order to ensure their support and cooperation; and establish stability of personnel and funding (Wata-

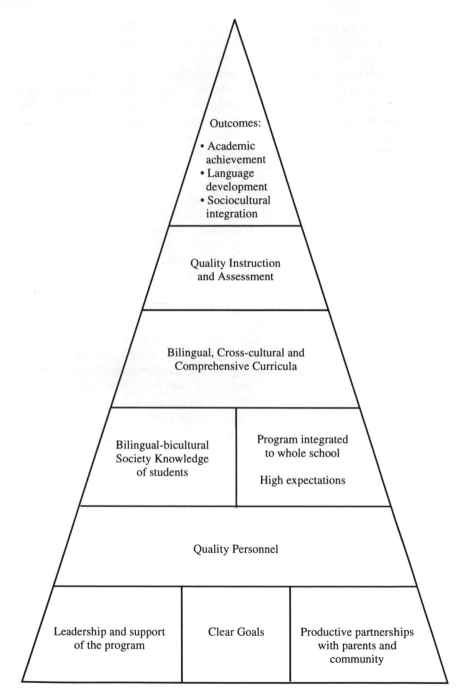

Fig. 6.1. Quality bilingual education pyramid.

homigie & McCarty, 1994). They also need to be up to date on current research and innovations and contribute to that body of knowledge with their own experience.

The educational principles recommended in this book can be used by either full bilingual programs serving one language group or by schools in which there are a variety of languages. Many of the recommendations can be applied by schools with multicultural populations even if they do not have a bilingual education program. Except for the conditions related to use of native language in curriculum and instruction, all other points should be applied by schools with bilingual students regardless of their ability in English. Bilingual individuals remain bilingual and bicultural even after they are proficient in English. Therefore, implementing the recommendations in this book would greatly increase their chances to succeed in school.

Evaluation should be directed primarily toward fostering each student's development. Traditional evaluations of bilingual education programs have focused on success rates in mainstreaming students. They have looked at students' outcomes, mainly in English, reading, and math. Schools must evaluate students' outcomes with respect to all three goals: academic achievement, language development, and sociocultural integration. They should use tools that fairly consider students' language skills and cultural backgrounds. Evaluation should not be limited to students' outcomes because such results depend on program quality. Results should be interpreted in terms of the school's characteristics and how well the school adheres to conditions of quality bilingual education. This book provides a framework for evaluation that focuses on the many aspects of schooling. A thorough description of the school organization and climate, staff qualifications, curricular content, and classroom instruction renders raw data. Scrutiny of such data under the framework outlined in Table 6.2 profiles a school's strengths and weaknesses.

Identification of schools' strengths and weaknesses are necessary to improve programs and to interpret students' outcomes. Only after schools determine that they have provided all the conditions for good education can they claim that students or families are responsible for poor student outcomes.

Many factors influence bilingual students' proficiency in English and development of the home language. Conditions such as respect for students' language and culture, uncontentious integration with native speakers of English, a clear goal of language development understood by staff and community, and intensive use of the languages in instruction facilitate students' efforts to become proficient in English without losing the home language. Poor results in language assessment cannot be attributed only to students' unwillingness to develop the languages or to the quality of language instruction in the bilingual program. Most of the conditions for successful language development are in the hands of the school as a whole.

Although academic achievement depends on students' desire and ability to succeed, schools can do much to facilitate the process. Quality curricula delivered by well-prepared personnel in a manner and/or language that the bilingual students can understand is essential. Adjustment to American culture without rejecting the home culture is a difficult goal. Schools that create an atmosphere respectful of

TABLE 6.2

Framework for School Evaluation

	F................................U
Quality School	
1. Clear goals	
2. Bilingual and bicultural society	
3. Bilingual program integrated with the whole school	
4. Students are well known by the staff	
5. Administration provides leadership and supports the program	
6. All staff set high expectations and support the students	
7. Quality personnel willing to work with students	
8. Productive relationships with parents and communities	
Quality Curricula	
9. Native languages are used to promote:	
(a) literacy	
(b) content area learning	
10. English is promoted and developed for:	
(a) social interaction	
(b) academic use	
11. Languages are used to maximize instruction	
12. Use of language in curriculum and instruction is well planned and consistent	
13. Curriculum makes use of students' cultures to promote learning	
14. Curriculum incorporates explicit teaching of American culture, including necessary background knowledge	
15. Bilingual students participate in a comprehensive curriculum that benefits from current educational innovations	
16. Materials are of high quality, varied, and in the language of the students as well as English	
17. Assessment is fair and authentic and has as a purpose improved teaching and learning	
Quality Instruction	
18. Instruction respects students, their language, and culture	
19. Instruction is engaging, challenging, and supportive	
20. Special strategies are used when teaching in English and when teaching students with limited schooling	
21. Class objectives include language, culture, and content	
22. Students play an active role in learning	
23. Optimal strategies are used for grouping students	
24. Assessment is integrated with instruction	
25. Resources are varied	
26. Families and community participate in the classroom	
27. Teachers coordinate to focus on each other's strengths	

Note. F = fulfilled; U = unfulfilled.

languages and cultures, incorporate the home culture in the curriculum, and provide instruction in American culture should be successful in training students to function in both cultural contexts.

This approach to evaluation of specific features within schools is a thorough but flexible model of evaluation (Brisk, 1996). Schools do not have to adhere to a particular model of bilingual education; rather they need to accumulate as many features of quality education as possible to enhance positive student outcomes. Only when evaluation is less concerned with proving the effectiveness of particular bilingual education models than it is in measuring the effectiveness of particular schools will it serve students.

CONCLUSION

The question I set out to answer in this book is what educators need to do to achieve quality bilingual education for language minority students. First, they need to overcome many of the ideologically based practices that have isolated the education of bilingual students from the movement toward general educational improvement. By doing so, they can implement programs with the positive characteristics defined in research and experience, and promote meaningful assessment of students when programs are evaluated.

Advocates for bilingual students need to pursue their work on two fronts. The first front is the political struggle to support native languages in education, not just for the sake of language learning, but to provide comprehensible content education. More important, however, is improvement of the quality of education afforded to these students. The political struggle will avoid going back to earlier policies of imposing English at the expense of other languages. Research and implementation focused on what is actually happening in the schools will ensure that the bilingual programs deserve our support because they provide good education.

Appendix: Teaching Strategies

CRITICAL AUTOBIOGRAPHIES

The purpose of this approach is to have students look critically and objectively at events in their lives. Through this analysis they will understand that what happens to them as bilingual individuals struggling for social and cultural adjustment is largely governed by circumstances outside themselves.

1. Introduction of the Project

A. *Younger students:* Explain that they are going to write about their lives in different countries or about the culture of their parents. Give an explanation as to the kinds of stories about themselves and their families that they could write.

B. *Older students*: Introduction of the concept of a biography and autobiography. Have them read biographies and autobiographies. Discuss them. Do other activities to familiarize them with this type of genre.

2. Exploration of Themes

There are many factors that affect the lives of bilinguals: linguistic, cultural, political, economic, sociological, and psychological. In writing the autobiographies, students should discuss them objectively to try to understand why things are the way they are. This exploration can be done during prewriting activities and during writing and revising. For example, one first-grade teacher suggested to a Korean bilingual student that he was going to write a chapter book including each one of these major themes. A seventh-grade teacher prepared worksheets with questions to raise some of these issues for discussion in class. Another teacher asked her students to tell her about their life in Russia, Israel, and the United States. They wrote a book for each country. As they were discussing the countries, the teacher asked questions to probe deeper into issues. Older students conducted research in the library. It is important to go deeper than the common autobiography in which students tell where they were born, lived, and so on. Many of these issues can be embedded in a social studies curriculum. With younger students, it is good to get parents involved.

3. Write Autobiographies Using a Process Approach to Writing

For younger students, they can draw, then dictate to the teacher what they want written down. They can then go through the revision process together. (It helps to record discussions while they are drawing, in order to add things to their text.)

4. Publication of Books

Students produce chapter books or several books. The key to bringing about change is the discussion and other activities that help analyze the situation. The books themselves are mere products, but the process is what makes the difference.

REFERENCES

Benesch, S. (1993). Reading and writing in critical autobiographies. In J. G. Carson & I. Leki (Eds.), *Reading in composition classroom* (pp. 247–257). Boston: Heinle & Heinle.

Brisk, M. E., & Zandman, D. (1995). A journey through immigration: Writing a critical autobiography. *Chelkat Lashon,* 19–20, 87–117.

Wallerstein, N. (1983). *language and culture in conflict.* Reading, MA: Addison-Wesley.

Walsh, C. E. (1993). Becoming critical: Rethinking literacy, language, and teaching. In J. V. Tinajero & A. F. Ada (Eds.), *The power of two languages* (pp. 49–57). New York: Macmillan/McGraw-Hill.

CROSS-AGE PROJECT

The purpose of this approach is to help older students with difficulties by making them teachers of younger students in precisely the area in which they ar experiencing difficulty.

1. Choose two classes, three or more grade levels apart.
2. Explain to both classes what the project is all about.
3. Start working with the older students (teachers-to-be) doing the following: (a) model the chosen method or approach; (b) train, explain, and discuss with students the method; and (c) let them rehearse with each other and do any preparation needed.
4. At all times the older learners should keep a journal in which they reflect, first about the training and later about the actual experience as teachers.
5. Teacher reads and responds to the journal.
6. When your "teachers" are ready to start implementation.
7. Pair the older and younger students. Divide them in two groups. Each group stays with one of the two teachers involved.

8. Allow for any other projects that result from the situation.
9. Plan other activities such as parties and field trips, that they can do together.
10. Meet with the "teachers" periodically to discuss how the implementation is going.

REFERENCES

Hoffman, D. M., & Heath, S. B. (1986). *Inside learner: Guidebook on interactive reading and writing in elementary classrooms.* Unpublished manuscript, Stanford University.
Freeman, Y. S., & Freeman, D. E. (1993). *Whole language for second language learners.* Portsmouth, NH: Heinemann.

DIALOGUE JOURNALS

1. Tell students that: (a) their dialogue journal is a place where they and the teacher will talk about anything they want to talk about; (b) the journals will not be evaluated or graded in any way; and (c) the journals are private and no one else will read them.
2. Each student has a notebook that is kept in the classroom.
3. You may give a brief handout to older students to clarify concepts and any other requirements, especially with second language students. For example, here is a handout used by a teacher of adult basic ESL students:

A dialogue journal is a very special kind of writing. It helps you learn to think and write in English. Every day you will write for 10 minutes. I will take your journals at the end of class, write back to you, and give you your journal at the beginning of next day's class.

Here are some things to remember:

1. Please use a black pen and write on one side of the paper only.
2. Please include the date each time you write.
3. Write as much as you like, but please write at least five lines a day.
4. Your journal is confidential. This means I will not show or tell anyone what you write.

4. If teaching an elementary self-contained class, have students read their journals (your responses to their previous entries) the first thing, and give them time to write their responses. Then allow them to return the journal during the day if they have more to say to you.
5. Encourage students to write to you about real issues that are important to them, seeking or giving genuine information, solving real problems, and so on.

6. The normal unequal status of the teacher and student is minimized, because both parties are equally engaged in the interaction, introducing and elaborating on topics, and so on. One person does not dominate or control the interaction with directives or questions. The teacher is as involved in the content of the interaction as the student.

7. Both participants are free to choose topics as they become important, without fear of censure. Topics are never predetermined by the teacher.

8. Communication is frequent and continuous, occurring at least once a week for at least a couple months. Every day for the whole academic year or semester is optimal.

9. Focus on meaning, not form. Do not correct. Seek only to clarify meaning. Mistakes are okay as long as meaning is negotiated.

10. Keep the communication private. This will help students feel free to express themselves and not fear correction or exposure. Journals become confidence builders and emotional outlets for students experiencing difficulties.

REFERENCES

Freeman, Y. S., & Freeman, D. E. (1989). Whole language approaches to writing with secondary students of English as a second language. In D. M. Johnson & D. H. Roen (Eds.), *Richness in writing* (pp. 177–192). New York: Longman.

Johnson, D. M., & Roen, D. H. (Eds.). (1989). *Richness in writing: Empowering ESL students.* New York: Longman.

Kreeft, J. (1984). Dialogue writing—Bridge from talk to essay writing. *Language Arts, 61*(2), 141–150.

Peregoy, S. F., & Boyle, O. F. (1996). *Reading writing, & learning in ESL: A resource book for K–12 teachers.* New York: Longman.

THE ICEBREAKER

- Pair students.
- Give each a piece of paper. Fold the page lengthwise.
- Ask them to write five questions they would like to know about their partners on the left column.
- Have then exchange papers and write the answers on the right side of the page.
- Exchange papers again.
- Have them read the answers and choose one they would like to know more about.
- Have them write five additional questions in relation to that answer.
- Exchange papers again and answer the additional questions.
- Have them return papers to the partner.
- Partners introduce each other based on what they learned.

RESPONSE TO LITERATURE JOURNALS

In the context of having students read and discuss a book, add the feature of having students write their reactions to the book in a journal.

- Model your own responses to a book the students have just read as a way of explaining how it should be done. Brainstorm with the students about the kinds of things they could have written about. Use questions to help. For example, how had they wished the story had ended, what did they think of the characters, what did they like and why?
- Give students a notebook.
- Ask them to write their reactions to the book or chapters assigned. Note: An elementary school teacher told the students to write "letters" to her about their readings.
- Indicate that they should not write a summary of what they read but they must write their personal reactions to the readings (i.e., feelings, ideas, or questions).
- Respond to the students' writings. Focus on what they are saying and in their questions.
- You can do this activity twice a week, on days that yo do not discuss the readings orally. In any event it is important to schedule it so that you will have time to respond to all their journals every time they write. Therefore, do not schedule it with more frequency than you can respond.
- Encourage students to meet and discuss their responses to the readings.

REFERENCES

Freeman, Y. S., & Freeman, D. E. (1989). Whole language approaches to writing with secondary students of English as a second language. In D. M. Johnson & D. H. Roen (Eds.), *Richness in writing* (pp. 177–192). New York: Longman.

Wollman-Bonilla, J. F. (1989). Reading journals: Invitations to participate in literature. *The Reading Teacher, 43,* 112–120.

SHARED READING

Materials

Good literature. If working with a large group of students you need to obtain or produce big books when working with children or transparencies when working with older students and adults.

Production of Big Book

1. Obtain 5 to 10 pieces of stock (32 × 42) or a large pad, and felt pens in black, brown, and colors.
2. Trace lines 1½ inches apart for story line. Copy wording in the book exactly as in the original in format and content. Leave space for margins and illustrations.
3. Illustrations: Copy or trace illustrations from original (no need to do them all) or have students draw on a separate piece of paper, then paste it to the book. After third grade you can do away with illustrations.
4. Staple together, including a title page.
5. Store hanging from hooks or skirt hangers.
6. Place on an easel for reading.

Procedure

1. Read aloud the story from original book.
2. Read the story from the big book or transparencies using a pointer to show where you are reading. Read with fluency and expression.
3. Allow students to join in if they want to. Repeat this procedure as many times as needed.
4. Let individual students read to the class also using the pointer.
5. Have a small version of the original available so that the students can borrow it to read on their own or in pairs.
6. Use the reading to do different types of exercises, such as close procedure, looking for specific words, letters, and so on.
7. Have students develop their own big books using the original story as a pattern.

REFERENCES

Holdaway, D. (1984). Developmental teaching of literacy. In D. Holdaway, *Stability and change in literacy learning* (pp. 33–47). Exeter, NH: Heinemann.

Peregoy, S. F., & Boyle, O. F. (1996). *Reading writing, & learning in ESL: A resource book for K–12 teachers.* New York: Longman.

SHARING TIME

The purpose of this activity is to give students practice in talking about something to an audience. It must be student directed.

1. Choose a semiprivate corner of the room, maybe use the one you use for reading aloud, where you have a chair for the teacher and a rug for the students. Explain to the students that every day they will gather around a leader and talk about something. It can be something that happened to them on the way to school, over the weekend, a TV program they saw, and so forth.
2. Choose a leader of the day and have the child sit on the teacher's chair. Start with those students who are more sure of themselves. The first day the teacher may want to model the role of the leader, by taking the leader's chair and telling something that happened to him or her.
3. Give the rules (which you may want to review occasionally):
   - One person shares at a time.
   - Leader chooses the person.
   - Children have to raise their hand if they want to talk.
   - If they misbehave they will get a warning (given by the leader, who also decides what "misbehaving" is).
   - At second warning they go to their seats.

REFERENCE

Michaels, S., & Foster, M. (1985). Peer–peer learning: Evidence from a student-run sharing time. In A. Jaggar & M. T. Smith-Burke (Eds.), *Observing the language learner* (pp. 143–158). Newark, DE: International Reading Association.

References

Abi-Nader, J. (1990). "A house for my mother": Motivating Hispanic high school students. *Anthropology and Education Quarterly, 21,* 41–58.

Ada, A. F. (1988). The Pájaro Valley experience. In T. Skutnabb-Kangas & J. Cummins (Eds.), *Minority education: From shame to struggle* (pp. 223–238). Clevedon, UK: Multilingual Matters.

Alva, S. A. (1991). Academic invulnerability among Mexican-American students: The importance of protective resources and appraisals. *Hispanic Journal of Behavioral Sciences, 13,* 18–34.

Alvarez, D. S., Hofstetter, C. R., Donovan, M. C., & Huie, C. J. (1994). Patterns of communication in a racial/ethnic context: The case of an urban public high school. *Urban Education, 29,* 133–149.

Ambert, A. (Ed.). (1991). *Bilingual education and English as a second language: A research handbook 1988–1990.* New York: Garland.

Andersson, T., & Boyer, M. (1970). *Bilingual schooling in the United States.* Washington, DC: U.S. Government Printing Office.

Andersson, T., & Boyer, M. (1978). *Bilingual schooling in the United States* (2nd ed.). Austin, TX: National Educational Laboratory Publishers.

Arvizu, S. F., Hernández-Chavez, E., Guskin, J., & Valadez, C. (1992). Bilingual education in community contexts: A two-site comparative research design. In M. Saravia-Shore & S. F. Arvizu (Eds.), *Cross-cultural literacy: Ethnographies of communication in multiethnic classrooms* (pp. 83–130). New York: Garland.

ASPIRA v. Board of Education of the City of New York, 72 Civ. 4002 (S.D.N.Y. August 29, 1974); 58 F.R.D. 62 (S.D.N.Y. 1973).

Au, K. H., & Jordan, C. (1981). Teaching reading to Hawaiian children: Finding a culturally appropriate solution. In H. Trueba, G. Guthrie, & K. H. Au (Eds.), *Culture and the bilingual classroom: Studies in classroom ethnography* (pp. 139–152). Rowley, MA: Newbury House.

August, D., & García, E. E. (1988). *Language minority education in the United States.* Springfield, IL: Thomas.

Bacon, H., Kidd, G. D., & Seaberg, J. J. (1982). The effectiveness of bilingual instruction with Cherokee indian students. *Journal of American Indian Education, 21*(2), 34–43.

Baker, C. (1993). *Foundations of bilingual education and bilingualism.* Philadelphia: Multilingual Matters.

Baker, K. A., & de Kanter, A. A. (1981). *Effectiveness of bilingual education: A review of the literature.* Washington, DC: Office of Planning and Budget, U.S. Department of Education.

Ballard, B., & Clanchy, J. (1991). Assessment by misconception: Cultural influences and intellectual traditions. In L. Hamp-Lyons (Ed.), *Assessing second language writing in academic contexts* (pp. 19–35). Norwood, NJ: Ablex.

Ballenger, C. (1992). Because you like us: The language of control. Making School Reform Work. *Harvard Educational Review,* 49–58.

Bartolomé, L. I. (1993). Effective transitioning strategies: Are we asking the right questions. In J. V. Tinajero & A. F. Ada (Eds.), *The power of two languages: Literacy and biliteracy for Spanish-speaking students* (pp. 209–219). New York: Macmillan/McGraw-Hill.

Beebe, L., & Giles, H. (1984). Speech accommodation theories: A discussion in terms of second language acquisition. *International Journal of the Sociology of Language, 46,* 5–32.

Ben-Zeev, S. (1977). The influence of bilingualism on cognitive strategy and cognitive development. *Child Development, 48,* 1009–1018.

Bermudez, A. B., & Márquez, J. A. (1994). Preserving home–school linguistic and cultural continuity. In R. Rodríguez, N. J. Ramos, & J. A. Ruiz-Escalante (Eds.), *Compendium of readings in bilingual education: Issues and practices* (pp. 274–282). San Antonio: Texas Association for Bilingual Education.

Berry, J. W. (1983). Acculturation: A comparative analysis of alternative forms. In R. J. Samuday & S. L. Woods (Eds.), *Perspectives in immigrant and minority education* (pp. 65–78). Lanham, MD: University Press of America.

Bhatnagar, J. (1980). Linguistic behaviour and adjustment of immigrant children in French and English schools in Montreal. *International Review of Applied Psychology, 29,* 141–159.

Bilingual Education. (1983). *Aquí* [video]. Needham, MA: WCVB, Channel 5.

Bloomfield, L. (1933). *Language.* New York: Holt.

Bossers, B. (1991). On thresholds, ceilings and short-circuits: The relation between L1 reading, L2 reading and L2 knowledge. *Reading in two languages. AILA REVIEW, 8,* 45–60.

Bou-Zeineddine, A. (1994). *The effect of the prewriting discussion language, Arabic/English on six adult students' writing in English.* Unpublished doctoral dissertation, Boston University, Boston, MA.

Boyer, E. L. (1995). *The basic school: A community for learning.* Princeton, NJ: The Carnegie Foundation for the Advancement of Teaching.

Bradley v. Milliken, 402 f. Supp. 1096, 1144 (E.D. Mich. 1975).

Brisk, M. E. (1978). Bilingual education legislation: The Boston desegregation case. In H. La Fontaine, B. Persky, & L. Golubchick (Eds.), *Bilingual education* (pp. 67–71). Wayne, NJ: Avery.

Brisk, M. E. (1981a). Language policies in American education. *Journal of Education, 163*(1), 3–15.

Brisk, M. E. (1981b). Teaching bilinguals to read: Approaches for linguistic minority children. In M. Danesi (Ed.), *Issues in Language* (pp. 63–73). Lake Bluff, IL: Jupiter Press.

Brisk, M. E. (1990). *The many voices of education for bilingual students in Massachusetts.* Quincy: Massachusetts Department of Education.

Brisk, M. E. (1991a). Cross cultural barriers: A model for schooling bilingual and English-speaking students in harmony. *Equity and Choice, 7*(2), 18–24.

Brisk, M. E. (1991b). *The many voices of bilingual students in Massachusetts.* Quincy: Bureau of Equity and Language Services, Massachusetts Department of Education.

Brisk, M. E. (1991c). Toward multilingual and multicultural mainstream education. *Journal of Education, 173*(2), 114–129.

Brisk, M. E. (1994a). *Portraits of success: Resources supporting bilingual learners.* Boston: Massachusetts Association for Bilingual Education.

Brisk, M. E. (1994b, June). *Restructuring schools to incorporate linguistically diverse populations.* Paper presented at the International Conference on Immigration, Language Acquisition and Patterns of Social Integration, The Hebrew University, Jerusalem.

Brisk, M. E. (1996). *The multicultural middle college high school: An attempt at creating an innovative bilingual high school.* Providence, RI: Educational Alliance, Brown University.

Brisk, M. E., & Bou-Zeineddine, A. (1993, April). *"It feels so good:" Native language use in ESL.* Paper presented at the TESOL Convention, Atlanta, GA.

Brisk, M. E., David, L., Martínez, J., Rodriguez, A. B. P., & Solá, M. (1982). Three complementary studies. In B. MacDonald & S. Kushner (Eds.), *Bread and dreams: A case study of bilingual schooling the U.S.A.* (pp. 175–214). Norwich, UK: Center for Applied Research in Education.

Brisk, M. E., & Zandman, D. (1995). A journey through immigration: Writing a critical autobiography. *Chelkat Lashon, 19–20,* 87–117.

Campbell, R. N. (1984). The immersion approach to foreign language teaching. In Office of Bilingual Education, *Studies on immersion education* (pp. 114–143). Sacramento: California State Department of Education.

Campos, S. J., & Keatinge, R. H. (1988). The Carpintera language minority student experience. In T. Skutnabb-Kangas & J. Cummins (Eds.), *Minority education: From shame to struggle* (pp. 299–307). Clevedon, UK: Multilingual Matters.

Cárdenas, B., & Cárdenas, J. A. (1972). *The theory of incompatibilities: A conceptual framework for responding to the educational needs of Mexican-American children.* San Antonio, TX: Intercultural Development Research Association.

Carle, E. (1987). *The very hungry caterpillar.* New York: Philomel Books.

Carrasco, R. L., Acosta, C. T., & de la Torre-Spencer, S. (1992). Language use, lesson engagement, and participation structures: A microethnographic analysis of two language arts lessons in a bilingual first grade classroom. In M. Saravia-Shore & S. F. Arvizu (Eds.), *Cross-cultural literacy: Ethnographies of communication in multethnic classrooms* (pp. 391–436). New York: Garland.

Carter, T. P., & Chatfield, M. (1986). Effective schools for language minority students. *American Journal of Education, 97,* 200–233.

Carter, T. P., & Maestas, L. C. (1982). *Effective bilingual schools serving Mexican American students.* Sacramento: California State University School of Education.

Casanova, U., & Arias, M. B. (1993). Contextualizing bilingual education. In M. B. Arias & U. Casanova (Eds.), *Bilingual education: Politics, practice and research* (pp. 1–35). Chicago: University of Chicago Press.

Castañeda v. Pickard, 648 F.2d 989 (5th cir. 1981).

Cazabon, M., Lambert, W. E., & Hall, G. (1993). *Two-way bilingual education: A progress report on the Amigos program.* Santa Cruz, CA: The National Center for Research on Cultural Diversity and Second Language Learning.

Cazden, C. B. (1988). *Classroom discourse: The language of teaching and learning.* Portsmouth, NH: Heinemann.

Cazden, C. B., Carrasco, R. L., Maldonado-Guzman, A. A., & Erickson, F. (1980). The contribution of ethnographic research to bilingual bicultural education. In J. Alatis (Ed.), *Current issues in bilingual education: Georgetown University Round Table on Languages and Linguistics* (pp. 64–80). Washington, DC: Georgetown University Press.

Center for Law and Education. (1975). *Bilingual-bicultural education: A handbook for attorneys and community workers.* Cambridge, MA: Harvard Graduate School of Education.

Chamot, A. U. (1995). Implementing the cognitive academic language learning approach: CALLA in Arlington, Virginia. *Bilingual Research Journal, 19*(3–4), 379–394.

Chamot, A. U., & O'Malley, J. M. (1986). *A cognitive academic language learning approach: An ESL content-based curriculum.* Washington, DC: National Clearinghouse for Bilingual Education.

Child, I. L. (1943). *Italian or American? The second generation in conflict.* New Haven, CT: Yale University Press.

Christian, C., Spanos, G., Crandall, J., Simich-Dudgeon, C., & Willetts, K. (1990). Combining language and content for second-language students. In A. M. Padilla, H. H. Fairchild, & C. M. Valadez (Eds.), *Bilingual education: Issues and strategies* (pp. 141–156). Newbury Park, CA: Sage.

Christian, D. (1994). *Two-way bilingual education: Students learning through two languages.* Santa Cruz, CA: The National Center for Research on Cultural Diversity and Second Language Learning.

Clayton, J. B. (1993). *Your land, my land: The process of acculturation for four international students in an elementary school setting in the United States.* Unpublished doctoral dissertation, Boston University, Boston.

Cleghorn, A., & Genesee, F. (1984). Languages in contact: An ethnographic study of interaction and an immersion school. *TESOL Quarterly, 18,* 585–625.

Coady, M. (1994). *Understanding the process of acculturation: The case study of a bilingual adolescent in the United States.* Unpublished masters thesis, Boston University, Boston.

Cohen, A. D. (1976). The case for partial or total immersion education. In A. Simões, Jr. (Ed.), *The bilingual child/El niño bilingüe* (pp. 65–89). New York: Academic Press.

Cohen, D. K. (1970). Immigrants and the schools. *Review of Educational Research, 40,* 13–27.

Coleman, J. S., Cambell, E., Hobson, C., McPartland, J., Mood, A., Weinfeld, F., & York, R. (1966). *Equality of educational opportunity.* Washington, DC: U.S. Government Printing Office.

Collier, V. P. (1989). How long? A synthesis of research on academic achievement in a second language. *TESOL Quarterly, 23,* 509–531.

Collier, V. P. (1992). A synthesis of studies examining long-term language minority student data on academic achievement. *Bilingual Research Journal, 16,* 187–212.

Collier, V. P., & Thomas, W. P. (1989). How quickly can immigrants become proficient in school English? *Journal of Educational Issues of Language Minority Students, 5,* 26–38.

Commins, N. L. (1989). Language and affect: Bilingual students at home and at school. *Language Arts, 66,* 29–43.

Conklin, N. F., & Lourie, M. A. (1983). *A host of tongues: Language communities in the United States.* New York: The Free Press.

Corder, S. P. (1983). A role for the mother tongue. In S. M. Gass & L. Selinker (Eds.), *Language transfer in language learning* (pp. 85–97). Rowley, MA: Newbury House.

Cortés, C. (1986). The education of language minority students: A contextual interaction model. In Bilingual Education Office, *Beyond language: Social & cultural factors in schooling language minority students* (pp. 3–33). Sacramento, CA: State Department of Education.

Crandall, J. (Ed.). (1987). *ESL through content-area instruction: Mathematics, science, social studies.* Englewood Cliffs, NJ: Prentice-Hall.

Crawford, J. (1989). *Bilingual education: History, politics, theory, and practice.* Trenton, NJ: Crane.

Crawford, J. (1992). *Hold your tongue.* Reading, MA: Addison-Wesley.

Crawford, J. (1995). Endangered Native American languages: What is to be done, and why?. *Bilingual Research Journal, 19,* 17–38.

Cummins, J. (1979). Linguistic interdependence and the educational development of bilingual children. *Review of Educational Research, 40,* 222–251.

Cummins, J. (1980). The entry and exit fallacy in bilingual education. *NABE Journal, 4*(3), 25–59.

Cummins, J. (1981). The role of primary language development in promoting educational success for language minority students. In Bilingual Education Department (Ed.), *Schooling and language minority students: A theoretical framework* (pp. 3–49). Sacramento: California State Department of Education.

Cummins, J. (1984). *Bilingualism and special education: Issues in assessment and pedagogy.* Clevedon, UK: Multilingual Matters.

Cummins, J. (1989). *Empowering minority students.* Sacramento: California Association for Bilingual Education.

Cummins, J. (1991). Interdependence of first- and second-language proficiency in bilingual children. In E. Bialystok (Ed.), *Language processing in bilingual children* (pp. 70–89). New York: Cambridge University Press.

Cummins, J. (1994). Knowledge, power, and identity in teaching English as a second language. In F. Genesee (Ed.), *Educating second language children* (pp. 33–58). Cambridge, UK: Cambridge University Press.

Cummins, J., & Sayers, D. (1995). *Brave new schools: Challenging cultural illiteracy.* New York: St. Martin's Press.

Curiel, H., Rosenthal, J. A., & Richek, H. G. (1986). Impacts of bilingual education on secondary school grades, attendance, retention and drop out. *Hispanic Journal of Behavioral Sciences, 8*(4), 357–367.

Darcy, N. T. (1953). A review of the literature on the effects of bilingualism on the measurement of intelligence. *Journal of Genetic Psychology, 82,* 21–57.

Darling-Hammond, L. (1994). Performance-based assessment and educational equity. *Harvard Educational Review, 64,* 5–30.

Davis, T. M. (1994). *Open doors 1993–94: Report on international educational exchange.* New York: Institute of International Education.

Dawe, L. C. (1983). Bilingualism and mathematical reasoning in English as a second language. *Educational Studies in Mathematics, 14,* 325–353.

DeAvila, E. A., Duncan, S. E., & Navarrete, C., (1987). *Finding out/Descubrimiento.* Northvale, NJ: Santillana.

DeAvila, E. A., & Duncan, S. E. (1982). *Finding out/Descubrimiento.* San Rafael, CA: Linguametrics Group.

deJong, E. J. (1993). *The evaluation of bilingual education: Evaluation designs and their implications.* Unpublished qualifying paper, School of Education, Boston University, Boston.

De La Garza, J. V., & Medina, M., Jr. (1985). Academic achievement as influenced by bilingual instruction of Spanish-dominant Mexican American children. *Hispanic Journal of Behavioral Sciences, 7*(3), 247–259.

Delgado-Gaitán, C. (1991). Involving parents in the schools: A process of empowerment. *American Journal of Education, 100,* 20–46.

DeVillar, R. A., & Faltis, C. J. (1991). *Computers and cultural diversity: Restructuring for school success.* Albany: State University of New York Press.

Dillon, S. (1995, October 24). Report faults bilingual education in New York. *The New York Times,* p. A1.

Doebler, L. K., & Mardis, L. J. (1980). The effects of a bilingual education program for Native American children. *NABE Journal, 5*(2), 23–28.

Dorian, N. C. (1982). Language loss and maintenance in language contact situations. In Lambert & B. Freed (Eds.), *The loss of language skills* (pp. 44–59). Rowley, MA: Newbury House.

Duncan, S. E., & DeAvila, E. A. (1979). Bilingualism and cognition: Some recent findings. *NABE Journal, 4*(1), 15–50.

Durán, R. P. (1989). Testing of linguistic minorities. In R. L. Linn (Ed.), *Educational measurement* (3rd ed., pp. 573–587). New York: Macmillan.

Duranti, A., & Ochs, E. (1995). *Syncretic literacy: Multiculturalism in Samoan American families.* Santa Cruz, CA: The National Center for Research on Cultural Diversity and Second Language Learning.

Edelsky, C. (1991). *With literacy and justice for all: Rethinking the social in language and education.* London: Falmer Press.

Edmonds, R. R. (1979). Effective schools for the urban poor. *Educational Leadership, 37*(1), 15–27.

Eggington, W. G. (1987). Written academic discourse in Korean: Implications for effective communication. In U. Connor & R. B. Kaplan (Eds.), *Writing across languages: Analysis of L2 text* (pp. 153–168). Reading, MA: Addison-Wesley.

Ehlert, L. (1987). *Growing vegetable soup.* New York: Harcourt Brace Jovanovich (HBJ Big Books).

Engle, P. L. (1975). *The use of vernacular languages in education: Language medium in early school years for minority language groups.* Washington, DC: Center for Applied Linguistics.

Enright, D. S., & McCloskey, M. L. (1988). *Integrating English: Developing English language and literacy in the multilingual classroom.* Reading, MA: Addison-Wesley.

Epstein, N. (1977). *Language, ethnicity, and the schools: Policy alternatives for bilingual-bicultural education.* Washington, DC: Institute for Educational Leadership, George Washington University.

Erickson, F. (1993). Transformation and school success: The politics and culture of educational achievement. In E. Jacob & C. Jordan (Eds.), *Minority education: Anthropological perspectives* (pp. 27–51). Norwood, NJ: Ablex.

Escamilla, K. (1994a). Goals 2000 and language-minority students: Skeptical optimism. *NABE News, 17*(7), 3.

Escamilla, K. (1994b). Issues in bilingual program evaluation. In R. Rodríguez, N. J. Ramos, & J. A. Ruiz-Escalante (Eds.), *Compendium of readings in bilingual education: Issues and practices* (pp. 74–83). San Antonio: Texas Association for Bilingual Education.

Escamilla, K. (1994c). The sociolinguistic environment of a bilingual school: A case study introduction. *Bilingual Research Journal, 18*(1–2), 21–47.

Evans v. Buchanan, Civ. Nos. 1816–1822 (D. Del. May 19, 1976).

Faltis, C. J. (1993). *Joinfostering: Adapting teaching strategies for the multilingual classroom.* New York: Merrill/Macmillan.

Faltis, C. J. (1994). Doing the right thing: Developing a program for immigrant and bilingual secondary students. In R. Rodriguez, N. J. Ramos, & J. A. Ruiz-Escalante (Eds.), *Compendium of readings in bilingual education: Issues and practices* (pp. 39–47). San Antonio: Texas Association for Bilingual Education.

Ferguson, C. A., & Heath, S. B. (1981). *Language in the U.S.A.* New York: Cambridge University Press.

Fern, V. (1995). Oyster School stands the test of time. *Bilingual Research Journal, 19,* 497–512.

Fernandez, R. M., & Nielsen, F. (1986) Bilingualism and Hispanic scholastic achievement: Some baseline results. *Social Science Research, 15,* 43–70.

Ferro, S. (1983). *Language influence on mathematics achievement of Cape Verdean students.* Unpublished doctoral dissertation, Boston University, Boston.

Figueiredo, J. M. (1985). *Reasons for leaving school: The perceptions of the Azorean Portuguese immigrant dropouts.* Unpublished doctoral dissertation, Boston University, Boston.

Fishman, J. A. (1966). *Language loyalty in the US: The maintenance and perpetuation of non-English mother tongues by American ethnic and religious groups.* The Hague: Mouton.

Fishman, J. A. (1976). *Bilingual education: An international sociological perspective.* Rowley, MA: Newbury House.

Fishman, J. A. (1988). "English only": Its ghosts, myths, and dangers. *International Journal of the Sociology of Language, 74,* 124–140.

Fishman, J. A., Gertner, M. H., Lowy, E. G., & Milán, W. G. (1985). *Ethnicity in action: The community resources of ethnic languages in the United States.* Binghamton, NY: Bilingual Presss/Editorial Bilingüe.

Fishman, J. A., & Markman, B. R. (1979). *The ethnic mother-tongue school in America: Assumptions, findings, directory.* New York: Ferkauf Graduate School, Yeshiva University.

Fitzgerald, J. (1993). Views on bilingualism in the United States: A selective historical review. *Bilingual Research Journal, 17*(1–2), 35–56.

Flanagan, M. (1984). *A study of a half-day ESOL program for second language learners in grades one through six.* Unpublished doctoral dissertation, Boston University, Boston.

Floden, R. (1991). What teachers need to know about learning. In M. Kennedy (Ed.), *Teaching academic subjects to diverse learners* (pp. 181–202). New York: Teachers College Press.

Freeman, Y. S., & Freeman, D. E. (1992). *Whole language for second language learners.* Portsmouth, NH: Heinemann.

Freire, P. (1970). *Pedagogy of the oppressed.* New York: Seabury.

Freire, P. (1973). *Education for critical consciousness.* New York: Continuum.

Fulton-Scott, M. J., & Calvin, A. D. (1983). Bilingual multicultural education vs. integrated and non-integrated ESL instruction. *NABE Journal, 7*(3), 1–12.

García, E. E. (1988). Attributes of effective schools for language minority students. *Education and Urban Society, 20*(4), 387–398.

García, E. E. (1991). Effective instruction for language minority students: The teacher. *Journal of Education, 173*(2), 130–142.

García, E. E. (1993). Project THEME: Collaboration for school improvement at the middle school for language minority students. In National Clearinghouse for Bilingual Education (Ed.), *Proceedings of the third national research symposium on limited English proficient student issues: Focus on middle and high school issues* (Vol. 1, pp. 323–350). Washington, DC: U.S. Department of Education.

Gardner, H. (1983). *Frames of mind: The theory of multiple intelligences.* New York: Basic Books.

Gardner, R. C. (1982). Social factors in language retention. In R, Lambert & B. Freed (Eds.), *The loss of language skills* (pp. 24–39). Rowley, MA: Newbury House.

Gardner, R. C., & Lambert, W. E. (1972). *Attitudes and motivation in second-language learning.* Rowley, MA: Newbury House.

Gault, A., & Murphy, J. (1987). The implications of high expectations for bilingual students. *Journal of Educational Equity and Leadership, 7*(4), 301–317.

Genesee, F. (1984). Historical and theoretical foundations of immersion education. In Office of Bilingual Education, *Studies on immersion education* (pp. 32–57). Sacramento: California State Department of Education.

Genesee, F. (1987). *Learning through two languages: Studies of immersion and bilingual education.* Cambridge, MA: Newbury House.

Genesee, F., & Hamayan, E. V. (1994). Classroom-based assessment. In F. Genesee (Ed.), *Educating second language children* (pp. 212–239). Cambridge, UK: Cambridge University Press.

Genishi, C. (1981). Codeswitching in Chicano six-year-olds. In R. P. Duran (Ed.), *Latino language and communicative behavior* (pp. 133–152). Norwood, NJ: Ablex.

Gerner de García, B. (1993). Language use in Spanish-speaking families with deaf children. *Dissertation Abstracts International, 53*/12, 4278. (University Microfilms No. 93- 12851)

Gerner de García, B. (1995). ESL applications for Hispanic deaf students. *Bilingual Research Journal, 19,* 453–467.

Gersten, R. (1985). Structured immersion for language minority students: Results of a longitudinal evaluation. *Educational Evaluation and Policy Analysis, 7*(3), 187–196.

Gersten, R. (1996). Literacy instruction for language-minority students: The transition years. *The Elementary School Journal, 96,* 227–244.

Gersten, R., Woodward, J., & Schneider, S. (1992). *Bilingual immersion: A longitudinal evaluation of the El Paso program.* Washington, DC: The READ Institute.

Gibson, M. A. (1993). The school performance of immigrant minorities: A comparative view. In E. Jacob & C. Jordan (Eds.), *Minority education: Anthropological perspectives* (pp. 113–128). Norwood, NJ: Ablex.

Gilson, E. H. (1986). Introduction of new writing systems: The Turkish case. In N. Schweda-Nicholson (Ed.), *Languages in the international perspective* (pp. 23–40). Norwood, NJ: Ablex.

Glazer, N. (1975). *Affirmative discrimination: Ethnic inequality and public policy.* New York: Basic Books.

Glazer, N. (1993, December). Where is multiculturalism leading us?. *Phi Delta Kappan,* 319–323.

Glazer, N., & Cummins, J. (1985). Viewpoints on bilingual education. *Equity and Choice, 2,* 47–52.

Gleick, J. (1987). *Chaos: Making a new science.* New York: Viking.

Goals 2000: Educate America Act—Message from the President of the United States. H. Doc. No. 70, House, April 22, 1993.

Goddard, H. H. (1917). Mental tests and the immigrant. *Journal of Delinquency, 2,* 243–277.

Goho, T., & Smith, D. (1973). *A college degree: Does it substantially enhance the economic achievement of chicanos?* (Occasional paper No. 503). Las Cruces: New Mexico State University.

Goldenberg, C. (1993). The home–school connection in bilingual education. In M. B. Arias & U. Casanova (Eds.), *Bilingual education: Politics, practice and research* (pp. 225–250). Chicago, IL: University of Chicago Press.

Goldenberg, C. Reese, L., & Gallimore, R. (1992). Effects of literacy materials from school on Latino children's home experiences and early reading achievement. *American Journal of Education, 100,* 497–536.

Goldenberg, C. Reese, L., & Gallimore, R. (1995). Effects of literacy materials from school on Latino children's home experiences and early reading achievement. In G. Gonzalez & L. Maez (Eds.), *Compendium of research on bilingual education* (pp. 135–157). Washington, DC: National Clearinghouse for Bilingual Education.

Gonzalez, B., & Cress, D. (1994, March). *A qualitative analysis of bilingual children's experiences with alternative assessments: Results from the urban district assessment consortium.* Paper presented at the Massachusetts Association for Bilingual Educations, Leominster, MA.

Gonzalez, N., Moll, L. C., Floyd-Tenery, M., Rivera, A., Rendon, P., Gonzalez, R., & Amanti, C. (1993). *Teacher research on funds of knowledge: Learning from households.* Santa Cruz, CA: National Center for Research on Cultural Diversity and Second Language Learning.

Goodman, K. (1986). *What's whole in whole language?* Richmond Hill, Ontario: Scholastic TAB.

Grabe, W., & Kaplan, R. B. (1989). Writing in a second language: Contrastive rhetoric. In D. M. Johnson & D. H. Roen (Eds.), *Richness in writing: Empowering ESL students* (pp. 263–283). New York: Longman.

Graves, D. H. (1983). *Writing: Teachers & children at work.* Portsmouth, NH: Heinemann.

Grosjean, F. (1989). Neurolinguists, beware! The bilingual is not two monolinguals in one person. *Brain and Language, 36,* 3–15.

Hakuta, K. (1986). *Mirror of language: The debate on bilingualism.* New York: Basic Books.

Hakuta, K., & D'Andrea, D. (1992). Some properties of bilingual maintenance and loss in Mexican background high-school students. *Applied Linguistics, 13,* 72–99.

Hakuta, K., & Diaz, R. M. (1985). The relationship between degree of bilingualism and cognitive ability: A critical discussion and some new longitudinal data. In K. E. Nelson (Ed.), *Children's language* (Vol. 5, pp. 319–344). Hillsdale, NJ: Lawrence Erlbaum Associates.

Hatch, E. M. (1978). *Second language acquisition: A book of readings.* Rowley, MA: Newbury House.

Hatch, E. M. (1983). *Psycholinguistics: A second language perspective.* Rowley, MA: Newbury House.

Heath, S. B. (1976). A national language academy: Debate in the new nation. *International Journal of the Sociology of Language, 47*(11), 9–43.

Heath, S. B. (1977). Our language heritage: A historical perspective. In J. K. Phillips (Ed.), *The language connection: From the classroom to the world* (pp. 23–51). Skokie, IL: National Textbook Company.

Heath, S. B. (1981). English in our language heritage. In C. A. Ferguson & S. B. Heath (Eds.), *Language in the U.S.A.* (pp. 6–20). Cambridge, UK: Cambridge University Press.

Heath, S. B. (1983). *Way with words: Language, life and work in communities and classrooms.* Cambridge, UK: Cambridge University Press.

Heath, S. B. (1985, November). *Keynote address.* Presented at the Massachusetss Association for Bilingual Education Conference, Boston.

Heath, S. B. (1986). Sociocultural contexts of language development. In California Association for Bilingual Education, *Beyond langue: Social and cultural factors in schooling language minority students* (pp. 143–186). Los Angeles: Evaluation, Dissemination and Assessment Center.

Hernández, J. S. (1991). Assisted performance in reading comprehension strategies with non-English proficient students. *The Journal of Educational Issues of Language Minority Students, 8,* 91–112.

Hernández, S. M., & Santiago, I. S. (1983). Toward a qualitative analysis of teacher disapproval behavior. In R. V. Padilla (Ed.), *Theory, technology, and public policy on bilingual education* (pp. 99–111). Rosslyn, VA: National Clearinghouse for Bilingual Education.

Hernández-Chavez, E. (1978). Language maintenance, bilingual education, and philosphies of bilingualsim in the United States. In J. E. Alatis (Ed.), *International dimensions of bilingual education* (pp. 527–550). Washington, DC: Georgetown University Press.

HEW. (1975). Memorandum on evaluation of voluntary compliance plans designed to eliminate educational practices which deny non-English language dominant students equal educational opportunity. Reprinted in *Bilingual–bicultural education: A handbook for attorneys and community workers* (p. 225). Cambridge, MA: Center for Law and Education.

Hewlett-Gómez, M., & Solis, A. (1995). Dual language instructional design for educating recent immigrant secondary students on the Texas–Mexico border. *The Bilingual Research Journal, 19,* 429–452.

Hinds, J. (1987). Reader versus writer responsibility: A new typology. In U. Connor & R. B. Kaplan (Eds.), *Writing across languages: Analysis of L2 text* (pp. 141–152). Reading, MA: Addison-Wesley.

Holdaway, D. (1979). *The foundations of literacy.* New York: Ashton Scholastic.

Holm, A., & Holm, W. (1990). Rock Point: A Navajo way. *Annals of the American Academy of Political and Social Science, 508,* 170–184.

Homza, A. (1995). Developing biliteracy in a bilingual first-grade writing workshop. *Dissertations Abstract International,* 56/06, 2148. (University Microfilm No. 95-33133)

House No. 1447. (1995). *An Act Relative to Bilingual Education.* Boston: The Commonwealth of Massachusetts.

Ianco-Worrall, A. D. (1972). Bilingualism and cognitive development. *Child Development, 43,* 1390–1400.

Imhoff, G. (1990). The position of U.S. English on bilingual education. In C. B. Cazden and C. E. Snow (Eds.), *English plus: Issues in bilingual education* (pp. 48–61). Newbury Park, CA: Sage.

Jacob, E., & Jordan, C. (1993). Understanding minority education: Framing the issues. In E. Jacob & C. Jordan (Eds.), *Minority education: Anthropological perspectives* (pp. 3–13). Norwood, NJ: Ablex.

Jacobson, R. (1990). Allocating two languages as a key feature of a bilingual methodology. In R. Jacobson & C. Faltis (Eds.), *Language distribution issues in schooling* (pp. 3–17). Clevedon, UK: Multilingual Matters.

Jacobson, R. (1994). Bilingual education: Some international implications for bilinguality. In R. Rodríguez, N. J. Ramos, & J. A. Ruiz-Escalante (Eds.), *Compendium of readings in bilingual education: Issues and practices* (pp. 14–21). San Antonio: Texas Association for Bilingual Education.

Johnson, G. W. (1949). *Our English heritage.* Philadelphia: Lippincott.

Jones, B. V., Palincsar, A. S., Ogle, D. S., & Carr, E. G. (1987). *Strategic teaching and learning: Cognitive instruction in the content areas.* Alexandria, VA: Association for Supervision and Curriculum Development in cooperation with the Central Regional Educational Laboratory.

Jordan, C., Tharp, R. G., & Baird-Vogt, L. (1992). "Just open the door:" Cultural compatibility and classroom rapport. In M. Saravia-Shore & S. Arvizu (Eds.). *Cross-cultural literacy: Ethnographies of communication in multiethnic classrooms* (pp. 3–18). New York: Garland.

Keller, G. D., & Van Hooft, K. S. (1982). A chronology of bilingualism and bilingual education in the United States. In J. A. Fishman & G. D. Keller (Eds.), *Bilingual education for Hispanic students in the United States* (pp. 3–19). New York: Teachers College, Columbia University.

Kessler, C., & Quinn, M. E. (1987). ESL and science learning. In J. Crandall (Ed.), *ESL through content-area instruction* (pp. 55–87). Englewood Cliffs, NJ: Prentice-Hall.

Keyes v. Denver School District No. 1, 413 U.S. 189 (1973).

Kleinfeld, J. S. (1979). *Eskimo school on the Andreafsky: A study of effective bicultural education.* New York: Praeger.

Kloss, H. (1977). *The American bilingual tradition.* Rowley, MA: Newbury House.

Krashen, S., & Biber, D. (1988). *On course: Bilingual education's success in California.* Sacramento: California Association for Bilingual Education.

Krashen, S., Scarcella, R. C., & Long, M. H. (1982). *Child-adult differences in second language acquisition.* Rowley, MA: Newbury House.

Krasnick, H. (1983). *From communicative competence to cultural competence* (Selected papers form the Annual Convention of TESOL, Toronto). (ERIC Document Reproduction Service No. ED 275 153)

LaCelle-Peterson, M. W., & Rivera, C. (1994). Is it real for all kids? A framework for equitable assessment policies for English language learners. *Harvard Educational Review, 64,* 55–75.

Lambert, W. E. (1977). The effects of bilingualism on the individual: Cognitive and sociocultural consequences. In P. A. Hornby (Ed.), *Bilingualism: Psychological, social, and educational implications* (pp. 15–27). New York: Academic Press.

Lambert, W. E. (1986). Pairing first- and second- language speech and writing in ways that aid language acquisition. In J. Vaid (Ed.), *Language processing in bilinguals: Psycholinguistic and neuropsychological perspectives* (pp. 65–96). Hillsdale, NJ: Lawrence Erlbaum Associates.

Lambert, W. E., & Cazabón, M. (1994). *Students' views of the Amigos program.* Santa Cruz, CA: The National Center for Research on Cultural Diversity and Second Language Learning.

Lambert, W., & Tucker, R. (1972). *Bilingual education of children: The St. Lambert experiment.* Rowley, MA: Newbury House.

Lau v. Nichols, 414 U.S. 563 (1974).

Lee, J. F. (1986). On the use of the recall task to measure L2 reading comprehension. *Studies in Second Language Acquisition, 8,* 201–212.

Leibowitz, A. H. (1976). Language and the law: The exercise of political power through official designation of language. In W. M. O'Barr & J. F. O'Barr (Eds.), *Language and politics* (pp. 449–466). The Hague: Mouton.

Leibowitz, A. H. (1980). *The Bilingual Education Act: A legislative analysis.* Washington, DC: National Clearinghouse for Bilingual Education

Leone, B. (1995). A K–5 bilingual resource room: The first year. *Bilingual Research Journal, 19,* 551–569.

Leong, C. K. (1978). Learning to read in English and Chinese: Some psycholinguistic and cognitive considerations. In D. Feitelson (Ed.), *Cross-cultural perspectives on reading and reading research* (pp. 157–173). Newark, DE: International Reading Association.

Lerner, M. (1957). *America as a civilization: Life and thought in the United States today.* New York: Simon & Schuster.

Lewis, E. G. (1977). Bilingualism and bilingual education: The ancient world to the Renaissance. In B. Spolsky & R. L. Cooper (Eds.), *Frontiers of bilingual education* (pp. 22–93). Rowley, MA: Newbury House.

Lindholm, K. J. (1990). Bilingual immersion education: Criteria for program development. In A. M. Padilla, H. H. Fairchild, & C. M. Valadez (Eds.), *Bilingual education: Issues and strategies* (pp. 91–105). Newbury Park, CA: Sage.

Lindholm, K. J. (1991). Theoretical assumptions and empirical evidence for academic achievement in two languages. *Hispanic Journal of Behavioral Sciences, 13*(1), 3–17.

Lindholm, K. J., & Aclan, Z. A. (1991). Bilingual proficiency as a bridge to academic achievement. Results from bilingual/immersion programs. *Journal of Education, 173*(2), 99–113.

Liu, S. S. F. (1978). Decoding and comprehension in reading Chinese. In D. Feitelson (Ed.), *Cross-cultural perspectives on reading and reading research* (pp. 144–156). Newark, DE: International Reading Association.

Lombardo, M. E. (1979). *The construction and validation of the listening and reading components of the English as a Second Language Assessment Battery.* Unpublished doctoral dissertation, Boston University, Boston.

Lucas, T. (1993a). Secondary schooling for students becoming bilingual. In M. B. Arias & U. Casanova (Eds.), *Bilingual education: Politics, practice and research* (pp. 113–143). Chicago: University of Chicago Press.

Lucas, T. (1993b). What have we learned from research on successful secondary programs for LEP students? A synthesis of findings from three studies. In National Clearinghouse for Bilingual Education (Ed.), *Proceedings of the third national research symposium on limited English proficient student issues: Focus on middle and high school issues* (Vol. 1, pp. 81–111). Washington, DC: U.S. Department of Education.

Lucas, T., Henze, R., & Donato, R. (1990). Promoting the success of Latino linguistic minority students in high schools. *Harvard Educational Review, 60,* 315–340.

Lucas, T., & Katz, A. (1994). Reframing the debate: The roles of native languages in English-only programs for language minority students. *TESOL Quarterly, 28,* 537–561.

Lyons, J. J. (1990). The past and future directions of federal bilingual education policy. In C. B. Cazden & C. E. Snow (Eds.), *English plus: Issues in bilingual education* (pp. 66–80). Newbury Park, CA: Sage.

Lyons, J. J. (1994). Clinton signs Elementary/Secondary Education Act. *NABE News, 18*(2), p. 1.

MacDonald, B., Aldeman, C., Kushner, S., & Walker, R. (1982). *Bread and dreams: A case study of bilingual schooling in the U.S.A.* Norwich, UK: Centre for Applied Research in Education, University of East Anglia.

Macedo, D. P. (1981). *Stereotyped attitudes toward various Portuguese accents* (Thought Provoking Paper No. 4). Washington, DC: National Clearinghouse for Bilingual Education.

Mace-Matluck, B. J. (1990). The effective schools movement: Implications for Title VII and bilingual education projects. In L. Malavé (Ed.), *Annual Conference Journal NABE '88–89* (pp. 83–95). Washington, DC: National Association for Bilingual Education.

Macías, R. F. (1994). Bilingual staff still needed. *Linguistic Minority Research Institute, 4*(2), 1–2.

Mackey, W. (1968). The description of bilingualism. In J. A. Fishman (Ed.), *Readings in the sociology of language* (pp. 554–584). The Hague: Mouton.

Mackey, W. (1972). *Bilingual education in a binational school.* Rowley, MA: Newbury House.

Mackey, W., & Beebe, V. N. (1977). *Bilingual schools for a bicultural community.* Rowley, MA: Newbury House.

Marsh, L. (1995). A Spanish dual literacy program: Teaching to the whole student. *The Bilingual Research Journal, 19,* 409–428.

Massachusetts General Laws, Ch. 71 (1993).

Massachusetts State Department of Education. (1990). *Two-way integrated bilingual education.* Malden: Author.

McArthur, E. K. (1993). *Language characteristics and schooling in the United states, A changing picture: 1979 and 1989.* Washington, DC: National Center for Education Statistics.

McCollum, P. A. (1993, April). *Learning to value English: Cultural capital in a two-way bilingual program.* Paper presented at the meeting of the American Educational Research Association, Atlanta, GA.

McConnell, B. (1983). Individualized bilingual instruction: A validated program model effective for both Spanish and Asian language students. In R. V. Padilla (Ed.), *Theory, technology, and public policy on bilingual education* (pp. 137–148). Roslyn, VA: NCBE.

McDiarmid, G. W. (1991). What teachers need to know about cultural diversity: Restoring cultural diversity: Restoring subject mattter to the picture. In M. M. Kennedy (Ed.), *Teaching academic subjects to diverse learners* (pp. 257–269). New York: Teachers College Press.

McKay, S. L., & Wong, S. C. (Eds.). (1988). *Language diversity: problem or resource?* Cambridge, MA: Newbury House.

McLaughlin, B. (1984). *Second language acquisition in childhood* (Vol. 2). Hillsdale, NJ: Lawrence Erlbaum Associates.

McPartland, J., & Braddock, J. M. (1993). A conceptual framework on learning environments and student motivation for language minority and other underserved populations. In National Clearinghouse for Bilingual Education (Ed.), *Proceedings of the third national research symposium on limited English proficient student issues: Focus on middle and high school issues* (Vol. 1, pp. 1–42). Washington, DC: U.S. Department of Education.

Medeiros, L. A. S. (1983). *Azorean-Portuguese students: Influence of socio-environmental factors of reading proficiency in the native language.* Unpublished doctoral dissertation, Boston University, Boston.

Medina, M., Jr. (1993). Spanish achievement in a maintenance bilingual education program: Language proficiency, grade and gender comparisons. *Bilingual Research Journal, 17,* 57–81.

Medina, M., Jr., & Escamilla, K. (1992a). English acquisition by fluent- and limited-Spanish-proficient Mexican Americans in a 3–year maintenance bilingual program. *Hispanic Journal of Behavioral Sciences, 14,* 252–267.

Medina, M., Jr., & Escamilla, K. (1992b). Evaluation of transitional and maintenance bilingual programs. *Urban Education, 27*(3), 263–290.

Mehan, H., Hubbard, A., Lintz, A., & Villanueva, I. (1994). *Tracking untracking: The consequences of placing low track students in high track classes.* Santa Cruz, CA: National Center for Research on Cultural Diversity and Second Language Learning.

Meier, D. (1995). *The power of their ideas: Lessons for America from a small school in Harlem.* Boston: Beacon Press.

Met, M. (1994). Teaching content through a second language. In F. Genesee (Ed.), *Educating second language children* (pp. 159–182). Cambridge, UK: Cambridge University Press.

Met, M., & Galloway, V. (1992). Research in foreign language curriculum. In P. Jackson (Ed.) *Handbook of research on curriculum* (pp. 852–890). New York: Macmillan.

Meyer v. Nebraska, 262 U.S. 390, 401–403 (1923).

Milk, R. D. (1993). Bilingual education and English as a second language: The elementary school. In M. B. Arias & U. Casanova (Eds.), *Bilingual education: Politics, practice and research* (pp 88–112). Chicago: University of Chicago Press.

Minicucci, C., & Olsen, L. (1992). *Meeting the challenge of language diversity: An evaluation of programs for pupils with limited proficiency in English.* Berkeley, CA: BW Associates.

Minow, M. (1990). *Making all the difference: Inclusion, exclusion, and American law.* Ithaca, NY: Cornell University Press.

Miramontes, O. (1994). ESL policies and school restructuring: Risks and opportunities for language-minority students. In R. Rodríguez, N. J. Ramos, & J. A. Ruiz-Escalante (Eds.), *Compendium of readings in bilingual education: Issues and practices* (pp. 48–58). San Antonio: Texas Association for Bilingual Education.

Mohan, B. A. (1986). *Language and content.* Reading, MA: Addison-Wesley.

Moll, L. C. (1988). Some key issues in teaching Latino students. *Language Arts, 65*(5), 465–472.

Moll, L. C. (1992). Bilingual classrooms studies and community analysis: Some recent trends. *Educational Researcher, 21*(2), 20–24.

Moll, L. C., Amanti, C., Neff, D., & González, N. (1992). Funds of knowledge for teaching: Using a qualitative approach to connect homes and classrooms. *Theory Into Practice, 31*(2), 132–141.

Moll, L. C., & Diaz, S. (1993). Change as the goal of educational research. In E. Jacob & C. Jordan (Eds.), *Minority education: Anthropological perspectives* (pp. 67–79). Norwood, NJ: Ablex.

Moll, L. C., & González, N. (1994). Lessons from research with language-minority children. *Journal of Reading Behavior, 26,* 439–456.

Moran, C., Tinajero, J. V., Stobbe, J., & Tinajero, I. (1993). Strategies for working with overage students. In J. V. Tinajero & A. F. Ada (Eds.), *The power of two languages: Literacy and biliteracy for Spanish-speaking students* (pp. 117–131). New York: Macmillan/McGraw-Hill.

Morgan v. Kerrigan. 401 F. Supp. 216,242 (D. Mass., 1975). aff'd 523 F. 2d. 917 (1st cir., 1975).

National Association for Bilingual Education. (1992). *Professional standards for the preparation of bilingual/multicultural teachers.* Washington, DC: Author.

National Council on Education Standards and Testing. (1992). *Raising standards for American education: A report to Congress, the Secretary of Education, the National Education Goals Panel, and the American people.* Washington, DC: U.S. Government Printing Office.

National Education Goals Panel. (1991). *The national educational goals report: Building a nation of learners.* Washington, DC: Author.

National Education Goals Panel. (1992). *The national educational goals report: Building a nation of learners.* Washington, DC: Author.

National Education Goals Panel. (1994). *The national education goals report: Building a nation of learners.* Washington, DC: U.S. Government Printing Offices.

National Governors Association, Task Force on Education. (1990). *Educating America: State strategies for achieving the national education goals.* Washington, DC: Author.

Nieto, S. (1992). *Affirming diversity: The sociopolitical context of multicultural education.* New York: Longman.

Northcutt, L., & Watson, D. (1986). *S.E.T.: Sheltered English teaching handbook.* Carlsbad, CA: Northcutt, Watson, Gonzales.

Oakes, J. (1985). *Keeping track: How schools structure inequality.* New Haven, CT: Yale University Press.

Ogbu, J. U. (1993). Frameworks—Variability in minority school performance: A problem in search of an explanation. In E. Jacob & C. Jordan (Eds.), *Minority education: Anthropological perspectives* (pp. 83–111). Norwood, NJ: Ablex.

Ogbu, J. U., & Matute-Bianchi, M. E. (1986). Understanding sociocultural factors: Knowledge, identity, and school adjustment. In Bilingual Education Office, *Beyond language: Social & cultural factors in schooling language minority students* (pp. 73–142). Sacramento: California State Department of Education.

Olsen, R. E. W-B. (1993, April). *A survey of LEP and adult ESL student enrollments in U.S. public schools.* Paper presented at TESOL conference, Atlanta, GA.

O'Malley, J. M., & Pierce, L. V. (1996). *Authentic assessment for English language learners: Practical approaches for the K–12 classroom.* Reading, MA: Addison-Wesley.

Ostler, S. E. (1987). English in parallels: A comparison of English and Arabic prose. In U. Connor & R. B. Kaplan (Eds.), *Writing across languages: Analysis of L2 text* (pp. 169–185). Reading, MA: Addison-Wesley.

Otheguy, R. (1994). *Comments on the Board of Education's "Educational progress of students in bilingual and ESL programs: A longitudinal study, 1990–1994.* Unpublished manuscript.

Ovando, C. J. (1994). Insights on diversity: Reflections of an involuntry voluntary immigrant. *Bilingual Research Journal, 18,* 115–117.

Paratore, J. R., Homza, A., Krol-Sinclair, B., Lewis-Barrow, T., Melzi, G., Stergis, R., & Haynes, H. (1995). Shifting boundaries in home and school responsibilites: The construction of home-based literacy portfolios by immigrant parents and their children. *Research in the Teaching of English, 29,* 367–389.

Peal, E., & Lambert, W. E. (1962). The relationship of bilingualism to intelligence. *Psychological Monographs, 76*(27), 1–23.

Pearlman, J. (1990). Historical legacies: 1840–1920. In C. B. Cazden & C. E. Snow (Eds.), *English plus: Issues in bilingual education* (pp. 27–37). Newbury Park, CA: Sage.

Pease-Alvarez, C., & Vasquez, O. (1994). Language socialization in ethnic minority communities. In F. Genesee (Ed.), *Educating second language children* (pp. 82–102). New York: Cambridge University Press.

Pease-Alvarez, L., Garcia, E. E., & Espinosa, K. (1991). Effective instruction for language minority students: An early childhood case study. *Early Childhood Research Quarterly, 6*(3), 347–363.

Penfield, W., & Roberts, L. (1959). *Speech and Brain-Mechanisms.* Princeton, NJ: Princeton University Press.

Peirce, B. N. (1995). Social identity, investment, and language learning. *TESOL Quarterly, 29,* 9–31.

Philips, S. (1972). Participant structures and communicative competence: Warm Springs children in community and classrooms. In C. B. Cazden, V. P. John & D. Hymes (Eds.), *Functions of language in the classroom* (pp. 370–394). New York: Teachers College Press.

Pintner, R., & Keller, R. (1922). Intelligence tests for foreign children. *Journal of Educational Psychology, 13,* 214–222.

Porter, R. P. (1990). *Forked tongues.* New York: Basic Books.

Porter, R. P. (1994, May 18). Goals 2000 and the bilingual student. *Education Week,* p. 44.

Portes, A., & Zhou, M. (1993). The new second generation: Segmented assimilation and its variants. In P. I. Ross (Ed.), *Interminority affairs in the United States: Pluralism at the crossroads* (pp. 74–96). Newbury Park, CA: Sage.

Purkey, S. C., & Smith, M. P. (1983). Effective schools: A review. *The Elementary School Journal, 83*(4), 427–452.

Radencich, M. C., McKay, L. J., & Paratore, J. R. (1995). Keeping flexible groups flexible: Grouping options. In M. Radencich & L. J. McKay (Eds.), *Flexible groupings for literacy in the elementary grades* (pp. 25–41). Needham, MA: Allyn & Bacon.

Radencich, M. C., McKay, L. J., Paratore, J. R., Plaza, G. L., Lustgarten, K. E., Nelms, P., & Moore, P. T. (1995). Implementing flexible grouping with a common reading selection. In M. Radencich & L.

J. McKay (Eds.), *Flexible groupings for literacy in the elementary grades* (pp. 43–65). Needham, MA: Allyn & Bacon.

Ramirez, A. G. (1985). *Bilingualism through schooling.* Albany: State University of New York Press.

Ramirez, J. D. (1992). Executive summary. *Bilingual Research Journal, 16,* 1–62.

Reyes, M. de la Luz, Laliberty, E. A., & Orbanosky, J. M. (1993). Emerging biliteracy and cross-cultural sensitivity in a language arts classroom. *Language Arts, 70,* 659–668.

Richards, J. B. (1987). In H. T. Trueba (Ed.), *Success or failure?: Learning and the language minority student* (pp. 109–130). Cambridge, MA: Newbury House.

Ríos v. Read, 73 F. R. D. 589 (E. D. N. Y. 1977).

Rivera, C., & Zehler, A. M. (1991). Assuring the academic success of language minority students: Collaboration in teaching and learning. *Journal of Education, 173,* 52–77.

Rodriguez, A. B. P. (1983). *Parental factors as motivational correlates among Puerto Rican bilingual children in special education.* Unpublished dissertation, Boston University, Boston.

Rodriguez, R. (1982). *Hunger of memory: The education of Richard Rodriguez.* Boston: D. R. Godine.

Romaine, S. (1995). *Bilingualism.* New York: Basil Blackwell.

Rossell, C. H. (1990). The research on bilingual education. *Equity and Choice, 6,* 29–36.

Rossell, C. H., & Ross, M. (1986). The social science evidence on bilingual education. *Journal of Law and Education, 15*(4), 385–419.

Ruiz, R. (1993). Critical research issues in bilingual secondary education. In National Clearinghouse for Bilingual Education (Ed.), *Proceedings of the third national research symposium on limited English proficient student issues: Focus on middle and high school issues* (Vol. 2, pp. 383–420). Washington, DC: U.S. Department of Education.

Saer, O. J. (1923). The effects of bilingualism on intelligence. *British Journal of Psychology, 14,* 25–28.

San Miguel, Jr., G. (1988). Bilingual education policy development: The Reagan years, 1980–1987. *NABE Journal, 12*(2), 97–112.

Saravia-Shore, M., & Arvizu, S. (1992). *Cross-cultural literacy: Ethnographies of communication in multiethnic classrooms.* New York: Garland.

Saville-Troike, M. (1984). What really matters in second language learning for academic achievement? *TESOL Quarterly, 18,* 199–219.

Sayers, D. (1989). Bilingual sister classes in computer writing networks. In D. M. Johnson & D. H. Roen (Eds.), *Richness in writing: Empowering ESL students* (pp. 120–133). New York: Longman.

Schmidt, P. R. (1995). Working and playing with others: Cultural conflict in a kindergarten literacy program. *The Reading Teacher, 48*(5), 404–412.

Schnalberg, L. (1995, August 2). Board relaxes bilingual education policy in California. *Education Week, 14*(41), 1.

Schneider, S. (1990, December). *Integrating whole language with a sheltered English curriculum.* Paper presented at the annual meeting of the National Reading Conference, Miami, FL.

Schumann, J. (1978). *The pidginization process: A model for second language acquisition.* Rowley, MA: Newbury House.

Secada, W., & Lightfoot, T. (1993). Symbols and the political contest of bilingual education in the United States. In M. B. Arias & U. Casanova (Eds.), *Bilingual education: Politics, practice and research* (pp. 36–64). Chicago: University of Chicago Press.

Segalowitz, N. (1977). Psychological perspectives on bilingual education. In B. Spolsky & R. Cooper (Eds.), *Frontiers of bilingual education* (pp. 119–158). Rowley, MA: Newbury House.

Selinker, L. (1972). Interlanguage. *IRAL, 10,* 201–231.

Serna v. Portales Municipal Schools. 351 F. Supp. 1279 (D.N.M. 1972).

Short, D. J. (1993). *Integrating language and culture in middle school American history classes.* Santa Cruz, CA: National Center for Research on Cultural Diversity and Second Language Learning.

Short, D. J. (1994). Expanding middle school horizons: Integrating language, culture, and social studies. *TESOL Quarterly, 28,* 581–608.

Singleton, D. (1992). Second language instruction: The when and the how. In J. F. Matter (Ed.), *Language teaching in the twenty-first century: AILA review* (pp. 46–54). Amsterdam: The Free University Press.

Siu, S. (1992). *Toward an understanding of Chinese-American educational achievement* (Center on Families, Communities, Schools and Children's Learning. Report No. 2). Baltimore: Johns Hopkins University.

Sizer, T. R. (1984). *Horace's compromise: The dilemma of the American high school.* Boston: Houghton Mifflin.

Sizer, T. R. (1992). *Horace's school: Redesigning the American high school.* Boston: Houghton Mifflin.

Sizer, T. R. (1995, January 8). What's wrong with standard tests. *Education Week, 58.*

Skutnabb-Kangas, T. (1979). *Language in the process of cultural assimilation and structural incorporation of linguistic minorities.* Rosslyn, VA: National Clearinghouse for Bilingual Education.

Slavin, R. E. (1970). *Cooperative learning: Theory, research, and practice.* Englewood Cliffs, NJ: Prentice-Hall.

Smith, H. L., & Heckman, P. E. (1995). The Mexican-American war: The next generation. In E. E. García & B. McLaughlin (Eds.), *Meeting the challenge of linguistic and cultural diversity in early childhood education* (pp. 64–84). New York: Teachers College Press.

Snow, C. (1990). Rationales for native language instruction: Evidence from research. In A. M. Padilla, H. H. Fairchild & C. M. Valadez (Eds.), *Bilingual education: Issues and strategies* (pp. 60–74). Newbury Park, CA: Sage.

Snow, C., Barnes, W., Chandler, J., Goodman, I., & Hemphill, L. (1989). *Unfulfilled expectations: Family and school effects on literacy.* Cambridge, MA: Harvard University Press.

Snow, C., Cancino, H., Gonzalez, P., & Shriberg, E. (1989). Giving formal definitions: An oral language correlate of school literacy. In D. Bloome (Ed.), *Classrooms and literacy* (pp. 233–249) Norwood, NJ: Ablex.

Soto, L. D. (1993). Native language for school success. *Bilingual Research Journal, 17,* 83–97.

Spanos, G. (1993). ESL Math and science for high school students: Two case studies. In National Clearinghouse for Bilingual Education (Ed.), *Proceedings of the third national research symposium on limited English proficient students issues: Focus on middle and high school issues* (Vol. 1, pp. 383–420). Washington, DC: U.S. Department of Education.

Spolsky, B. (1972). *The language education of minority children.* Rowley, MA: Newbury House.

Spolsky, B. (1978). American Indian education. In B. Spolsky & R. L. Cooper (Eds.), *Case studies in bilingual education* (pp. 332–361). Rowley, MA: Newbury House.

Spolsky, B. (1989). *Conditions for second language learning.* Oxford, UK: Oxford University Press.

Stein, C. B., Jr. (1986). *Sink or swim: The politics of bilingual education.* New York: Praeger.

Stergis, R. (1995). *Connections between bilingual program parents and their children's schooling.* Unpublished doctoral dissertation, Boston University, Boston.

Suarez-Orozco, M. M. (1987). Towards a psychosocial understanding of Hispanic adaptation to American schooling. In H. T. Trueba (Ed.), *Success or failure?: Learning and the language minority student* (pp. 156–168). Cambridge, MA: Newbury House.

Suarez-Orozco, M. M. (1993). "Becoming somebody": Central American immigrants in U.S. inner-city schools. In E. Jacob & C. Jordan (Eds.), *Minority education: Anthropological perspectives* (pp. 129–143). Norwood, NJ: Ablex.

Suarez-Orozco, M. M., & Suarez-Orozco, C. E. (1993). Hispanic cultural psychology: Implications for education theory and research. In P. Phelan & A. L. Davidson (Eds.), *Renegotiating cultural diversity in American schools* (pp. 108–138). New York: Teachers College Press.

Sung, B. L. (1987). *The adjustment experience of Chinese immigrant children in New York City.* New York: Center for Migration Studies.

Swain, M. (1984). Large-scale communicative language testing: A case study. In S. J. Savignon & M. S. Berns (Eds.), *Initiatives in communicative language teaching* (pp. 185–209). Reading, MA: Addison-Wesley.

Swain, M., & Barik, H. C. (1976). Bilingual education for the English Canadian: Recent developments. In A. Simões, Jr. (Ed.), *The bilingual child/El niño bilingüe* (pp. 91–111). New York: Academic Press.

Taylor, D. M. (1987). Social psychological barriers to effective childhood bilingualism. In P. Hornel, M. Palij, & D. Aaronson (Eds.), *Childhood bilingualism: Aspects of linguistic, cognitive and social development* (pp. 183–195). Hillsdale, NJ: Lawrence Erlbaum Associates.

Teitelbaum, H., & Hiller, R. J. (1977). Bilingual education: The legal mandate. *Harvard Educational Review, 47,* 138–170.

Teresa P. v. Berkeley Unified School District, 724 F. Supp. 698 (U.S. Dist. 1989).

Thomas, W. P., & Collier, V. P. (1996). Language minority student achievement and program effectiveness. *NABE News, 19*(6), 33.

Tikunoff, W. J. (1983). *Significant bilingual instructional features study.* San Francisco, CA: Far West Laboratory.

Tikunoff, W. J., & Vasquez-Faría, J. A. (1982). Successful instruction for bilingual schooling. *Peabody Journal of Education, 59*(4), 234–271.

Title VII. The Bilingual Education Act. (1968). (20 U.S.C. 880b-1). P. L. 90–247.

Tollefson, J. W. (1991). *Planning language, planning inequality.* New York: Longman.

Tomlinson, S. (1989). Ethnicity and educational achievement in Britain. In L. Eldering & J. Kloprogge (Eds.), *Different cultures same school* (pp. 15–37). Amsterdam: Swets & Zeitlinger.

Torres-Guzman, M. E. (1992). Stories of hope in the midst of despair: Culturally responsive education for Latino students in an alternative high school in New York City. In M. Saravia-Shore & S. Arvizu (Eds.), *Cross-cultural literacy: Ethnographies of communication in multiethnic classrooms* (pp. 477–490). New York: Garland.

Torres-Guzmán, M. E., & Goodwin, A. L. (1995). Urban bilingual teachers and mentoring for the future. *Education and Urban Society, 28,* 48–66.

Transitional Bilingual Education. Chapter 71A. (1971). Annotated Laws of Massachusetts: Education (pp. 269–278).

Trix-Haddad, F. (1981). First language illiteracy—Second language reading: A case study. In S. Hudelson (Ed.), *Learning to read in different languages* (pp. 32–44). Washington, DC: Center for Applied Linguistics.

Trueba, H. (1989). *Raising silent voices.* Cambridge, MA: Newbury House.

Tzeng, O. J. L. (1983). Cognitive processing of various orthographies. In M. Chu-Chang (Ed.), *Asian- and Pacific-American perspectives in bilingual education: Comparative research* (pp. 73–96). New York: Teachers College Press.

United Nations Educational, Scientific and Cultural Organization. (1953). *The use of vernacular languages in education.* Paris: Author.

U.S. Commission on Civil Rights. (1971a). *Report I. Ethnic isolation of Mexican Americans in the public schools of the Southwest.* Washington, DC: U.S. Government Printing Office.

U.S. Commission on Civil Rights. (1971b). *Report II. The unfinished education: Outcomes for minorities in the five Southwestern states.* Washington, DC: U.S. Government Printing Office.

U.S. Commission on Civil Rights. (1972a). *Report III. The excluded student.* Washington, DC: U.S. Government Printing Office.

U.S. Commission on Civil Rights. (1972b). *Report IV. Mexican American education in Texas: A function of wealth.* Washington, DC: U.S. Government Printing Office.

U.S. Commission on Civil Rights. (1973). *Report V. Teachers and students.* Washington, DC: U.S. Government Printing Office.

U.S. Commission on Civil Rights. (1974). *Report VI. Toward quality education for Mexican Americans.* Washington, DC: U.S. Government Printing Office.

U.S. Department of Health, Education, and Welfare. (1975, August 11). *Task force findings specifying remedies available for eliminating past educational practices ruled unlawful under Lau v. Nichols.* U.S. Government: Federal Register.

U.S. General Accounting Office. (1987). *Bilingual education: A new look at the research evidence.* Washington, DC: U.S. Government Printing Office.

U.S. v. Texas, 342 F. Supp. 24, 27–38 (E.D. Tex. 1971).

Valdesolo, E. T. (1983). *The effect of bilingualism on the ability to formulate scientific hypothesis.* Unpublished doctoral dissertation, Boston University, Boston.

Vazquez, J. (1989). *Bilingual education programs for return migrant students in Puerto Rico: Perceptions of participants, parents and teachers.* Unpublished doctoral dissertation, Boston University, Boston.

Veltman, C. (1983). *Language shift in the United States.* New York: Mouton.

Von Maltitz, F. W. (1975). *Living and learning in two languages.* New York: McGraw-Hill.

Vygotsky, L. S. (1978). *Mind in society: The development of higher psychological processes* (M. Cole, V. John-Steiner, S. Scribner, & E. Souberman, Eds. & Trans.). Cambridge, MA: Harvard University Press.

Waggoner, D., & O'Malley, J. M. (1985). Teachers of limited English proficient children in the United States. *NABE Journal, 9*(3), 25–42.

Walsh, C. E. (Ed.). (1991). *Literacy as praxis: Culture, language, and pedagogy.* Norwood, NJ: Ablex.

Watahomigie, L. J., & McCarty, T. L. (1994). Bilingual/bicultural education at Peach Springs: A Haulapai way of schooling. *Peabody Journal of Education, 69*(2), 26–42.

Weber, G. (1971). *Inner-city children can be taught to read: Four successful schools.* Washington, DC: Council for Basic Education. (ERIC Document Reproduction Service No. ED 057 125)

Werner-Smith, A. M., & Smolkin, L. B. (1995). An ESL/bilingual/bicultural pre-collegiate program for Southeast Asian refugee high school students. *The Bilingual Research Journal, 19,* 395–408.

Willig, A. C. (1985). A meta-analysis of selected studies on the effectiveness of bilingual education. *Review of Educational Research, 55*(3), 269–317.

Wong Fillmore, L. (1979). Individual differences in second language acquisition. In C. J. Fillmore, D. Kempler, & W. S-Y. Wang (Eds.), *Individual differences in language ability and language behavior* (pp. 203–228). New York: Academic Press.

Wong Fillmore, L. (1982). Language minority students and school participation: What kind of English is needed. *Journal of Education, 164,* 143–156.

Wong Fillmore, L. (1989). Teaching English through content: Instructional reform in programs for language minority students. In J. H. Esling (Ed.), *Multicultural education and policy: ESL in 1990* (pp. 125–143). Toronto: Institute for Studies in Education.

Wong Fillmore, L. (1991). When learning a second language means losing the first. *Early Childhood Research Quarterly, 6,* 323–346.

Wong Fillmore, L. (1992). Learning a language from learners. In C. Kramsch & S. McConnell-Ginet (Eds.), *Text and context: Cross-disciplinary perspectives on language study* (pp. 46–66). Lexington, MA: Heath.

Wong Fillmore, L., & Valadez, C. (1986). Teaching bilingual learners. In M. Wittrock (Ed.), *Handbook of research on teaching* (3rd ed., pp. 648–685). New York: Macmillan.

Wurzel, J. (1981). Value orientation differences in an urban school and their implications for the amelioration of conflict in the classroom. *Journal of Education, 163*(1), 56–69.

Wurzel, J. (1988). Multiculturalism and multicultural education. In J. Wurzel (Ed.), *Toward multiculturalism: A reader in multicultural education* (pp. 1–13). Yarmouth, ME: Intercultural Press.

Zanger, V. V. (1987). *The social context of second language learning: An examination of barriers to integration in five case studies.* Unpublished doctoral dissertation, Boston University, Boston.

Zanger, V. V. (1993). *Face to face: Communication, culture and collaboration.* Boston: Heinle & Heinle.

Zappert, L. T., & Cruz, B. R. (1977). *Bilingual education: An appraisal of empirical research.* Berkeley, CA: Berkeley Unified School District.

Author Index

Subject Index